Outside
MAGAZINE'S

GUIDE TO
FAMILY
VACATIONS

ALSO AVAILABLE:

Outside Magazine's Adventure Guide to Northern California

Outside Magazine's Adventure Guide to New England

Outside Magazine's Adventure Guide to the Pacific Northwest

Outside Magazine's Adventure Guide to the Mid-Atlantic
(available spring 1998)

Outside Magazine's Adventure Guide to
Southern California & the Baja Peninsula *(available spring 1998)*

Outside MAGAZINE'S

GUIDE TO
FAMILY VACATIONS

Macmillan • USA

Macmillan Travel
A Simon & Schuster Macmillan Company
1633 Broadway
New York, NY 10019

MACMILLAN is a registered trademark of Macmillan, Inc.

Outside Magazine and the *Outside* Magazine logo are registered trademarks of *Outside* Magazine, a publication of Mariah Media Inc., and their use is expressly licensed.

Find Macmillan online at **http://www.mgr.com/travel** or on America Online at Keyword: **Frommer's**. Find Outside Online at **http://outside.starwave.com**

All text from *Outside* Magazine's Family Vacations issues, reprinted with permission of the authors, and edited by Leslie Weeden.

Produced by Gowanus Books
Cover by Susan Scandrett, *Outside* Magazine
Interior Design by designLab, Seattle
Trip-Finder Map by Rew Adams
Illustrations by Rew Adams and Meg Kimmel

Photography Credits: Balsams Grand Resort Hotel *(pages 1, 149);* Paula Carroll Fullmer *(pages viii, 182);* Greg Dianich/EcoStock *(page 227);* Earl Harper/EcoStock *(page 63);* Carol Harold/EcoStock *(page 119);* Hawk's Cay Resort and Marina *(page 141);* Scott Hill *(page 219);* Nantahala Outdoor Center *(pages 51, 89, 239);* Dennis Peppler *(page 195);* Amy Peppler Adams *(pages 19, 71, 105, 165, 209, 233);* Catherine Schirmer *(page 41);* Strathcona Park Lodge *(page 81).*

Manufactured in the United States of America

CONTENTS

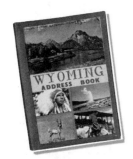

12 Learning Vacations:
Summer 101   141

13 Multisport Resorts:
Independence Days   149

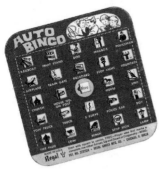

1

An African safari? With a 3-year-old? Are you completely insane?"

That was the response, from in-laws to pediatrician, when we announced our vacation plans. While we'll admit to having entertained our own doubts, where is it written that adventure ends when parenthood begins?

Traveling En Famille

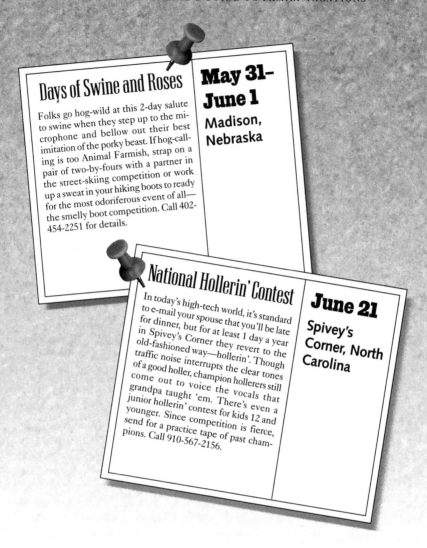

Days of Swine and Roses

May 31–June 1
Madison, Nebraska

Folks go hog-wild at this 2-day salute to swine when they step up to the microphone and bellow out their best imitation of the porky beast. If hog-calling is too Animal Farmish, strap on a pair of two-by-fours with a partner in the street-skiing competition or work up a sweat in your hiking boots to ready for the most odoriferous event of all—the smelly boot competition. Call 402-454-2251 for details.

National Hollerin' Contest

June 21
Spivey's Corner, North Carolina

In today's high-tech world, it's standard to e-mail your spouse that you'll be late for dinner, but for at least 1 day a year in Spivey's Corner they revert to the old-fashioned way—hollerin'. Though traffic noise interrupts the clear tones of a good holler, champion hollerers still come out to voice the vocals that grandpa taught 'em. There's even a junior hollerin' contest for kids 12 and younger. Since competition is fierce, send for a practice tape of past champions. Call 910-567-2156.

Bouncing along in a Land Rover (not equipped with seat belts) en route to our campsite in a remote corner of Hwange National Park in Zimbabwe, we passed elephants, giraffes, impalas, zebras, warthogs, and kudu. I don't know what was more thrilling—the endless African sky or the look of amazement on our daughter Roxie's face. But our doubts resurfaced later that night, when the thunder cracked so hard it felt like it would split the earth. As rain poured out of the sky and our tent trembled wildly, each drop that pelted us was another disapproving finger wagging. My husband, Bill, and I lay awake in the dark, soggy and terrified. Roxie, meanwhile, slept through

Moose Dropping Festival

June 12–13
Talkeetna, Alaska

Twenty-five years ago, two bored Talkeetna housewives had the revelation that moose droppings make fabulous jewelry. Today, Talkeetnans still mine these nuggets for the annual Moose Dropping Festival, where even candy is shaped to fit the theme. (Rumor has it that the candy tastes better than fudge.) Although there's plenty happening for kids, most will say their favorite event is to cheer on their moms in the Mountain Mother Contest where women chop wood, carry groceries through an obstacle course, shoot a longbow, and cast a fishing reel—all with a 15-pound baby doll on their backs. Call 907-733-2487.

Mighty Mud Mania

June 18
Scottsdale, Arizona

Looking for good, clean family fun? Try Scottsdale's 22nd annual Mighty Mud Mania, a daylong mudfest including mud obstacle courses, mud pools, mud slides, and mudcastle building. If visions of a mud-filled car at the end of the day are holding you back, don't worry—the Scottsdale firefighters are on hand to hose everyone down. And after a whole day of mud-in-the-face, eyes, ears, nose, and mouth, the kids may not track mud onto the carpet for months. Call 602-994-2771.

the whole thing. We awoke the next day to find her—born and raised in Manhattan—affectionately fondling a dung beetle. When she learned that this cute bug lays eggs in little balls of "poop" that it rolls itself, she could not have been more pleased.

And so were we. Adventure was still possible.

Of course, heading out isn't quite the same as it used to be. Before Roxie, we'd point to a map, figure out the logistics, and go. Now, we plan; spontaneity is the first casualty of parenthood. We've learned to pack provisions that take into account every conceivable contingency—hunger, boredom, canceled flights, rain, mood swings. Then

Milbridge Days Celebration

July 26–27

Milbridge, Maine

Teams practice for years to perfect their technique in the Great Grease Codfish Relay Race, the most exciting event at Milbridge Days Celebration. The relay includes dressing up in firemen's gear and running with a 20-pound greased, dead codfish through a stream of high-powered water from fire hoses. Although the codfish race takes center stage, the blueberry pancake breakfast, parade, and lobster cookout make the weekend truly unforgettable. Call 207-546-2422.

Boom Days

August 1–3

Leadville, Colorado

Leadville's Boom Days are the closest you'll ever come to the Old West. With folks in turn-of-the-century costume competing in hand mucking, spike driving, and jackleg drilling events, and burros and their riders being auctioned off at the famous Burro Race Calcutta, you'll drive away wishing you were riding in a horse and buggy. The bank even buries money for the best event of all—the kid's Sand Pile Money Grab. For more information, call 800-933-3901.

there are concerns about finances—which grow exponentially with family size—as well as the need for activities that accommodate a variety of ages, abilities, and interests. Sometimes it seems easier to just stay home.

But all that planning can become part of the fun. When we took a trip to Saddleback Lake in northern Maine last summer, we filled the living room with the gear we'd be packing—life jackets, baseball mitts, mosquito repellent, and maps. Just the sight of equipment gets the juices going, and anticipation about our trip grew: Roxie got interested in the area's history and geology. If your kids are included from the beginning, they'll have a stake in the outcome.

For us it's worth it—even with the addition of kid number two. We've

Hope Watermelon Festival

August 14–17

Hope, Arkansas

Sure, it's the hometown of President Clinton, but it's also revered as the watermelon capital of the world. Here you'll find the country's most mammoth melons, and just when they're at their ripest some 60,000 visitors flock to participate in the madness. With watermelon eating, watermelon decorating, and watermelon seed-spitting contests, as well as a Watermelon 5k run, it's no wonder President Clinton feels left out when foreign policy keeps him away. For additional information, call 501-777-3640.

taken Roxie (now 6) and Eli (15 months) to Maine, Florida, Cape Cod, and Colorado—where we went rock climbing at Garden of the Gods. Next summer we're going camping in Arizona with friends and their 8-year-old, and when Eli's older we'll try a horsepacking trip, something I've always dreamed of doing. Neither Bill nor I have spent much time on a horse, but we figure we'll learn to ride the same time the kids do. Traveling with children doesn't have to mean lowering our sights.

As for Roxie, I credit our trips with instilling in her a keen inquisitiveness—along with an abiding interest in bugs. And Eli? I was heartened when he uttered his first word. "Go," he said, as he sped off toward the door. "GO!"

—JULIE SALAMON

Family Travel Quiz

② On an average evening at home, you:

(a) Strap on the in-lines, skate 12 miles to the drive-thru at Taco Tom's, sit in on drums for "Bruised Food" (your son's garage band), and still make it to the gym in time for the Terrific Torso class.

(b) Monitor the Weather Channel, peruse the Land's End catalog, floss your teeth, set the alarm system, and climb into bed by 10:02 P.M.

(c) Drop off your daughter at hockey practice, your son at T'ai Chi, and the dog at assertiveness training—then dash off eight more pages of your novel-in-progress.

(d) Fantasize about selling the house and sailing a papyrus boat to Rangiroa.

Start

① On vacation, you would find it most difficult to survive without:

(a) Half a gallon of Nuprin and an industrial-strength neoprene knee brace.

(b) PoolPal swim diapers, water wings safety devices, and an emergency life ring.

(c) The headphones for the family's four separate-but-equal Discman players.

(d) Your Bowie knife, pot-grabber, and prize recipe for bannock.

3 **In a restaurant you look for:**

(a) Knife-wielding tableside Japanese cooks who can slice radishes into roses faster than you can say "wasabi."

(b) Noodles, not pasta.

(c) A menu as thick as the L.A. phonebook.

(d) A chef who can work magic with organic daikon.

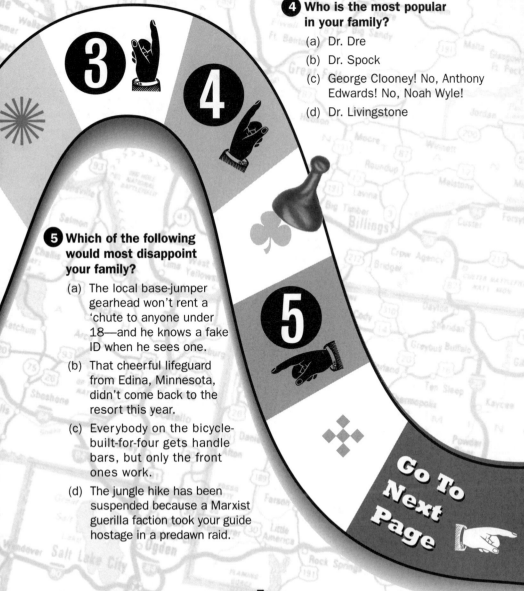

4 **Who is the most popular in your family?**

(a) Dr. Dre

(b) Dr. Spock

(c) George Clooney! No, Anthony Edwards! No, Noah Wyle!

(d) Dr. Livingstone

5 **Which of the following would most disappoint your family?**

(a) The local base-jumper gearhead won't rent a 'chute to anyone under 18—and he knows a fake ID when he sees one.

(b) That cheerful lifeguard from Edina, Minnesota, didn't come back to the resort this year.

(c) Everybody on the bicycle-built-for-four gets handle bars, but only the front ones work.

(d) The jungle hike has been suspended because a Marxist guerilla faction took your guide hostage in a predawn raid.

Go To Next Page

6 **One of your greatest fears is that:**

(a) Your son will come home with Jenny McCarthy tattooed over his newly pierced left nipple.

(b) The bad hair day memorialized on your passport photo very likely will cause a border guard to mistake you for Moammar Ghadaffi.

(c) Someone in your family will violate the no-politics rule at the dinner table and blurt out, "You know, that Pat Buchanan really has a point."

(d) Your children will finally realize tofu hot dogs taste like wet Kleenex.

7 **Your family would be most excited about visiting:**

(a) Any Club Med that offers an intensive Circus Workshop.

(b) The Universal Studios set where they filmed "Murder, She Wrote."

(c) Any place that has a video-game arcade, a 150-foot jungle water-fall, an art-house theater, and tandem bikes for rent.

(d) The site where the Donner Party was stranded.

9 When the television is on in your home it's likely to be tuned to:

(a) "Hercules: The Legendary Journeys."

(b) Reruns of "Marcus Welby, M.D."

(c) The program listings, searching for something everyone can agree on.

(d) The Discovery Channel's "Ecosystems of the Korup Forest."

Go To Next Page

8 You would most likely bring home which of the following souvenirs?

(a) The in-flight magazine (who has time to shop?).

(b) One of those cool snow-domes from the hotel gift shop.

(c) Puffer-fish skeletons found on solitary beach walks.

(d) Tanka paintings and a yak-bone dagger.

| WHO ARE YOU? | BEST TRIPS FOR YOUR FAMILY |

If you answered mostly (a), you're...

Action Addicts

+ Strathcona Park Lodge, British Columbia, page 150

+ Any multisport sampler trip, page 158

+ Molokai Ranch, Molokai, Hawaii, page 226

+ Colorado River rafting, page 97

+ Dirt Camp, Moab, Utah, page 55

Your family is in perpetual motion. It requires round-the-clock entertainment—particularly for the jaded teenagers, whose DNA coding includes the phrase, "all family vacations shall stink." Any palatable (let alone successful) vacation destination must offer a full quiver of adrenaline-producing weapons. Your sole vacation-survival goal is to fend off boredom—and impromptu encounters with local law enforcement.

If you answered mostly (b), you are...

Security Freaks

+ Hyatt Regency, Kauai, Hawaii, page 221

+ Keystone Resort, Colorado, page 154

+ Radisson's Arrowwood Resort, Minnesota, page 155

+ C Lazy U Ranch, Colorado, page 138

+ American Indian Culture Trip, Southwest U.S., page 206

Nothing is left to chance when you travel. Reservations? Double-confirmed. Traveler's checks serial numbers? Stashed—in four different locations (two in an opposite hemisphere in case continental drift runs amok). You might have small children and thus are extremely attuned to precise scheduling. You're not looking for thrills—just a swimming pool with well-marked ends ("knee-deep" and "shallow") and a restaurant with high booster seats and low prices. When you do venture off the well-worn path, tour guides lead the way. You would be quite happy dying at a ripe old age having never gone anywhere—or done anything—that required innoculation.

WHO ARE YOU?   BEST TRIPS FOR YOUR FAMILY

If you answered mostly (c), you're...

Independent Contractors

◆ Anywhere in Alaska, page 209

◆ Cape Breton Island road trip, Nova Scotia, page 191

◆ Nantahala Outdoor Center, North Carolina, page 159

◆ Ludlow's Island Resort, Minnesota, page 157

◆ Glacier National Park, Montana, page 111

Your family has extremely diverse opinions about almost everything, and the word "compromise" long ago was deleted from the spellchecker on your family PC. In order to satisfy everyone—even your persnickety in-laws who may be tagging along—you must ruffle the feathers of no one. Vacation destinations must allow everyone to pursue their own interests—even if they're not sure what they are. You consider group tours a new level of personal hell.

- -

If you answered mostly (d), you are...

Adventure Junkies

◆ African safari, page 228

◆ High Arctic Spring Caribou Basecamp, page 203

◆ Australian Outback and Great Barrier Reef trip, page 229

◆ Outward Bound's Colorado mountaineering school, page 147

◆ Chilko, Chilcotin, and Fraser river system, British Columbia, page 91

If it didn't cause a stir at the security gate, you'd lead the family through airport concourses with an Indiana Jones hat and bullwhip. When you travel you are resourceful, spontaneous, and willing to try almost anything. Your children thrive on new experiences and know how to handle themselves. You've taught them to take only pictures, leave only footprints—and never, ever drink from an aseptic juice box. You all like to immerse yourself completely in a culture and its culinary customs when you travel—even if that means burping some of it up later on.

—MEG LUKENS NOONAN

- -

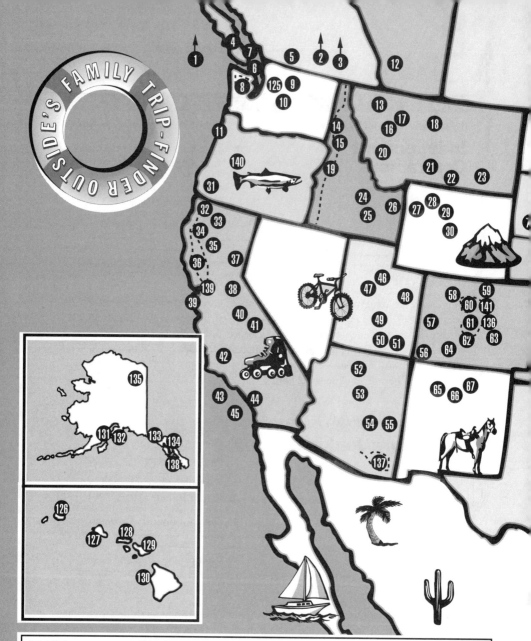

THE LOW-DOWN CHART	Age Guidelines	Muscle Factor	Word from the Wise
Backpacking	You can march out of the delivery room and onto the trail if you're so inclined. Just know that the younger the child, the more logistics are involved—and the more patience and energy required from you.		Think diversionary tactics. Tell stories, sing songs. And there's no shame in bribery: Hershey bars can work wonders with tired kids.
Boardsailing	It's ideal for teens, who at times long for less togetherness. But because of its physical demands, it's not an option for anyone under 10. Twelve is even better. Let your teens cut loose with this oh-so-cool, challenging sport.		It's a hard sport to learn, and lessons don't come cheap. So if you must, stick to snorkeling or rent Jet Skis.
Canoe-Camping	It's a bit like asking what age is best to ride in a car. Anyone can just sit there. And as with an extended car trip, wise parents bring along games and distractions to keep the young ones occupied.		Keep your PFDs strapped on tight, and invest in dry bags. The right gear is essential for comfort and safety.
Fishing	If your kid is old enough to grasp a pole, fishing is possible. Adult supervision is mandatory, however, for kids under 8. As for fly fishing, wait until age 12.		PC-types should repeat after me: Catch and release. It's the activity itself, not the end result, that really matters.
Horseback Riding	The key is leg length. By age 8, kids' legs reach far enough down the horse's side to control it. A western saddle is the closest you can come to a Barcalounger; falling off is harder than you think.		Dude ranches are used to the foibles of city slickers. So wait until you're in their capable hands instead of trying out some rent-by-the-hour outfit.
In-Line Skating	Who hasn't seen pint-size grommets in evening-gown-length NHL jerseys buzzing around like Jeremy Roenick? These kids are maybe 4.		Don't forget pads (knee and elbow), wrist guards, and helmet.
Mountain Biking	Even bigger terrain requires riding skill and leg power. Eight is a good age to begin; 9-year-olds can really crank. By 10, kids will be waiting for you at the top of a rise while you eat their dust.		Bring more water than you think you'll need. And don't forget helmets, eye protection, and a tire-repair kit.

White Knuckle Quotient	Kid Endorsement	Our Final Say	Most You'll Spend
	"I'm usually not up for going. But once I'm out there, my Dad and I quiz each other on trees and animal tracks. At the top of the mountain, I look around and figure this isn't so bad." —Tim Junker, 11	The cheapest, simplest route into the big outdoors. And there's no one so house-proud as family tent campers who've copped the perfect spot and are all set up for a night of roasting marshmallows.	
	"There's power in your sails, but you ride the force of the waves. You can go fast or jump. Whatever. The ocean is incredible. I was 100 yards offshore in Maui and rode next to a humpback whale." —Levi Siver, 15	Don't be intimidated by all the buff board gods and goddesses. Boardsailors welcome initiates to the fold. Great family sport; great family equalizer.	
	"The canoe part is fun. I like to paddle. But the camping is really great. We use two small tents instead of one big one. I don't even mind the work—washing dishes and stuff." —Annie Dickens, 12	Gliding down a peaceful waterway and accessing wilderness without sweating is relaxing for parents, but no kid is bored for long when water is involved.	
	"What I like best is when you feel the tug of the fish on the line. Then you have to reel it in really fast. Waiting can get boring. But not too boring, I guess, because I keep on fishing. And I like it." —Jebb Norton, 6	Any family trip around the water will be enhanced by the swapping of fish tales around the campfire. Your kids will get hooked, and practice that fly-cast in the backyard.	
	"Riding big horses up big mountains is so much fun. You get to act like a cowboy. And it builds confidence when an animal as huge as a horse actually pays attention to you." —Megan Berwick, 17	Don't be chicken. It's only a horse, and, remember, you're the one who's more highly evolved. Besides, the best way to really appreciate the West is from the back of a hoofed one.	
	"Skating really gets your blood pumping—you can do it anywhere, and you just know that when you drop down that ramp, the chicks are digging it." —Chad Long, 16	A family that rolls together grows old together. You don't have to ride ramps—that's called aggressive skating. But any kind of skating, including bopping down the roads, is a great workout, and anyone can dig that.	
	"Face it. If you're a kid and you're going to ride a bike, you want it to be a mountain bike so you can crank down a trail or jump a bump." —Vincent Sanchez, 14	Kids do go nuts for this. If you're game to try, you very well might get hooked, too. The scenery is stunning, the action nonstop. Best of all, the sport comes as naturally as...well, riding a bike.	

(continues)

15

THE LOW-DOWN CHART *(cont.)*

	Age Guidelines	Muscle Factor	Word from the Wise
Road Cycling	Let your child acquire enough leg length to graduate to a slightly larger bike. Otherwise, with a small pedal crank, he'll be spinning at 900 rpm compared with your 70. Outfitters say age 8 and up.		Plan trips that stick to those low-traffic Blue Highways. And do your first tour under the auspices of an outfitter; that support van can be a godsend for a tired kid—or for you!
Rock Climbing	Some 4-year-olds scuttle up rock walls like geckos, but panic when they reach the top. By 8, kids can tackle a multi-pitch route. Confidence is an important factor, so start them on some easy routes.		Climb with reputable guides. Is the equipment state-of-the-art, or are you on belay with baling twine?
Sailing	The boat's motion rocks infants to sleep. Besides PFDs, toddlers require a leash—which sounds worse than it is—or protective netting on the boat. Older kids will love amphibious living.		Bareboating may be the grail for part-time sailors, but the not-so-salty should practice their chops on either a crewed charter or with a stint at a sailing school.
Sea Kayaking	Don't count on real paddling help until age 13 or so. Infants and toddlers can go on these trips (ferried in an extra cockpit hole); a slightly older child can share a double and better appreciate the experience.		If you can't read a compass or a map, commission a guide. Kayaks are easy to pilot, but the sea is nothing to trifle with.
Snorkeling	Blowing water out, then breathing air in through a snorkel is tougher than it sounds. While some 6-year-olds can do it, 8 is a better age to take the first plunge. Even then, expect some coughing jags initially.		Slather on the sunscreen—SPF 15 at a minimum. And educate your kids on what to avoid—jellyfish stings and coral cuts hurt.
Whitewater Rafting	Five is the minimum age most guides will accept. For bouncier Class III rivers, age 7 is best. The jump to Class IV is considerable; kids should be 12 or older. Class V and above: Forget it!		On guided trips expect five-star dining—salmon in béarnaise sauce and chardonnay. And don't foget the PFDs.

White Knuckle Quotient	Kid Endorsement	Our Final Say	Most You'll Spend
	"I like to ride fast, and that's easier on smooth roads—plus my Dad and I can talk. I concentrate on riding, but since the road is pretty solid, I can take time to look up and see the sights, too." —Baker Giduz, 9	They call it touring because you become one with the scenery. Low-key, do-at-your-own-pace. Pull the littlest family member in a bike trailer.	
	"Scary? Nah. Someone's holding you on a rope so you can't fall. I like the little holds and I like climbing and climbing and not paying attention and, all of a sudden, you're really high up." —Taylor Anderson, 6	At home, sign up for a class at your local climbing gym. These gyms are crawling with kids and instructors who know how to teach kids; your own will be transformed into wall rats in no time.	
	"Other sailing kids are all over the place, so you don't get bored. We play volleyball and build bonfires on the beach at night. I like to go diving and fish for dinner."—Carolyn Neale, 14	*Swiss Family Robinson* without the shipwreck. (That family sure got along.) The smells and sounds are like New Age relaxation therapy, which could get dull but for the sea—a formidable playground.	
	"The boats are so quiet that you can sneak up and see all these animals up close. When I get tired, I've been known to lie back in the boat, go to sleep, and let my mom do all the work." —Justin Paige, 10	There is no ecosystem more diverse than where land meets water; in a kayak, you're smack in the middle of it all. You might want to take some paddling lessons before you go.	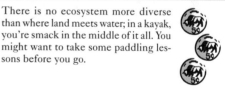
	"My family went to Maui, and a boat took us out to this place where sea turtles hang out. The ocean is like this whole different world. It's really quiet and the fish are bright and colorful." —Austin Tenn-McClellan, 8	On a sailing trip or a beach vacation, snorkeling is mandatory. Immerse yourself in the ocean for a whole new view of the world—this one silent and spectacularly colored.	
	"If you love to get wet, you've *got* to try this. The rapids are scary and fun, and I always scream when I'm going through them. And you get to camp at night. That's the *best*." —Molly Norton, 8	As family vacations go, rafting is sublime: a perfect mix of adventure, quiet, and, pampering.	

17

2

In our family, certain hikes are like yardsticks, marks on a doorjamb as the children grow. One of the first, when our daughters were about 3 and 5 years old, was the half-mile ramble from my grandmother's rickety High Sierra cabin along the lake to the general store, with its jars of fluorescent salmon eggs and crayon-colored snow cones. We marched over the worn granite, balanced on the old plank bridges, crunched the sugar pine needles underfoot.

Backpacking

Walk This Way

When that one became old hat, my wife and I led the way on ever longer and more exotic walks. In the opposite direction, away from civilization, is Stair Rock, into which CCC workers chipped steps during the Depression and from which we jumped into bottomless, sapphire water. Next was the hike to The Lookout on a back trail that gains 400 feet of altitude and provides a breathless, bird's-eye view. It can get hot at The Lookout; we had to bring water and share it in the scented cedar shade.

When the girls were old enough to carry small backpacks and walk for half a day, we packed lunches and struck out for The Inlet, where the river that filled the lake pooled and warmed on pink feldspar sand.

Some of the sites we discovered we named ourselves in acts of ownership and pure celebration. Others, like Cleopatra's Bath, are actually on the map. Cleo's is a kind of graduation hike, a full 3 miles from the cabin up an indistinct trail. I pulled the map out when the girls were maybe 8 and 10 years old, and we made the connection between that granite dome over there and these nesting lines on the page. We got semi-lost. We bushwhacked. We inched along cracks in the rock above the creek. (I began carrying a piece of rope when I realized the girls had no fear of falling.)

When at last we clambered up the final pitch and beheld the glistening pools, it was as if we were the first to discover them, we full-grown trampers in the wilderness.

—PETER SHELTON

THE WEST COAST

Lightning Lakes
Manning Provincial Park,
British Columbia

The Trail: The Lightning Lakes chain—four lakes strung along a beautiful, 8-mile-long Cascade Mountain valley—provide plenty of ooh, just enough aah, and (most important for parents) nary an ugh. Many families use this pleasant, mostly flat (325-foot elevation gain) valley trail for a half-day hike around Lightning Lake to Flash Lake (3.5 miles), where gargantuan peaks loom in the distance. For a 3-day backpacking trip, continue on to Strike Lake, and then hike another half-mile west to the Strike Lake camp, about 5 miles in.

Things to Do: Strike Lake is a noted trout producer, and you should have time after setting up camp to fish. The next day, hike 2 miles west to Thunder Lake, a quiet, almost eerie setting of barren mountains and lush lowlands.

Local Wisdom: Thunder Lake is a steep-sided valley with rock-avalanche danger and is occasionally closed. Don't go too early in the season; snow often lingers until well into May.

The Way There: From Vancouver, B.C., follow Highway 1 east about 93 miles to Hope. Continue east about 43 miles on Highway 3 to Manning Park Lodge in Manning Provincial Park. Just beyond, turn south on Gibson Pass Road and go about 2 miles, forking left where the signs indicate the Lightning Lake Day Use Area. Follow the trail from the parking lot around either side of Lightning Lake.

Resources: For hiking maps and trail information, contact **B.C. Parks Visitor Information Center** (604-840-8836). **Kanala Wilderness Adventures** (604-674-2774) in Clearwater, B.C., is a local outfitter.   —RON C. JUDD

DON'T FORGET

compass
pot-grabber
candle lantern
rope to hang food
moleskin
cooking spices
instant cocoa
safety pins

Olympic National Park Coastal Trail
Washington

The Trail: Sometimes the best way to ditch crowds on a trail is to stay off the trail altogether. That's not a practical option for families in most wild places. But it definitely is in Olympic National Park, where many stretches of a magnificent 57-mile strip of unspoiled ocean beach are easily negotiable.

One of the best and most accessible trips on this wild coastline is the 18.5-mile, 3- to 4-day hike between Rialto Beach and Sand Point. The strip can be hiked in either direction, depending on arrangements you've made for transportation at the southern (Rialto Beach) or northern (Sand Point, near Ozette Campground) trailhead. The flat grade and stunning scenery make this a good family outing. But often-blustery weather, a couple of tricky passages, and the general rigors of walking in soft sand put this hike out of reach of small children—it's best for ages 12 and up.

If the weather cooperates, the multiday walk is unforgettable: This stretch of beach is often called "The Shipwreck Coast," and several monuments to lost lives are among the few signs of modern man you'll encounter along the way. Wildlife (raccoons, sea lions, whales, deer, elk, and shore birds) is plentiful.

Local Wisdom: Some headlands along the way can only be skirted at low tide, making an accurate tide table a must. Most of the route is on sand, but the path

HIRED HANDS

REI Adventures (800-622-2236) leads a 7-day backpacking trip along the Cascade Mountains trails that circle Mt. Rainier. Hikers learn about minimum-impact travel and navigation as they trek past dense forests and immense glaciers. Departures are July 13 and 27 and August 10 and 31; cost is $750 plus a $15 membership fee; minimum age is 14.

Super Natural Adventures (800-263-1600) offers a 7-day/6-night trip to Mt. Assiniboine, Alberta, that provides backcountry experience at a more leisurely pace. The trip begins with 1½ days of short hikes before heading out on a 3-day hike through meadows of wildflowers. The cost is $689 per person for ages 13 and up; trips leave July 15, August 19, and September 6.

American Wilderness Experience (800-444-0099) explores Idaho's Salmon River country with a River of No Return Wilderness and Nature Discovery Seminar, followed by 7 days of backpacking in the region. Cost is $1,005 per person; the trip begins July 12.

climbs over headlands in at least four places, depending on the tides. Consult park rangers about any missing rope ladders or other obstructions you might encounter, as well as overnight permits (required) and special campsite restrictions around Sand Point.

The Way There: To reach the north (Sand Point) trailhead from Port Angeles (about 3 hours west of Seattle), follow Washington 112 west just beyond Sekiu, turn south on Ozette Lake Road, proceed about 20 miles and park at the lot near Ozette Ranger Station. To reach the southern (Rialto) trailhead, take U.S. 101 56 miles south from Port Angeles to Forks and follow signs 14 miles west to Rialto Beach. If the road (storm-damaged last year) is open to Rialto Beach, park there. If not, park 2 miles east at Mora Campground or at the boat launch area about three-quarters of a mile from Rialto Beach.

Resources: For general information and a pamphlet on coastal hiking, call **Olympic National Park** (360-452-0330). A good guidebook is David Hooper's *Exploring Washington's Wild Olympic Coast* (The Mountaineers Books, $10.95). "Custom Correct Maps" (available at most local stores: $2.50 per map) have accurate information about headlands and tides.

—RON C. JUDD

Monte Cristo
Central Cascades, Washington

The Trail: Washouts can sometimes lead to breakthroughs. When the sole road into the historic mining village of Monte Cristo (now a ghost town) washed out in 1980, the Forest Service let it "go wild" and revert to trail. The road is smooth and mostly flat (300-foot elevation gain), with rugged Cascade peaks on all sides. Popular among mountain bikers, this fat-tire highway is also gaining favor among hiking parents, who find it a memorable but gentle backcountry introduction for children of all ages. First-time overnighters should either walk the 4 scenic miles along the South Fork of the Sauk River to a string of excellent riverside campsites or camp in the newly established shelter near the old village.

Things to Do: Trout fishing in the river can be decent (out-of-staters and anyone 15 and older need a state license), and kids enjoy exploring the ghost town. Three nearby trails climb into a spectacular alpine valley: Gothic Basin (6 miles round-trip), Poodle Dog Pass and Silver Lake (3.5 miles), and Glacier Basin (5 steep, rugged miles). Check with the Forest Service to verify trail conditions; flooding is not uncommon, and snow can last until late summer.

Local Wisdom: These day hikes are among the best bang-for-the-mileage-buck in the Cascades, but they head straight up and are rocky in places. Small children are happier poking around the valley.

The Way There: From Seattle (about 90 minutes away), follow I-5 north to exit 194. Drive 6 miles east on U.S. 2 to Washington 9 (near Snohomish) and follow it north to Washington 92. Turn right and head 8 miles east to Granite Falls. At the end of town, turn left on the Mountain Loop Highway and drive 11 miles to the **Forest Service's Verlot**

Public Service Center (maps and info available), and another 19.5 miles to the parking area at Barlow Pass. Trail permits are not required.

Resources: For trail and road conditions, call the **Verlot Public Service Center** at 360-691-7791. Green Trails map No. 111, "Sloan Peak," is a good topo; so is the Darrington Ranger District map ($3). *Pacific Northwest Hiking* ($18.95, Foghorn Press) describes this and dozens of other nearby trails.

—RON C. JUDD

Manzana Trail
Los Padres National Forest, central California

The Trail: Tell your kids you're taking them to a new school, then surprise them with this: The Lower Manzana Trail wanders along Manzana Creek through a canyon of meadows, sandstone narrows, and deep pools, leading to an abandoned schoolhouse in a former pioneer community that flourished here from the 1880s until just after the turn of the century. This 16-mile, fairly level round-trip is a perfect 3-day, first-time trip for kids. The San Rafael Mountains are steep and brushy and covered with prickly chaparral, so most activities here center on the creek.

Spend one night in the primitive campsites at Potrero Camp (1 mile) or Coldwater Camp (3.5 miles), and at least one at Manzana Schoolhouse Camp (8 miles).

Things to Do: Trout can be found along the entire route, but the best fishing is upstream in the headwaters at Manzana Narrows (California fishing license required). Occasional pools are head-deep and perfect for cold-water plunges.

Local Wisdom: Manzana Creek is heaven until late June or early July, when deerflies and horseflies show up. Also, watch out for poison oak and rattlesnakes, which emerge in the summer months.

The Way There: To reach the trailhead, take California 154 to Armor Ranch Road, approximately 20 miles north of Santa Barbara. Take a right and proceed until the road turns into Happy Canyon Road. Head into the forest as the road becomes Sunset Valley Road, which dead-ends at the trailhead. Leave your car at Nira Campground (no permit required).

Resources: Contact the **Santa Barbara Ranger District Office** (805-967-3481) or the **Los Padres National Forest Supervisor's Office** (805-683-6711). An excellent annotated map is the "San Rafael Wilderness and Vicinity Recreational Map," available at either ranger station.   —ANDREW RICE

San Miguel Island
Channel Islands, California

The Trail: Sixty miles by boat from Ventura off the Southern California coast, San Miguel Island is a wild and starkly lovely place. For years it was used as a Navy gunnery range, but now San Miguel is uninhabited and part of Channel Islands National Park. Eight miles long and four miles wide, the island represents a meeting of land and sea unlike anything on the mainland. Visitors land at Cuyler Harbor on the east end, a half-moon cove of perfect sand and outrageously blue water with seals basking on the offshore rocks. Because of the fragile ecology, all hikers must be accompanied by a ranger.

The most popular hike on the island is the 14-mile round-trip from Cuyler Harbor to Point Bennett, a sandy point on the island's northwest end that is famous as the only place in the world where you can see six different pinniped species at once. As many as 20,000 northern elephant seals, harbor seals, stellar sea lions, California sea lions, and Guadalupe fur seals all gather here. You'll probably be able to get close, but don't forget the binoculars—it always seems they're doing something really interesting at the other end of the beach.

On the hike back from Point Bennett, you'll see the unique caliche forest, a miniature petrified forest left behind when calcium carbonate present in blowing soil reacted with ancient plants' organic acid, leaving behind these eerie casts of their long-gone trunks and branches. Other wildlife here includes the diminutive island fox, a fearless variety found only in the Channel Islands, and countless species of sea and land birds.

Things to Do: You can camp in primitive sites near the rangers' residence on the bluff overlooking Cuyler Harbor, but no potable water is available and fires are prohibited. Bring a good tent, as the wind blows constantly. The beach below camp is a perfect place to search for shells and pretty stones (though it's illegal to remove them).

For bedtime stories after sundown, borrow a book on island history from the ranger. Many ships have gone down here, and the history is filled with dramatic tales of tragedy, treachery, and heroic deeds.

Local Wisdom: San Miguel lies directly on the geographic demarcation between southern and northern California, and the weather varies accordingly: It can be sunny one day and pea-soup fog the next. You can always count on the wind to blow, but the island is gorgeous in any conditions.

The Way There: Most visitors to San Miguel arrive via the Island Packers' boat from the Park Service dock in Ventura (adults, $90 round-trip; $80 for kids 12 and under; 805-642-1393). It's at least 5 hours from Ventura, so be prepared for a long and potentially rough haul. Along the way you might see gray and blue whales, basking sharks, and dolphins. Private boats need a Park Service permit to land, and campers need a free camping permit. Both permits are available at **Channel Islands National Park headquarters** at the Ventura harbor; call 805-658-5711.

Resources: Call the **Park Service** at 805-658-5730 or Island Packers for additional information.

—ANDREW RICE

Stuart Fork Trail
California

The Trail: The 513,100-acre Trinity Alps Wilderness is the second-largest wilderness in California—a rugged, isolated area of more than 55 lakes, barren granite mountain ridges, deep canyons, and lush meadows between the Trinity and Salmon Rivers in California's northwest corner.

From Bridge Camp Campground in a forested canyon, the Stuart Fork Trail to Morris Meadow follows a fairly gentle course up the canyon of the Stuart Fork of the Trinity River, where the deep evergreen forest opens up to vistas of snow-covered granite spires. Families with children as young as 6 like this trail for a 3- or 4-day backpacking trip.

There are primitive campsites within 2 miles of the trailhead, but it's worth trekking on to just beyond Oak Flat (4 miles from the trailhead), where you'll find several places to pitch your tent just before a river crossing. In late summer pools here are usually still deep enough for a swim, and there's good fishing for rainbow trout.

The next day, carry on to Morris Meadow, 8.7 miles from the trailhead, where the jagged granite peaks of Sawtooth Ridge rise almost 3,000 feet above the north edge of the meadow. Smaller patches of meadow extend into the forest, and numerous campsites with fire rings are tucked into the woods.

Things to Do: An ambitious day hike from Morris Meadow is the 10.6-mile round-trip to Emerald Lake in the headwaters of the Stuart Fork. Though the Forest Service rates this hike as easy to moderate, the length makes it unsuitable for most kids under the age of 9 or 10.

Local Wisdom: Although these are coastal mountains, snow often lingers until late June or mid-July. High trails are sometimes closed by snow into July,

STAYING SAFE: TEACH YOUR CHILDREN WELL

Lost Kids In February 1981, 9-year-old Jimmy Beveridge and his two brothers, age 7 and 15, headed out on a hike one-half mile from their campsite in Palomar Mountain State Park northeast of San Diego. Jimmy dashed off and took a shortcut; 4 days later his body was found 2 miles from the campground. Rain and fog had moved in suddenly; he had died of hypothermia. Following this tragedy, renowned tracker Ab Taylor and writer Tom Jacobs developed a program called "Hug-A-Tree" to teach children four basic principles for staying safe in the wilderness:

1. **If you get lost, stay in one place.** This reduces the distance searchers need to cover and conserves your energy.

2. **Take a whistle and a large plastic garbage bag with you whenever you leave camp.** To stay dry, make a hole in the side or one corner of the bag for your face to poke out, thus keeping your head covered to retain more heat. Whistles are louder than yelling and require less energy; three toots are the universal signal to searchers.

3. **Make yourself big.** It's hard to see people from a helicopter, so wear bright clothes. Find a clearing and make an SOS sign in the dirt using sticks, leaves, and/or rocks. You can also use a mirror as a signal device.

4. **Leave a footprint behind.** Have each child make a footprint on a piece of aluminum foil. This can save precious search time by eliminating false trails.

Teach kids to avoid getting lost by staying on the trail and picking out land-marks. If your child does become lost, call the sheriff as quickly as possible. Some-times children are afraid to answer rescuers calling their name. The shouting can make them think adults are angry, or, even in an emergency, they may take warn-ings against speaking with strangers to heart. Brief them in advance on how to respond to rescuers should they get lost.

For information, contact **Hug-A-Tree and Survive,** 6465 Lance Way, San Di-ego, CA 92120; 619-286-7536.   *—Debra Shore*

- -

Bear Attacks Bears are shy animals who tend to hightail it out of the vicinity when they hear you and your brood approaching. Experts suggest wearing bells and jingling down the trail to give bears time to vacate the premises.

If you do bump into one, don't run away; instead, stand your ground and talk. If the bear should charge, however, drop to the ground, assume a tight fetal position, and play dead. (Adults should use their bodies to cover young children.) Most bears will check you out, then lose interest.   *—Lisa Twyman Bessone*

Essential Backpack Recipes

Cooking up menus that the kids won't wrinkle their noses at is difficult enough; it can seem next to impossible when camping. But follow advice from the experts from outfitters whose backcountry cuisine has pleased even the pickiest palate. You may find your kids not only cleaning their plates, but asking for seconds. Each recipe feeds four.

Breakfast

Western Spirit Cycling
Crunchy Banana-Cranberry Oatmeal

4 c. water
1⅔ c. rolled oats
1⅓ c. dried cranberries
1 c. plain granola
2 T. brown sugar
¼ c. chopped nuts (optional)
1 banana, sliced (optional)

In a saucepan, bring water and oats to a boil, then move to cooler temperature and continue cooking until oats soften (about 12 minutes). Add cranberries and remove from heat after 2 minutes, or when mixture thickens. Stir in granola, sugar, nuts, and banana.

Lunch

Yellowstone Mountain Guides
Cowboy Lunch

1 c. whole wheat flour
4 T. powdered buttermilk or 1 c. milk
2 tsp. baking powder
½ tsp. baking soda
1 tsp. salt
1 c. cornmeal
2 T. molasses
2 T. honey
2 T. shortening
2 eggs
1 c. water
1 8-oz. can corn, drained

Mix dry ingredients. Heat Dutch oven over coals, add all wet ingredients to the dry ones, and stir just enough to moisten. Bake in oven with lots of coals on the lid for 20 to 25 minutes. Serve with a cup of soup and honey for the bread.

Dinner

Yellowstone Mountain Guides
Vivian's Delight

1½ lbs. lean hamburger
olive oil
1 medium onion, chopped
½ small head cabbage, chopped
½ 14-oz. can sauerkraut
½ bell pepper, diced
1 24-oz. can diced tomatoes
1 T. chopped garlic
2 tsp. caraway seeds
½ tsp. black pepper
1 T. oregano leaves

Brown hamburger in a little bit of olive oil; add onion, cabbage, sauerkraut, bell pepper, tomatoes, and spices. Add a little water if mixture is dry. Make baking-powder biscuits (see below). Place on top of mixture in a casserole. Bake at 425° for 10 to 12 minutes or until biscuits are golden.

Baking-Powder Biscuits

2 c. all-purpose flour
4 tsp. baking powder
2 tsp. sugar
½ tsp. cream of tartar
¼ tsp. salt
½ c. butter or margarine
⅔ c. milk (or use buttermilk and add
    ¼ tsp. baking soda)

Mix dry ingredients in a resealable bag prior to departure. In camp, cut in the butter. Add the milk all at once. Stir just until dough sticks together. Knead lightly and spoon or cut biscuits. Add to Dutch oven per recipe for Vivian's Delight (see above).

—Lorien Warner

and the rivers and creeks don't generally warm up enough for swimming until the middle or end of July.

The Way There: From Weaverville, take California 3 toward Clair Engle (Trinity) Lake. Drive north for about 14.5 miles until you cross a bridge over the Stuart Fork Arm of the lake. Immediately after this bridge turn left and drive through the **Trinity Alps Resort** (916-286-2205) 3.5 miles to the end of the road. A store at the resort is a good place to pick up supplies. For maps and information about the Trinity Alps Wilderness contact the **Weaverville Ranger District,** P.O. Box 1190, Weaverville, CA 96093 (916-623-2121). —ANDREW RICE

Snag Lake Loop
Lassen Volcanic National Park, northern California

The Trail: The sprawling lava plains, jutting cinder cones, and remarkably clear waters around Mount Lassen are like a living laboratory. This route, a moderate (1,000-foot elevation gain) 13.5-mile loop from Butte Lake, circles the lake, then turns south on a gentle 6-mile walk through light forest and grasslands to Snag Lake, where good camping is found near Grassy Creek. The loop then swings north, with great views of Prospect Peak, Cinder Cone, and the Fantastic Lava Beds. On the 6-mile journey back, the trail passes west of the spectacular Painted Dunes.

Things to Do: Trout fishing is good in both Butte and Snag Lakes, and the short (1 mile round-trip), steep side trip

to the summit of Cinder Cone (6,907 feet) on the trek home is a real winner.

Local Wisdom: Black bears are sometimes seen along the route, so either hang your food or use bear-proof containers.

The Way There: From Redding, follow California 44 east 72 miles to the gravel Butte Lake Road. Turn south and proceed 6.5 miles to the park entrance station ($5 per car). Just beyond, bear left and proceed a short distance to the parking lot on the lake's north shore. Free backcountry permits (required for campers) are available at Visitor Contact stations or the Hat Creek Valley Information Center in Old Station.

Resources: Trail maps ($3.95) and information are available from **Lassen Volcanic National Park** (916-595-4444). The USGS topographic quad is Prospect Peak. A good route description is found in *The Hiker's Guide to California* ($14.95, Falcon Press). —RON C. JUDD

THE SOUTHWEST

Mora Flats
Pecos Wilderness, New Mexico

The Trail: The trail from Iron Gate Campground to Mora Flats is an easy 3 miles, and there are numerous places to camp in the partially open grassy river flats stretching along the Río Mora. Set up base camp here (minimum 200 feet from the river) and explore the area on day hikes, or continue on a 15-mile loop to Beatty's Flats and Hamilton Mesa. The route involves several stream crossings and a steep climb to Hamilton Mesa, but the combination of cascading streams, broad grassy meadows, and spectacular views of the Truchas Peaks and Santa Barbara Divide makes this a great place to introduce children to backcountry camping. (Children as young as 8 can do it, but 11 is optimal.)

Things to Do: For horseback rides into the Pecos Wilderness across Hamilton Mesa, contact Huie Ley at the **Terrero**

THE HYSTERICAL PARENT

How far can I reasonably expect my child to hike? Before embarking on a multiday hiking trip, first try a few easy day hikes, gradually increasing the distance. And before you attempt wilderness camping, do a night or two of car-camping. The following outlines the different capabilities of each age group, with some tips on safety.

Age: 0–2 years. **Distance:** Depends entirely on how far a parent can haul the child in a baby pack. **Safety Strategies:** Provide a safe play area at the campsite; tie bells to the baby's shoe so the child can't crawl off without being missed.

Age: 2–4 years. **Distance:** One-half to 2 miles, stopping every 10 to 15 minutes. Too heavy to carry far, so patience is needed. **Safety Strategies:** Dress in bright colors (easy to spot if they get lost) and pin a whistle to clothes. Three blows means "I'm lost."

Age: 5–7 years. **Distance:** 3 to 4 miles over easy and rolling terrain; rest stops every 30 to 40 minutes. **Safety Strategies:** Carry a daypack with water, whistle, plastic bag, snacks, and jacket so your child can stay safe if lost on the trail and alone overnight.

Age: 8–9 years. **Distance:** 6 to 7 miles over variable terrain, a full day at an easy pace. Can carry a framed pack if taller than 4 feet. **Safety Strategies:** Begin teaching map use.

Age: 10–12 years. **Distance:** Full day, 8 to 10 miles over variable terrain. You should start to be concerned about your ability to keep up. **Safety Strategies:** Entering the know-it-all years, they find it hard to imagine getting into trouble.

Age: Teens. **Distance:** 8 to 12 miles; look for decreased mileage during growth spurts. **Safety Strategies:** Same as above, with added challenge of convincing teens that they aren't invincible.

—*Barbara Kennedy, M.D., is a pediatrician, an avid hiker, and the mother of four.*

General Store and Riding Stable, 12 miles north of Pecos ($45–$70 per person; call 505-757-6193 to reserve).

Local Wisdom: Beware the afternoon thunderstorms—often accompanied by large hailstones—in July and August. It's best to get up early and do the bulk of your hiking in the sunny morning hours.

The Way There: Drive 23 miles east of Santa Fe on I-25 to Pecos, then take New Mexico 63 north. Travel about 4.5 miles north of Terrero to Forest Road 223 (rough and rocky, but accessible in good weather), and continue another 4 miles to reach Iron Gate Campground.

Resources: The Santa Fe National Forest map ($4) is available from the **Pecos Ranger District office** (505-757-6121); the USGS topo maps are the Pecos Falls, Elk Mountain, and Cowles quads. The *Trail Guide to Geology of the Upper Pecos* is indispensable; also helpful is the *Trail Guide to the Pecos Wilderness*, produced by the Southwest Natural and Cultural Heritage Association. Both are available in Santa Fe bookstores and district ranger offices.
—DEBRA SHORE

THE ROCKIES

Blodgett Canyon
Selway-Bitterroot Wilderness, southwestern Montana

The Trail: From a distance, the Bitterroot Range of the Rockies is a seemingly impenetrable wall of 9,000-foot peaks dividing Idaho from Montana. But up close, the canyons and valleys that slither between the peaks can be downright inviting. Blodgett Canyon is especially gentle for first-timers, but the surrounding terrain—nearly vertical canyon walls—is macho enough to make even young campers feel like they've really been somewhere. Your chances of meeting up with deer, elk, and moose increase the farther you head into the canyon. And because good camping areas are found every few miles on this 15-mile lowland trail, hikers can head upstream until someone poops out, then set up camp.

Things to Do: Partner up for back rubs. Necks will be craning throughout the entire hike through Blodgett, where canyon walls jut straight up as high as 3,000 feet. Keep an eye out for mountain goats on the upper ridges and waterfalls cascading from the top. If wall-gazing gets old, you can cast a line for rainbow trout in Blodgett Creek.

Local Wisdom: This trail gets a fair amount of horse use. Yield to them and nod appreciatively: Horse groups help maintain the trail.

The Way There: From Missoula, drive about 48 miles south on U.S. 93 through the Bitterroot Valley toward Hamilton. Two miles north of Hamilton, turn west on the county road just before the Bitterroot River crossing. Proceed one-half mile west, 1.8 miles south, and about 3 more miles west to the trailhead (the way is well signed after you turn off U.S. 93). No permits are required.

Resources: For trail information, contact the Bitterroot National Forest's **Stevensville Ranger District** at 406-777-5461. The Selway-Bitterroot Wilderness Map, available from National Forest offices, is a good choice. The best topographic map is the USGS Printz Ridge quad. —RON C. JUDD

Buchanan Pass Trail
Indian Peaks Wilderness, Colorado

The Trail: To introduce your family to Rocky Mountain highs, hike from Monarch Lake about 4 miles along the leafy green Cascade Creek Trail, then follow the Buchanan Pass Trail and set up base camp about three-quarters of a mile farther, in an open area of small meadows and ponds. Then spend several days exploring the alpine lakes, waterfalls, and beaver ponds along the adjoining trails. A permit for the Buchanan Travel Zone lets you camp anywhere as long as you're at least 100 feet from a lake, stream, or trail.

Things to Do: Hike up the Buchanan Pass Trail to Fox Park (4 miles from the trailhead) to see wildflowers blanketing a meadow in a glacier-carved valley. Climb another 2 miles and 1,400 feet to Buchanan Pass for views of Sawtooth Mountain and the Middle St. Vrain Valley to the east. Or follow the Gourd Lake turnoff (2¼ miles from the trailhead) and hike 2.7 miles up to a lake (elevation 10,800 feet) in a natural amphitheater. Hike around the lake, explore its spurs, and check out the rainbows and cutthroats that fill it. Cascade Falls lies along the Cascade Creek Trail, about 1 mile past the trail

Inside Skinny

Trail Eats
Until someone makes a four-wheel-drive cooler that can follow you into the backcountry, pack space will be at a premium. These staples save precious space by serving double duty.

✦ **Kool-Aid:** As a drink mix, it disguises the taste of iodine-treated water; also makes a great flavoring for snow cones.

✦ **Grape-Nuts:** After breakfast you can use it to make pudding pie crusts or casserole toppings.

✦ **Jell-O:** Makes an excellent hot drink for kids.

✦ **Cup-A-Soup:** Mix with instant Potato Buds for a high-carbo side dish that doesn't taste like glue.

Sole Survival
Hiking boots need to be broken in before hitting the trail; the following techniques go far beyond just wearing them around the house:

1. Use shoe trees to accelerate the stretch-to-fit process.

2. Turn a hose on them, then wear until they dry to mold the boot's uppers to your foot.

3. Hold the boot at the heel and toe, then bend and straighten for a half-hour.

If you find that your boots still need tweaking, call Steve Komito at **Komito Boots** (800-422-2668). He can make any brand of hiking boots fit like a glove.

Stay the Course
Topo maps, compasses, and global positioning systems (GPS) can keep you from getting lost, but only if you know how to use them. A GPS is a handheld device that receives a signal from three satellites to buzz in on your exact location. The GPS 2000 from **Magellan** (800-707-5221) is priced for the beginning buyer at $200. Another recommended investment to help you get oriented is the book *Be Expert with Map and Compass*, by Björn Kjellstrom ($17; to order from Eastern Mountain Sports, call 603-924-6154).

junction with the Buchanan Pass Trail. It's another 4 miles to Crater Lake and a spectacular view of Lone Eagle Peak.

Local Wisdom: Remember to acclimate yourselves to the altitude; this hike starts at 8,300 feet.

The Way There: Follow I-70 west from Denver. Exit at U.S. 40 (the Winter Park exit) and head north toward Granby. Follow U.S. 34 north 6 miles to County Road 6, an unimproved road. Drive 9 miles to the parking area at Monarch Lake. Permits ($4 reservation fee) are required for overnight camping June 1 to September 15; contact the **Sulphur Ranger District** at 970-887-4100.

Resources: Arapaho and Roosevelt National Forest maps are available at Sulphur or Boulder Ranger District offices. Use USGS Monarch Lake, Isolation Peak quads, and the "Trails Illustrated Indian Peaks Wilderness" map ($8.95). —DEBRA SHORE

THE MIDWEST

Achenbach Trail
Theodore Roosevelt National Park, western North Dakota

The Trail: This is the wilderness that thrilled President Theodore Roosevelt more than a century ago. Beginning from the Squaw Creek Campground, the 16-mile prairie path climbs from Little Missouri River bottomland up through the Achenbach Hills, drops to the river again, climbs to eroded clay buttes dotted with juniper and sage-brush, and returns along the river bottom to the campground. This is one of the least-visited national parks in the U.S., so odds are you'll have the backcountry to yourselves. The best campsites lie along the river, tucked beneath gnarled old cottonwoods where Teddy himself probably bedded down. Get free backcountry permits at the visitor center. Because of fire danger, camp stoves are required.

Things to Do: Set everyone down atop Sperati Point (about 9.5 miles from the trailhead) and scan the broken prairie for glimpses of deer, bison, pronghorn, coyotes, prairie dogs, and golden eagles. Take a star chart and maybe even a small telescope—on a clear night you can see stars 1,500 light-years away.

Local Wisdom: There are two spots where you'll have to ford the sluggish Little Mo; check with rangers about water levels before starting out. Stay well clear of bison—they can outrun a horse and are dangerous when provoked—and watch out for rattlesnakes.

The Way There: The park is 170 miles west of Bismarck. Take the Belfield exit on I-94 and go north on U.S. 85 for 60 miles to the North Unit Visitor Center. The trailhead is at the southern end of Squaw Creek Campground, 5 miles west of the visitor center.

Resources: Books and maps may be purchased from the Theodore Roosevelt Nature and History Association in Medora, west of Belfield on I-94; you'll want the North Unit USGS topo map ($4). For more information, call the **North Unit Visitor Center** at 701-842-2333.
—LARRY RICE

Angleworm Trail
Boundary Waters Canoe Area Wilderness, Minnesota

The Trail: Remember *Blueberries for Sal,* the children's classic by Robert McCloskey? Your biggest challenge on the Angleworm Trail—an easy 2.5-mile approach on an old fire trail and a 9-mile loop around Angleworm Lake—is likely to be dragging your kids (or spouse) away from the abundant native blueberries, ripe in late July and August. A few stream crossings along the way involve some hopping and skipping, and on the northern end you'll pass through a stand of 80- to 100-year-old red and white pines. Plan to spend 2 nights and 3 days doing the loop. The permit system limits the number of campers, so you'll enjoy relative solitude and can choose among the eight designated campsites around the lake, or make your own campsite farther away from the trail.

Things to Do: Cast for northerns in Angleworm Lake or walleye in nearby Home Lake (state fishing license required). Look for the remnants of an old sawmill camp at one of the designated campsites along the lakeshore.

Local Wisdom: Don't leave any valuables in your car (there have been break-ins at the trailhead parking lot).

The Way There: From Duluth, take U.S. 53 to Minnesota 169. The trailhead is 17 miles north of Ely, off County Road 644.

Resources: Reserve in advance by calling the **Boundary Waters Canoe Area Wilderness Reservation Service** at 800-745-3399 ($9 reservation fee; maximum group size is nine). You can pick up permits the day before your trip at the **Ely permit station** (218-365-7681), where you can also purchase a detailed map of the Superior National Forest ($4).

—DEBRA SHORE

Superior Hiking Trail
Minnesota

The Trail: A steep and narrow footpath following the ridgeline overlooking Lake Superior, the trail stretches more than 200 miles from Two Harbors to the Canadian border. The 34.3-mile section from Caribou River Wayside to the Lutsen Ski Area is a rugged marvel (recommended for children 12 and over because of its many steep stretches) whose sharp relief affords spectacular views of the lake and surrounding country. The trail heads up the beautiful and dramatic gorge of the Caribou River, crossing rivers, ponds, bogs, and creeks amid vegetation like the carnivorous pitcher plant, sundew, sphagnum moss, orchids, and blue-flag iris.

Things to Do: Check out the glacial potholes in the Temperance River gorge, where the rock has been scoured into kettles. There are countless short spur trails that lead to overlooks like Carlton and Britton peaks, with views that encompass the vast forests of maple, birch, aspen, and mixed conifers. Watch for moose, waterfowl, bears, and even wolves. Fish for trout and salmon in the streams, and be sure to bring along pancake batter to mix with the wild blueberries during July and August.

33

Local Wisdom: Sometimes fog settles in for days, though it usually burns off in the morning. There are no rangers or patrols here as the trail was built and is maintained by volunteers. Expect a rich variety of insect life.

The Way There: From Duluth, follow Minnesota 61 north for 92 miles and park at the Lutsen Ski Area. Then take the Superior Shuttle back to your starting point at Caribou River State Wayside (Friday through Monday, late May to mid-October; $6–$15 per person depending on the distance).

Resources: For maps, guidebook, and trail information, call the **Superior Hiking Trail Association** (218-834-2700). For the **Superior Shuttle,** call 218-834-5511. —DEBRA SHORE

Porcupine Mountains Wilderness State Park
Michigan

The Trail: Amid towering old-growth hemlocks and white pines along a 12-mile loop from Lake of the Clouds, you're likely to spot black bears, eagles, peregrine falcons, blue herons, cranes, and foxes. July and August are best for camping: The insects subside somewhat after the Fourth of July, and blueberries and thimbleberries are ripe for picking. From the Lake of the Clouds parking lot, hike three-quarters of a mile to the lake. From here, the North Mirror Lake Trail climbs steeply for one-half mile (you can reverse the loop to descend, rather than climb, this sec-tion) and then flattens out. Mirror Lake (4 miles from Lake of the Clouds) lies in the heart of the wilderness, surrounded by rugged bluffs and tall pines. The 50-plus back-country campsites are first-come, first-served. Head back to Lake of the Clouds via the Correction Line Trail and the Big Carp River Trail. Use binoculars to scope out peregrine falcons in the cliffs.

Things to Do: On a side trail, hike 2 miles south of Mirror Lake to Summit Peak and its observation tower. Go waterfall-hunting (there are more than 90 in the park, many uncharted; check at the visitors center for leads).

Local Wisdom: Remember your bear-avoidance techniques: Hang your food at some distance from your campsite and allow no food in your tents. Check with rangers about park conditions. Windstorms often cause substantial blowdowns, and water levels vary with melt-off and rain.

The Way There: The park is 2½ hours from Marquette, Michigan. Take U.S. 41, which turns into Michigan 28, to Bruce Crossing; then head north on U.S. 45 to Ontonagon. From there, drive west 14 miles on Michigan 64 to the park's visitor center; continue another 7 miles on Michigan 107 to the Lake of the Clouds parking area. Permits ($6 per night) are required for backcountry camping (one to four persons). Register at the visitor center (10 A.M.–6 P.M.) or at park headquarters after hours; call 906-885-5275.

Resources: A detailed map is available from the park ($2.95); USGS quads for the Mirror Lake loop are Government Peak, Carp River, and Tiebel Creek. Get *The Porkies Companion*, by Bob Sprague and Mike Rafferty ($11.95), at park headquarters. —DEBRA SHORE

THE SOUTH

Hemmed-In Hollow Trail
Buffalo National River,
northwest Arkansas

The Trail: It's a 2-day, 10.8-mile round-trip to Hemmed-In Hollow, with the highest waterfall (175 feet) between the Appalachians and Rockies, via the Center Point Trailhead. The trail climbs and edges a high bluff, then enters the hills and sculpted side hollows, forests, and meadows of the Ponca Wilderness Area. Frequent overlooks offer broad panoramic views of the Ozarks and the Buffalo River valley. At Hemmed-In Hollow, the free-leaping waterfall spills over the lip of the bluff, straight down to the narrow canyon's rocky floor. You can explore around, behind, and below the falls, but be careful: The rocks are slippery. Camping is allowed anywhere at least 100 feet from the trail or river, but not around Hemmed-In Hollow itself. Backcountry permits aren't required, but it's a good idea to apprise rangers of your plans.

Things to Do: This is a good place to teach your kids to use a map and compass, as intersecting trails can sometimes become confusing. Budding naturalists can spot armadillos, road-runners, and tarantulas coexisting with white-tailed deer, bobcats, mink, beavers, elk, and black bears. Smallmouth bass is the game fish of choice (state fishing license required).

Local Wisdom: To reach Hemmed-In Hollow you'll hike 1,300 feet down to the river—the trip out is unexpectedly steep, especially for kids under 10. For a real appreciation of the area's heritage, sign up for a full-day "Ecotour," led by **Ozark Ecotours** ($45 including lunch; call 501-446-5898).

The Way There: Hemmed-In Hollow is a 3-hour drive northwest of Little Rock. The trailhead is on Arkansas 43, 22.5 miles south of park headquarters in Harrison.

Resources: Get the Trails Illustrated Topo Map "Buffalo National River: West Half" ($8.50) from the **Buffalo National River** (501-741-5443), as well as *Buffalo River Hiking Trails*, by Tim Ernst ($14.95; 800-838-4453). —LARRY RICE

Good Spring Loop Trail
Mammoth Cave National Park,
south-central Kentucky

The Trail: Visitors to Mammoth Cave National Park come primarily to tour the longest cave system in the world, with more than 350 miles of known passageways. By contrast, the park's surface world is one few people explore. This is a mistake, because the pit-marked, rolling terrain harbors one of the largest virgin forests in Kentucky, as well as 70 miles of hiking trails. The 8-mile Good Spring Loop Trail, a moderate 2-day route, winds up and down oak-covered ridges, along pebbly stream beds, and through breezeless hollows laced with small caves and waterfalls. Scattered sinkholes and limestone outcroppings help kids understand the worlds both above and below ground. There are three campsites, all with a nearby water source; backcountry permits (free) are required for all overnight trips.

Things to Do: At night, the ghostly hollows echoing with the call of whippoorwills and owls make a perfect setting for scary campfire tales. When you're done exploring the surface, go underground. Some thirteen ranger-guided cave trips cover 14 miles of trails. If you only have time for one, try the 3½-hour "Introduction to Caving" tour—you'll crawl, climb, and walk along passageways off the usual tour routes. Helmets and lights are provided by the park; you furnish knee-pads and gloves that you don't mind getting slimed. Tickets cost $17.50 for adults, $10 for children 8 to 12; call **Destinet** at 800-967-2283.

Local Wisdom: At the trailhead, visit the Good Spring Church cemetery, where the weathered tombstones attest to the hard life on the frontier—many died young. Raccoons can be a problem here if your camp isn't clean.

The Way There: The park is 95 miles south of Louisville. Exit I-65 at Park City or Cave City, 2 and 5 miles, respectively, from the park entrance. Get your backcountry permit at the visitor center, cross the Green River by ferry, and then drive about 3 miles to the trailhead.

Resources: Mammoth Cave National Park (502-758-2328) has maps, publications, and guidebooks.

—LARRY RICE

John Muir Trail
Tennessee/Kentucky

The Trail: Straddling the Tennessee/ Kentucky border, the Big South Fork National River and Recreation Area protects more than 100,000 acres of lushly vegetated ridges and valleys along the scenic and remote Cumberland Plateau, a large, flat-topped tableland rising more than 1,000 feet. The 50-mile John Muir Trail, named for the pioneering naturalist, starts at the O & W Bridge and ends at Pickett State Park. The trail shadows the Big South Fork River for much of its length, passing deep forests, historic homes, canyons, and waterfalls. Commanding bluffs provide panoramic overlooks of the Big South Fork countryside, and there's plenty of exploring to do among the sandstone arches and rock shelters. Plan on at least 4 days to explore the whole stretch; although there isn't much elevation change, you still have some distance to cover.

Things to Do: A great spot to camp is Fall Branch, reached by following the trail north along the west side of the Big South Fork River from the Leatherwood Ford trailhead parking area. A quarter-mile bushwhacking hike from the campsite is Angel Falls, a nasty Class III–IV rapid. Where the trail merges with the river, fisherkids can try their luck for bass and catfish. After a spell of tenting, you might want to sample the creature comforts of the **Charit Creek Lodge** (adults,

$46; children 10 and under, $36; breakfast and dinner included; 423-429-5704). The rustic, full-service establishment, accessible only by foot, mountain bike, or horse, is located 4.1 miles up Station Camp Creek Trail where it crosses the John Muir Trail, 20.4 miles in. There is no electricity, but cabins are equipped with kerosene lamps and woodstoves.

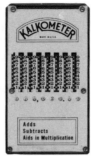

Local Wisdom: June to mid-July and September are the prime times; late July and August are usually hot and humid.

The Way There: The trailhead lies about 80 miles northwest of Knoxville. From Oneida, take Tennessee 297 west 15 miles to the Big South Fork visitor center (where you can get free backcountry use permits).

Resources: Good reference books are *Trails of the Big South Fork: A Guide for Hikers, Bikers, and Horse Riders* ($12.95), by Russ Manning and Sondra Jamieson, and *Hiking the Big South Fork* ($10.95), by Brenda D. Coleman and Jo Anna Smith. These, as well as "Trails Illustrated Big South Fork Map" ($8.95), are available from **Big South Fork National River and Recreation Area** (615-879-4890).   —LARRY RICE

THE NORTHEAST

Phelps Trail
Adirondack Park, New York

The Trail: Children always want what's biggest and best. An 18-mile out-and-back hike on the Phelps Trail takes them to New York's highest peak, 5,344-foot Mount Marcy. The first day is an easy to moderate climb of 3.5 miles, from the Garden parking area in Keene Valley, through thick forests and across several streams to Johns Brook Lodge. There, families can overnight in bunk rooms or lean-tos, or pitch tents near the trail. Head up Mount Marcy early the next morning; it's a moderate to steep 5.5-mile, 3,000-foot climb.

Things to Do: The 360-degree panorama of unbroken forest and mountain peaks from Mount Marcy leaves no doubt that you're inside the greatest public wilderness this side of the Mississippi. Plan on spending at least an hour on the rocky dome, helping your children pick out other peaks with a map and binoculars. The next day, climb one of the less-trafficked mountains: Johns Brook Lodge sits at the hub of a trail system fanning out to peaks such as Gothics, Saddleback, and the Wolfjaws; you can make day hikes for a week without running out of mountains.

Local Wisdom: Make your ascent of Marcy on a less crowded weekday. You'll need to arrive at the small Garden trailhead parking area before 9 A.M. to find a spot. If it's full, park in Keene, 1.6 miles away.

The Way There: From Albany and points south take I-87, the Adirondack Northway, to exit 30. Follow New York 73 north for 11 miles to Keene Valley and turn left in town at Adirondack

Park's wooden sign that directs you to the trailhead. Parties of ten and under do not need a permit to camp overnight. Lean-tos are made available on a first-come, first-served basis. Reservations are required for bunks at rustic (no electricity) **Johns Brook Lodge** (age 12 and up, $41; under 12, $18.50, including breakfast).

Resources: For Johns Brook Lodge reservations and information, contact the Adirondack Mountain Club's **Adirondack Loj** at 518-523-3441. The essential guide and map to the area is the club's *Guide to Adirondack Trails: High Peaks Region* ($16.95 for both). To order, call 800-395-8080.

—THURSTON CLARKE

The Basin-Cascade Trail
White Mountains National Forest,
New Hampshire

The Trail: This 3.1-mile trail leads through red spruce and balsam fir to Lonesome Lake, a shallow tarn at 2,734 feet and the site of the Appalachian Mountain Club's most family-friendly hut. The trail departs from The Basin, a deep granite pothole carved by the Pemigewasset River. After crossing a tricky log bridge near the half-mile mark, you come to Kinsman Falls and, one-half mile farther, the fiercer Rocky Glen Falls. The trek takes 3 to 4 hours, even with young children. The hut sleeps 44 in two bunkhouses; there's no camping except for the Lafayette Campground, which isn't far from the trailhead.

Things to Do: If you have older kids, you might make the 4-hour round-trip to the summit of 4,100-foot Cannon Mountain (and bask in superiority watching the sandal-footed tourists disembark from the tramway). Work your way back to the hut via Kinsman Ridge to Kinsman Pond (about 6.5 miles). Young kids enjoy circumnavigating the lake on a well-marked, boggy trail. At the hut, naturalists sometimes conduct family nature walks, pointing out chipmunks, red squirrels, black ducks, and abandoned beaver dams.

Local Wisdom: Black flies can be nasty from late May through July; protect yourself with long pants, long sleeves, bandannas, and hats.

The Way There: From Boston, about 2½ hours away, take I-93 north to Lincoln, New Hampshire, south of Franconia Notch. Just north of mile marker 106, exit at the sign for The Basin and follow signs to the parking lot.

Resources: For hut reservations (strongly recommended), call the **Appalachian Mountain Club** at 603-466-2727 (adult nonmember rate, $57–$62 per night; adult members, $50–$55; child nonmembers, $34–$39; child members, $27–$32). Find the trail on USGS Franconia and Lincoln maps. Good reference books are *Best Hikes with Children in Vermont, New Hampshire, and Maine*, by Cynthia C. Lewis and Thomas J. Lewis ($12.95, The Mountaineers), and *High Huts of The White Mountains*, by William E. Reifsnyder ($10.95, Appalachian Mountain Club Books).

—MEG LUKENS NOONAN

Hundred Mile Wilderness Trail
Maine

The Trail: The northernmost section of the 2,135-mile Appalachian Trail, known as the Hundred Mile Wilderness Trail, snakes through some of the least-developed forest in the country. From the small town of Monson in the south to the pinnacle of 5,267-foot Mt. Katahdin at trail's end, this area of central Maine is home to more than 10 million acres of boreal forest. That's the equivalent of five Yellowstones with a Yosemite thrown in for good measure. But unlike those two popular national parks, this region of Maine is not even designated a national forest, virtually guaranteeing obscurity. On any given day in summer you're more likely to see moose, beavers, and loons than other hikers. This remote trail is ideal for families who want to get lost in wave after wave of spruce, firs, and maples, the mass of green interrupted only by ponds and rivers. The trail takes roughly 12 days to complete, but you can cut the hike in half by stopping at Jo-Mary Road, near Cooper Brook Falls, where a string of lean-tos and campsites are spaced roughly a day's hike apart.

Things to Do: This up-and-down trail is a thigh-burner for everyone, especially children under 8, who might find the hiking far too strenuous. Indeed, the elevation gain northbound is close to 17,000 feet. Take breaks at spots like Gulf Hagas, a 2.5-mile gorge that's ideal for swimming and picnicking. All along the route are fishing holes teeming with brook or lake trout.

Local Wisdom: With its cool nights and warm days, late August is the best time to try the trail. The black flies are long gone, wild blueberries are in season, and the first tinges of fall color begin to light up the route.

The Way There: From Portland, take I-95 north to Exit 39 at Newport. Follow Maine 7 north, changing to Maine 23 north in Dexter. In Guilford, follow Maine 6 west to Monson. The trailhead is 4 miles north of Monson at the junction of Maine 6 and the Appalachian Trail. To hear about the highlights from Appalachian Trail through-hikers, spend a night at legendary **Shaw's Boarding House** (bunks, $15 per person; private rooms, $20–$45; 207-997-3597) in Monson, a favorite hikers' haunt. Shaw can also shuttle your car from Monson to Jo-Mary Road for $10 an hour (approximately $50).

Resources: For excellent topos and descriptions of the trail, write to the **Maine Appalachian Trail Club,** P.O. Box 283, Augusta, ME 04332, for a copy of their indispensable *Appalachian Trail Guide to Maine* ($24.95). For further information, contact the **Maine Publicity Bureau** at 800-533-9595.

—STEPHEN JERMANOK

3

Here's what most of us know intuitively: Children are born to be outside. For several thousand generations, children were happily born outside, raised outside, and were allowed to rage outside. So are we going to allow a few decades of electricity and "Sesame Street" to change all that? Nope. Parents are responsible for having transformed kids into indoor beings, and we are necessarily obligated to provide them an opportunity to feel at home with their natural birthright. It's good for them, and it's also a hell of a lot of fun for us.

My wife and I started taking our sons out in the canoe when they were infants, and by the time they were 2 or 3 we were going on camping trips. As soon as they were able to paddle, at about 5 or 6 years old, we let them, and we also asked for their help in setting up camp, building the fire, and preparing the meals. By the time they were 9 or 10, we no longer "took" them paddling. It was more like a partnership: Buddies out there on the water, playing it safe but having fun.

Canoe Camping
Now, Voyageurs!

Don't dwell on worst-case scenarios, but anticipate them and provide against them. For instance, if the boat dumps, will you be close enough to shore to recover? Are your first-aid kit and cell phone protected in a waterproof flotation box? Keep the uninterrupted stretches of paddling short, and make the periods of kick-back time long. When my sons were about 3 or 4, I'd place a little bucket of stones in front of them (kids love to throw stuff into water), and when the stones were gone, I knew it was time to head for shore. Which is where I would allow them to roam and rage. It's what children are born to do.   —RANDY WAYNE WHITE

THE SOUTHWEST

Green River
Utah

Canyons, slickrock waterfalls, weird rock formations, and American Indian ruins along the Green's last 120 miles excite even the most jaded teen. One of America's premier flatwater floats, the trip south, from the town of Green River to the Green's confluence with the mighty Colorado, is for parental units with backcountry experience and adventurous older children. There are just three places to bail out: Ruby Ranch, 25 miles downstream from the put-in; Mineral Bottom, 70 miles downstream and accessible via a dirt track; and Spanish Bottom, at the confluence. Two outfitters licensed to operate in Canyonlands National Park retrieve paddlers from Spanish Bottom (arrange in advance) and jet-boat them to Moab.

The key to enjoying the Lower Green: Don't rush it. Budget plenty of time for serendipity and exploration. The paddle from the put-in to Ruby Ranch takes in parched high-desert plains. Below the ranch, just after the San Rafael enters from the west, high sandstone walls rise hundreds of feet form the phantasmagorical gorge of Labyrinth Canyon.

Jaw-Dropper: Just below Mineral Bottom, the Green snakes through Stillwater Canyon. Sheer riverside walls tower 400 feet; the rim, stepped back in terraces, is another 1,500 feet higher.

Digression: A mile-long trail at Spanish Bottom gains 1,500 feet to reach the Doll House, a cluster of stone towers and other odd formations.

The Green in a Nutshell: Put-In/ Take-Out: Crystal Geyser/ Spanish Bottom. **Length:** 120 miles; 5 to 7 days. **Prime Time:** Mid-May to mid-June; temperatures are 100-plus in July and August. **Traffic:** Light. **Rapids/Portages:** None. **Facilities:** Wilderness camping along the Lower Green; permits for wilderness camping required in Canyonlands. **Outfitters: Tex's Riverways** (801-259-5101); **Tag-A-Long Expeditions** (801-259-8946). **Information: Canyonlands Na-**

tional Park (801-259-7164); **Utah's Canyonlands Region** (800-635-6622 or 801-259-8825). —DAVID DUNBAR

THE MIDWEST

Upper Missouri National Wild and Scenic River
Montana

The Upper Missouri National Wild and Scenic River is a place where one can easily imagine what it was like when Blackfeet Indians and 60 million bison roamed the endless plains. Extending for 149 miles from Fort Benton, Montana, to the U.S. 191 bridge at James Kipp Recreation Area, the Upper Missouri is part of the Lewis and Clark National Historic Trail, as well as one of the best canoe floats in the nation. The vistas along the river seem little changed from the way Lewis and Clark described them in 1805 during their epic 2½-year journey to the Pacific: The prairie buttes and bluffs of the Missouri Breaks are just as lonely, and the White Cliffs rising over the valley are just as stunning.

On an early summer float, you're likely to see bighorn sheep, deer, and pronghorn antelope, as well as elk, coyotes, beavers, bald and golden eagles, and all kinds of waterfowl. Take turns with the kids reading passages out loud from *The Journals of Lewis and Clark*, or a loose-leaf copy called *River History Digest* that's available on loan from the Bureau of Land Management or from your outfitter.

Jaw-Dropper: At 56 river miles from Fort Benton, look to the right for the

---

Inside Skinny

Rocker On
Like in-line hockey skates, canoe keels may or may not be rockered. Puckheads adjust wheel heights on their skates, making the middle two lower than the ones at each end. This technique, called rockering, enhances your ability to turn quickly—though speed suffers. The same is true of canoe keels: The more turned-up the ends, the greater the maneuverability, which is what the whitewater set looks for. Tourers, who want to eke as much speed as possible out of the calmer waters, tend to favor a straighter keel.

For Paddle Elitists...
To get psyched for your upcoming trip, read the works of Canadian author and conservationist Bill Mason. *Song of the Paddle* is a comprehensive guide to canoeing, camping, and outdoor living; *Path of the Paddle* is the definitive illustrated guide to the art of canoeing. The latter includes a foreword written by former Canadian Prime Minister Pierre Trudeau, another canoe enthusiast. Your local bookstore probably carries these classics. If not, the publisher (Key Porter Books, Toronto) suggests that your bookstore order them for you.

Eye of the Needle, a sandstone arch perched on a 200-foot cliff. Follow a brief, well-worn trail through an outcropping of steep rock to the rim of the White Cliffs.

Digression: The White Cliffs area, about a third of the way into the trip around mile 51, is a long stretch of sandstone spires and cliffs where gargoylelike stone formations jut out of the sloping hillsides. Here also are the Hole-in-the-Wall, Indian teepee circles, abandoned homesteader cabins, and Lewis and Clark historical campsites.

STAYING SAFE: BUG JUICES

Bugs like water—so expect some close encounters with this less-than-appealing slice of wildlife. Insect repellent is essential, of course, but it's not without controversy. The consensus in wilderness medical circles is that the first line of defense is to spray clothes and netting with Permethrin, a safe and effective insecticide derived from the chrysanthemum plant. But bugs can bite before they're killed by insecticides: Your family will also need repellent to keep bugs at bay.

Deet is the most effective—though, to many parents, the most repelling—concoction. It's toxic, and has caused seizures in children when overapplied at full strength. Dr. Eric A. Weiss, an assistant professor of emergency medicine at Stanford University's Medical Center and board member of the Wilderness Medical Society, thinks deet may suffer a bad rap. "Extrapolations from the severest cases are used to make generalizations about the product that aren't justified," Weiss says, adding that there's virtually no risk when a concentration of 17 to 20 percent deet is applied a few times a day. This will repel biting insects and, to a lesser extent, ticks (which transmit such diseases as Rocky Mountain spotted fever and Lyme disease). Cautious parents will want to apply deet products over sunscreen to minimize absorption into the skin and maximize the repellent's bug-shooing effects.

However, Buck Tilton, director of the Wilderness Medicine Institute, isn't prepared to endorse deet so heartily. "Deet is absorbed into the skin, and not all of that is discharged in the urine," he says. "It's stored in the body somewhere and it's too early to tell what that might mean." Nontoxic products, like Avon's Skin-So-Soft and those that contain citronella, are about 10 to 15 percent as effective as deet: They repel insects by coating the skin; once absorbed, their repelling abilities are lost, so reapply them every 30 minutes.

The Upper Missouri in a Nutshell: Put-In/Take-Out: The Wild and Scenic portion of the river begins at the upriver end of the town of Fort Benton, Montana, and runs 149 miles to the U.S. 191 bridge at James Kipp Recreation Area. **Length:** Float trips of various lengths are possible, from weekend jaunts to the 5- to 8-day journey that traverses the full 149 miles. **Prime Time:** Summer is a good time, but be prepared for extremes in weather. Midafternoon temperatures can exceed 90 degrees, while an evening thunderstorm can push temperatures down into the mid-40s. **Traffic:** Generally very light, but it can get crowded on holiday weekends. **Rapids/Portages:** None. The river can be run by canoeists of average ability. **Facilities:** There are excellent camping areas along the river on BLM land. Permits are not necessary. For variety, stop in at Virgelle, a charming ghost town along the river with a population of 3. Don Sorensen, the self-proclaimed mayor, runs what may be the most unusual B&B on the High Plains—a mercantile building built in 1912 and restored homestead cabins. Costs range from $20 per person for the cabins to $70 (for two) for lodging in the old general store. Call 800-426-2926 for reservations. **Outfitters:** For rentals, guides, or shuttle service, contact Missouri River Canoe Co. (800-426-2926). **Information: Bureau of Land Management, Lewistown District** (406-538-7461). Inquire about the *Floater's Guide to the Upper Missouri* (detailed maps loaded with descriptive text, $8).

—LARRY RICE

Voyageurs National Park
Minnesota

Two centuries ago this fur-rich country along the Canadian border was traversed only by Native Americans and French-Canadian *voyageurs* in their birch-bark canoes. Today, the 218,000-acre park adjoins a stretch of the "voyageurs highway" between Lake Superior and Lake of the Woods, and is the perfect setting for a family canoe outing.

With four major lakes and twenty-six smaller lakes, there are many routes within the park; however, the premier canoe trip is the circumnavigation of the Kabetogama Peninsula, a 75,000-acre roadless area, 26 miles long and about 6 miles across. The journey takes in most of the park's big lakes, meaning you and your young navigators will have some 500 islands and countless coves and bays to explore. The lake system is renowned as some of the best walleye water in the nation, and you can spot whitetail deer, beavers, river otters, bald eagles, black bears, moose, and wolves.

Jaw-Dropper: Paddle east upon exiting Black Bay Narrows (near the Rainy Lake Visitor Center), and you'll be greeted by large and small islands and limitless blue water. For the next few days you'll cruise along the rugged north shore of the Kabetogama Peninsula.

Digression: At the head of Anderson Bay is the 9.4-mile Cruiser Lake Hiking Trail, which bisects the peninsula. A series of ridges leads up to vistas of distant lakes and ponds, then drops down into dense ravines before reaching mile-long Cruiser Lake about 4 miles in.

Voyageurs in a Nutshell: Put-In/Take-Out: Roads approach the park from four points along U.S. 53 between Duluth and International Falls. A good place to start and end your trip is the Ash River Visitor Center on Kabetogama Lake. To get there, exit U.S. 53 onto County Road 129 (the Ash River Trail), and go east for about 11 miles. Follow signs to the Ash River Visitor Center. **Length:** The 75-mile circumnavigation of the Kabetogama Peninsula by canoe or kayak generally requires 6 to 8 days. A variety of shorter trips are also possible. **Prime Time:** Late July and August and the first 2 weeks of September are best; temperatures are generally comfortable and black flies are pretty much gone. **Traffic:** Since the area is a known fishing hotspot and motorboats are allowed in most waters, you'll be wise to avoid the weekends in midsummer. **Rapids/Portages:** Only two short portages are necessary: Gold Portage skirts a rapid between Kabetogama Lake and Rainy Lake; the other portage is at Kettle Falls, the site of a small turn-of-the-century dam. **Facilities:** More than 120 campsites are located on islands or near lakeshores and are accessible only by watercraft. Each is equipped with a table, tent pad, fire ring, and an

45

open-pit toilet; bring a water filter. There are also 250 other primitive sites in Voyageurs; no permits are required for backcountry camping. **Outfitters:** Contact the national park for a complete list of canoe concessionaires. **Information: Voyageurs National Park** (218-283-9821). **Recommended Reading:** *Voyageurs National Park Water Routes, Foot Paths and Ski Trails,* by Jim DuFresne, and *Voyageurs National Park,* by Greg Breining, both published by **Lake States Interpretive Association** (218-283-2103). —LARRY RICE

Niobrara River
Nebraska

This prairie waterway flows wide and shallow between high sandstone cliffs at the northern edge of the grass-covered Sand Hills of Nebraska. Before hitting the water, thrill the kids with windshield close-ups of bison, elk, and Texas longhorns in the exhibition pasture of the Fort Niobrara National Wildlife Refuge, just east of Valentine. Then launch your canoe at Cornell Bridge, near the refuge's western boundary, and start scanning the grasslands and wooded breaks for otters, beavers, red-tailed hawks, wild turkeys, and herons. The Niobrara is a biological crossroads where six ecosystems overlap. Ponderosa pine and cedar line the upper canyon walls, while gullies are forested with burr oak, ash, and black walnut.

Lots of families tie inner tubes behind their canoes and let the kids freeload. A Niobrara tube isn't a standard-issue butt-wetter; it's a gigantic tractor-tire inner tube with a canvas deck. Rocky Ford, site of a natural rock dam, tends to bang up canoes—but the 3-foot drop is perfect for tubing runs.

Jaw-Dropper: Okay, maybe only an eyebrow-archer, but more than

HIRED HANDS

The Chewonki Foundation (207-882-7323) leads a 6-day Down East canoe trip on the St. Croix River in northeastern Maine. You'll paddle a 33-mile stretch of Class I and II rapids, watching for nesting bald eagles and fishing for smallmouth bass. The trip runs from August 17 to 22, and costs $575 for adults, $475 for kids 12 and under (the minimum age is 10).

Wells Gray Park Backcountry Chalets (604-587-6444) operates a number of 6-day canoe trips on the Azure and Clearwater lakes of Wells Gray Provincial Park, in the southern Cariboo Mountains of eastern British Columbia. Trips run June 22, July 6 and 20, and August 17 and 31. The cost is C$600 per person, with 25 percent off for kids 13 and under.

Bear Cub Adventure Tours (518-523-4339) makes New York's Adirondack Park its stomping grounds, leading a 5-day trip up the Bog River to Lows Lake, a good basecamp for hiking and fishing. The custom trip costs $2,000 for a family of four.

ninety-three waterfalls spill into the Niobrara on this stretch, and some thirty are visible from the river in mid-summer. To amuse the kids, turn cataract-counting into a competitive sport.

Digression: About 12 miles downstream from Cornell Bridge, in Smith Falls State Park, a quarter-mile creekside trail heads up-canyon through sun-dappled stands of birch and pine to Smith Falls—at 67 feet, the highest in Nebraska.

The Niobrara in a Nutshell: Put-In/Take-Out: Cornell Bridge, 4 miles east of Valentine in the Fort Niobrara National Wildlife Refuge/Egelhoff's Narrows. **Length:** 30 miles; 2 days. **Prime Time:** Anytime except July—it's a scorcher. **Traffic:** Fairly heavy on summer weekends. **Rapids/Portages:** Rocky Ford (Class II), Kuhre's Rapids (Class III). **Facilities:** Nine commercial campgrounds and one public campground (Smith Falls State Park). **Outfitters: Dryland Aquatics** (800-337-3119 or 402-376-3119), **Brewers Canoers** (402-376-2046), and **Graham Canoe Outfitters** (402-376-3708). **Information: Niobrara/Missouri National Scenic Riverways** (402-336-3970), **Valentine Chamber of Commerce** (402-376-2969).—DAVID DUNBAR

Eleven Point River
Missouri

Flowing southeast through the Ozarks of southern Missouri, the Eleven Point offers some of the finest river-running and canoe camping in the Midwest. With clear water, forested banks, rocky bluffs, and countless springs, this National Scenic River meanders for much of its 44-mile length through a living tunnel of box elders, river birches, and sycamores. The surrounding hills and hollers shelter a variety of wildlife, from whitetail deer and beaver to bobcat and the occasional coyote. Bring binoculars to spot pileated woodpeckers, kingfishers, red-shouldered hawks, great blue herons, and wild turkeys.

Be sure to take along a mask, snorkel, and fins; underwater visibility is usually excellent. If the kids would rather catch fish than watch them, select their lures for rock and smallmouth bass. Along the river are Civil War–era grist mills, old moonshiner stills, and boom holes—where logs were loaded onto rail cars around the turn of the century.

Jaw-Dropper: The section of river from Cane Bluff to Greer Crossing (9.3 to 16.4 miles from the put-in) is marked by several towering bluffs, rising as high as 250 feet, where hikers can get a commanding view of the river.

Digression: More than thirty natural springs supply the Eleven Point, issuing from limestone formations full of caves and sinkholes. About 1 mile up the outlet 16 miles from Thomasville is Greer Spring, the second-largest spring in Missouri with an outflow of 220 million gallons of water a day.

The Eleven Point in a Nutshell: Put-In/Take-Out: Launch at Missouri 99 at Thomasville and pull out at The Narrows at the Missouri 142 bridge. **Length:** 44 miles; 3 to 4 days of easy floating. **Prime Time:** Early summer is best; the water is still high and the afternoon sun is warm. **Traffic:** Summer weekends can be hectic, so go midweek. **Rapids/Portages:** The water is generally smooth, though it has occasional twists, turns, and logjams. The trip is suitable for beginners. **Facilities:** Eight to ten "float camps" (equipped with table, latrine, tent pad, and fire ring) are staggered along the river, but many paddlers pitch their tents on gravel bars or in wooded bottoms. One especially good pullover is at Horseshoe Bend (about 26 miles below Thomasville), where the river curves around a narrow ridge among groves of oaks and shortleaf pine. The Forest Service also maintains four auto-access campgrounds. **Outfitters:** Canoe rental and shuttle service are available at **Hufstedler's Store & Canoe Rental** (417-778-6116) in Riverton, **Richards Canoe Rental** (417-778-6186) in Greer, and **Woods' Float & Canoe Rental** (417-778-6497) in Alton. You can rent a canoe for $26 per day; vehicle shuttles average $15 to $18. **Information: Eleven Point Ranger District** (573-325-4233); **Forest Supervisor, Mark Twain National Forest** (573-364-4621). A free river map is available.   —LARRY RICE

The Temagami
Ontario, Canada

In the rock-ribbed Canadian Shield, an intricate jigsaw of lakes and rivers frets the vast sweep of boreal forest. As a result, trippers can create improvisations on established canoe trails—especially in the Temagami region, about 300 miles north of Toronto, near the boundary of Ontario and Québec. With nearly 1,500 miles of routes in 2,000 square miles, you could spend decades paddling this watery maze without repeating yourself.

One novice 6-day in-and-out route starts at Mowat Landing, off Highway 58. Paddle southwest, portage around Mattawapika Dam, then continue on Lady Evelyn River into Lady Evelyn Lake. Next, head through Obasiga Narrows, then west into Sucker Gut Lake. From there, paddle north into Hobart Lake and follow Willow Island Creek, then Tupper Creek, finally ending up in Tupper Lake.

Digression: A 3-mile trail from Tupper Lake climbs Maple Mountain, which rises more than 1,000 feet above the surrounding lakeland. From a summit fire tower, 25-mile views extend in all directions.

The Temagami in a Nutshell: Put-In/Take-Out: Mowat Landing. **Length:** About 48 miles; 6 days. **Prime Time:** Anytime except early June, when

DON'T FORGET...
waterproof matches
bug repellent
pocket knife
mosquito head-net
flashlight
extra batteries
rain hat
marshmallows

the bugs are fiercest. **Traffic:** Moderate on lakes with road access; light elsewhere. **Rapids/Portages:** Two. **Facilities:** Campsites are plentiful along the whole route. **Outfitters: Smoothwater** (705-569-3539). **Information: Ontario Recreational Canoeing Association** (416-426-7170). —DAVID DUNBAR

THE SOUTH

Peace River
Florida

This aptly named blackwater river, suitable for children of all ages, flows south from Florida's central lake district, becoming estuarial long before it eases into the Gulf of Mexico at Charlotte Harbor, just north of Fort Myers. One of the state's longest waterways, the Peace is also one of its wildest—only the occasional bridge and power line intrude on your subtropical backcountry experience. Lined in places with powdery white sand, the river glides past mossy overhanging cypress trees, willow groves, and palmetto thickets.

Anglers land bass, bream, and catfish from the tea-colored water. Watch for herons, red-shouldered hawks, and snowy cattle egrets. You'll also tally otters, turtles, and deer.

The Peace supplies its own souvenirs. Get your kids to pack a shovel and sifter, look for gravely or rocky places low along the riverbank, then dig for the fossilized teeth of sharks, mammoths, and primitive horses—maybe even the vertebrae of prehistoric whales.

Jaw-Dropper: A 15-foot, knobbly backed "log" on the riverbank suddenly rises and jumps into the river with a tremendous splash: an alligator. Though a fair number of them patrol the Peace, no paddler has ever been attacked.

Digression: About 10 miles downstream from the Fort Meade Bridge, take a half-mile woodland walk along Paynes Creek to a state historic site where five Seminoles killed a pair of traders in 1849. Kids get a kick out of guides in period dress, a 6-pound cannon, and a 100-foot suspension footbridge over the creek.

The Peace in a Nutshell: Put-In/Take-Out: The state-designated Peace River Canoe Trail runs south, from the Fort Meade Bridge to the State Road 70 Bridge, west of Arcadia. **Length:** 67 miles, 4 or 5 days. **Prime Time:** Late May, early June; July and August are buggy and hot. **Traffic:** Crowded on spring weekends; quieter during the summer. **Rapids/Portages:** None. **Facilities:** Two commercial campgrounds; wilderness camping along most of the canoe trail. **Outfitters: Canoe Outpost** (941-494-1215), **Canoe Safari** (941-494-7865). **Information: Florida Department of Environmental Protection, Office of Greenways and Trails** (904-487-4784). —DAVID DUNBAR

THE NORTHEAST

Saco River
New Hampshire/Maine

One of New England's most popular canoeing rivers rises in the White Mountains of New Hampshire, flows southeast through a wide valley of farmlands and forests in Maine, and empties into the sea at Saco, south of Portland. A 40-mile stretch from Center Conway, New Hampshire, to Hiram, Maine, is just right for families with young children: The water's clean and shallow (2 to 4 feet deep in summer), and you can picnic and camp almost anywhere. If the kids get antsy, they can drop a line for brook trout and bass, dive into a riverbed swimming hole, or explore the miles of beaches that line the banks.

Jaw-Dropper: Even old canoe hands express amazement at finding such clear water and white sand in New England.

Digression: About 21 miles downstream from Center Conway, a mile-long channel leads to Lovewell Pond, where paddlers are rewarded with views of Mount Washington and other peaks in New Hampshire's Presidential Range.

The Saco in a Nutshell: Put-In/Take-Out: Center Conway, New Hampshire/Hiram, Maine. **Length:** 43 miles; 3 days. **Prime Time:** May and June; the water gets low in July. **Traffic:** Heavy on summer weekends. **Rapids:** One short section of Class I. **Portages:** An optional 20-yard end run around the remains of a wooden dam at Walker's Falls, and a mandatory 300-yard portage around the minihydro dam at Swan's Falls. **Facilities:** Four commercial campgrounds (just the basics) and two campgrounds operated by the Appalachian Mountain Club; camping permitted on unposted sandbars from the Maine state line to Hiram. **Outfitters: Saco Bound** (603-447-2177), **Canal Bridge Canoes** (207-935-2605), **Saco River Canoe & Kayak** (207-935-2369), **River Run** (207-452-2500), and **Woodland Acres Camp 'n Canoe** (207-935-2529). **Information: Appalachian Mountain Club** (603-466-2721).

—DAVID DUNBAR

4

My entire family bikes. It all started about 10 years ago when my dad bought a bike to stay in shape and persuaded my mom to try it. She did—and got totally psyched. Dad is still a fitness rider, but Mom loves to compete. She's rated Category III on the roads and races beginner on mountain bikes.

I take full credit for getting her into mountain biking: I was tour racing on the roads by the time I was 6. Then, 3 years ago (I was 11), I got my Cannondale N300, and that was it. There's nothing better than clicking into high gear and pedaling down hills. I live to catch air, and I even like the uphills (pain is good). Sure, I crash; I've even trashed a few helmets in my day. I ride hard (after all, I'll heal)—but not irresponsibly.

As a matter of fact, I actually find myself worrying about my parents when we

Mountain Biking All You Need Is Dirt

ride together. While I don't think twice about crashing, I really don't want them to get hurt (and they rarely do). But I find myself bombing along, getting way out ahead, then stopping until I have them in view.

I'm proud of them, especially my mom. I don't know many other riders who are as hard-core as my mom. There are times when she's been riding, dressed in her gear, and drops something off at school for me. The other kids think she's pretty cool. So do I.

—VINCENT SANCHEZ

THE WEST COAST

Methow Valley
Washington

If you quadrupled the lodging rates and invited Gerald Ford to stop by and crash a few times, Washington's Methow Valley could very well qualify as the Vail of mountain biking. It may seem a silly comparison, given that Vail is a posh ski town, the Methow an obscure valley hidden in the eastern shadow of the North Cascades. But families trekking to Methow for a week of mountain biking will find many of the same pleasant hard-play,

soft-touch attractions of a well-run ski resort—sans glitz.

The Methow, a not-so-well-kept secret for cross-country skiers, is a mountain-biking family's summertime dream. The valley's sprawling, 175-kilometer cross-country trail system was built with skiers in mind, but it's wide-open all summer for fat tires. For cycling parents, the big draw is accessibility. No need for loading the bikes on a trunk rack in the Methow. Though the trail network—maintained by the Methow Valley Sport Trails Association—extends throughout much of the upper valley, the lower-valley trails are within easy riding distance of accommodations like the highly regarded **Sun Mountain Lodge** (cabins, $145–$270; doubles, $140–$235; $18 extra for kids over 12; 800-572-0493), with its own 80 kilometers of trails.

Trail variety is overwhelming, with more than enough to keep even the most determined rider busy for weeks. Families can set out for an hour-long cruise to the Methow River or a 3-day, single-track expedition into the Cascades. Beginner routes lead through the dry pine forests to a series of beaver ponds, picnic sites, and scenic viewpoints. But advanced, gut-buster trails up Thompson Ridge are only a short ride away. Farther up the valley, a growing string of mountain chalets, riverside B&B's, and country inns, such as the **Mazama Ranch House** (doubles with kitchenettes, $80; cabins with kitchens, $95; $10 each additional person; kids under 12 free), are found along the Methow—nearly all of them either on or very near the trail network. Bike rentals ($20–$30 per day, $75–$100 per week), maps, and advice are available at **Winthrop**

Mountain Sports (509-996-2886). For one-stop lodging information, call **Methow Valley Central Reservations** (509-996-2148). —RON C. JUDD

Lake Tahoe
California

Lake Tahoe is home to the **Flume Trail**, a 17-mile climb from 7,000 to 8,300 feet along a narrow trail with a sheer drop-off that rewards bikers with unparalleled vistas of Lake Tahoe. Guidebooks warn that it's too tough for kids, while a Forest Service rep reports that kids do it all the time: Your judgment call. And if riding a cliff masquerading as single-track doesn't appeal to you, there's great riding here for all ability levels.

The West Shore Bike Path, a 10-mile paved trail, winds along the wooded West Shore of Lake Tahoe from Sugar Pine Point State Park to Tahoe City. Great views of the lake, nice beaches, and several small towns are accessible from the bike path, as are two connecting trails that branch north and east of Tahoe City. There's good off-road riding within a short distance from Sugar Pine Point: the McKinney-Rubicon Trail off Highway 89, dubbed a world-class off-road highway by locals; the more difficult 4-mile (one-way) Ellis Peak Trail that hooks up with it; and the varied trails at Squaw Valley Bike Park, where a cable-car ride to the High Camp Bath and Tennis Club provides easy access to trails for all riding levels. A suggested route for families here is the High Camp Loop, a wide trail that cruises through sprawling meadows with lake views. Prices at the park are $19 for one ride, $26 for all day; call 800-545-4350 or 916-583-5585.

Inside Skinny

You Are an Ambassador

Hikers and horseback riders tend to view all mountain bikers as bat-out-of-hell crankers oblivious to the sanctity of the trail. You can help dispel that notion by following these rules for safety, courtesy, and common sense.

✦ **Ride gently.** It's your job to protect and preserve the mountain-bike environment: Ride only in designated areas, restricting high-speed theatrics to trails earmarked for such abuse. Portage over sensitive wet areas and ride down the middle of puddles—skirting the mud widens the trail, and that's a no-no. Never cut off switchbacks. Repair damage you encounter (for instance, if a water bar—the barrier that prevents trail erosion by diverting water to the sides—is clogged, take a second to drag your heel over the offending mess and clear it out).

✦ **Be courteous.** Slow down to a walking speed when you encounter a hiker; come to a dead stop and establish verbal contact with an equestrian to keep from spooking the horse.

✦ **Yield.** When bikers meet along the trail, the downhiller should yield to the climbing rider (it's easier to restart when gravity's on your side).

Tool Time

The aspiration of every mountain biker worth his *derailleur* is a McGuyveresque level of self-sufficiency. We've heard of tire punctures repaired with heated tree sap or a PowerBar wrapper and wad of chewed gum, but you're better off buying a patch kit and tool set to start. Another good investment: *Pedro's Simple Trailside Repair Guide* (3D Press), a cheat sheet for repairing most common breakdowns that's printed on tear-resistant, waterproof paper. Call 800-378-4188.

Stupid Bike Tricks

Mountain bikers are frustrated Lettermans, known for packing a section of tread when skiing or climbing, then stamping phony tire marks in outlandish places.

Camping is available at **Sugar Pine Point** (campsites, about $15; call 800-444-7275 or 916-525-7982), which has piped water, flush toilets, pay showers, and a swimming beach and pier for day use. Another nearby option, the **Kaspian Campground** (campsites, $10; call 800-280-2267 or 916-544-5994), gets some highway noise but offers proximity to trails. From there you can follow the paved bike path or tackle Blackwood Canyon Road, a 4-mile gradual uphill grade followed by 3 miles of steep switchbacks toward Barker Pass. Where the pavement ends, the Ellis Peak Trail begins. This is not a ride for the faint of lung, but the views are spectacular. If you're feeling adventurous, you can always head for the Flume Trail—but pack your parachute. For more information, contact the **Lake Tahoe Visitors Center** at 916-544-7750.

—JAMES RODEWALD

Mammoth Mountain
California

Aside from the usual summer trappings at Mammoth—hiking, fishing, hot springs, horseback riding, the San Andreas Fault—the Big One has gained a reputation as the eastern Sierra's number one off-road destination. The **Mammoth Mountain Inn**, located at the base of its 11,053-foot granite namesake, offers 2- and 3-day instructor-guided tours through the mountain's 65-plus miles of single-track. After breakfast at the Mountainside Grill, riders of all levels take off from the hotel to conquer steep grinds or enjoy casual spins on fully suspended Schwinn mountain bikes. Included in weekend packages are a 2-hour lesson, bikes and

protective gear, breakfast, lodging, and tickets to the bike park, home of the 6-mile Kamikaze downhill run and the new Off the Top downhill, a kinder version of its predecessor. Prices begin at $214 per person; additional lessons cost $25 for a half-day session (for two to five people). Packages are available May 1 through October 31, weather permitting. For information, call 800-228-4947, ext. 3606, or 619-934-0606

—MICHAEL KESSLER

THE SOUTHWEST

Deer Valley Resort
Utah

If you're looking for panoramic views of Utah's Uinta and Wasatch Ranges, one of the best networks of lift-serviced mountain biking anywhere, and first-class lodging to limp back to at the end of the day, look no farther than the Deer Valley Resort. The centerpiece of Deer Valley's mountain biking is a 30-mile network of single-track and double-track for all abilities, serviced by the mid-mountain Sterling lift. It lets everyone off at the top of Bald Mountain, overlooking historic Park City. From there, take your pick of Naildriver Downhill and Homeward Bound to lose the 1,300 feet of vertical. More experienced riders can move on to Flagstaff Loop, Tour Des Suds, or the 30-plus-mile backcountry route to Salt Lake City along the Wasatch Crest Trail.

The mountain-bike school at the base of the lift offers instruction and riding tips to all levels of riders, from first-timers to NORBA racers. Rates range from about $25 per hour for a private lesson to about $90 for a half-day group session with up

STAYING SAFE: AVOIDING THE KILLER ENDO

Whether the cause be roots, rocks, loose dirt, or that old urban surprise, the car door swung into your path, every two-wheeler has seen one or two *endos*—the miserable experience of flying right over your handlebars. The trick is to keep such falls to a minimum, and when a fall is inevitable, to be prepared to roll with it. Just as a beginning skier wouldn't attempt a black diamond on a first run, a beginning mountain biker should graduate to trails of increasing difficulty. Build confidence slowly, and practice the following to stay in the saddle, or at least make leaving it unexpectedly a lot less painful:

✦ **Balance.** Your goal is to ride so slowly that your feet are in the pedals but the bike is almost standing still: That's how you scout a trail. Never attempt a downhill without scouting it first.

✦ **Braking.** There are important differences between the front and rear brakes. Slamming on the more powerful front brakes can catapult you over the handlebars; too much gusto at the rear might send you into a skid, which would stress both you and the trail. On steeps, learn to use both brakes, relying more on the rear brake and feathering the front.

✦ **Eye position.** Don't fixate on the front tire. Look ahead, 30 to 40 feet down the trail. You'll be prepared if you know what's coming.

✦ **Body position.** Keep your body low, and shift it back and forward as you encounter various terrain. Stand up, keeping your knees and elbows soft—they'll be your body's shock absorbers.

✦ **Falling.** Find a grassy spot and practice bailing off your bike. Don't cushion your fall with your arms; wrists are vulnerable to breaks. Instead, tuck and roll.

—Franklin Henry is a pro rider and instructor on the staff of Dirt Camp, based in Boulder, Colorado.

to eight riders. Rentals cost about $25–$35 per day. The lift opens as soon as conditions permit in June and operates Wednesday through Sunday until Labor Day. A full-day pass costs about $14; kids 12 and under are only allowed with a paying adult or a waiver signed by a parent.

Two-bedroom condos at Deer Valley ($155–$260 per night) have full kitchens and sleep four to six. For reservations call 800-424-3337. Park City's **Hidden Haven Campground,** with 35 tent sites, is about 8 miles away ($13.50–$17.50 per night; call 801-649-8935).

—DEREK TAYLOR

Dirt Camp
Moab, Utah

Even if no one in the family has gold-medal aspirations, mastering the tools of competitive mountain biking will make even the easiest of jeep trails a lot more fun. At any of Dirt Camp's sessions, those skills can be learned, even if not mastered (hey—Moab wasn't built in 6 days). Families can check into a spring or fall camp in Moab, when temperatures are less brutal than during the height of summer. Instructors provide individualized attention during rides, as well as afternoon clinics for developing basic skills like falling, bunny hops, body positioning on corners, and preparing your bike for a race. The Dirt Camp philosophy emphasizes fun: Nothing is mandatory—this is camp, not school.

On your own, take a family cruise to the spectacular double arches known as **Gemini Bridges**; the 8-mile round-trip is dirt road most of the way, with very little single-track. All lodging (at the Canyonlands Inn) and meals are included in the camp's cost ($1,425 per person), as are all rides, demos, and instruction. Kids should be 14 or older.

The Moab camps are Dirt Camp's signature offerings, but their menu is expanding: Other weeklong camps co-incide with annual mountain-biking extravaganzas such as Crested Butte's Fat Tire Bike Week and Moab's own Fat Tire Festival. And one special camp will feature the Volvo/Cannondale Race Team—if you're struggling to get a teenage fat-tire prodigy down with the family program, giving him or her the opportunity to get pointers from Alison Sydor, Myles Rockwell, or Missy Giove might just do the trick. And then there's the short course: Dirt Camp runs 2-day weekend sessions during the summer at Keystone, Colorado, and Northstar at Lake Tahoe ($289 per person).

For specific dates and other information, call 800-711-3478 or 303-499-3178; E-mail: dirtcamp1@aol.com.

—JAMES RODEWALD

THE FUN FILE: OUTBACK BOREDOM BUSTERS

Organize a Treasure Hunt. Let older kids write out and hide clues along the bike route for the younger ones to find. Don't forget paper, pen, and a prize.

Shoot Marbles. Just because you've left the city for the great outdoors doesn't mean you have to abandon all your citified ways. *The Marble Book* (Workman Publishing) teaches 54 games, like Bossout and Dropsies, and comes with 30 marbles plus 2 shooters.

Play the Harmonica. It's portable and, with some practice, it's easy to learn. As with mountain biking itself, 10 is a good age to take it up.

Have a Scavenger Hunt along the Trail. Before a ride, make a list of fifteen items that your bikers have to spot along the trail. For example, something with four legs, scarlet gila, something winged. Kids check off items as they see them.

I Spy. Pack paper and pencils. Collect twenty-five items from in and around camp, put them on a plate, then cover them with a towel. Other family members get 25 seconds to try to memorize all the items before the plate is covered up again. Whoever remembers the most wins. —*Lisa Twyman Bessone*

The Hill Country
Texas

Texas in the summer may sound like hell, but Kerr County, in the heart of Texas Hill Country west of Austin and San Antonio, is an exception. Even in the dog days, Hill Country nights are cool, with comfortable days and low humidity. The 5,400-acre **Hill Country State Natural Area** has more than 30 miles of trails, most of which are open to mountain biking. Three loop rides, all of which intersect and can be shortened to less difficult out-and-backs, make up the bulk of the great riding here. The 7-mile North Loop switches from single- to double-track as it climbs through forest to Cougar Canyon Overlook. The West Loop offers two options: the 5.3-mile smooth double-track, with no big hills or obstacles, and the 6.8-mile track through a panorama of hills. The 6.6-mile South Loop starts on a county road that leads to double-track, then single-track down a rocky slope that crosses deep woodland groves.

Though there's plenty of challenging terrain, beginners should be fine if they hike around the most difficult sections. Campsites are primitive (no water or electricity), but the preserve's proximity to Bandera (half-hour drive) and Kerrville (about 1 hour's drive) means easy access to civilization. Camping is by permit and is available only on Thursday, Friday, Saturday, and Sunday nights. The Hill Country State Natural Area (210-796-4413) is closed Tuesdays and Wednesdays.

Noncampers can stay at the funky **Horseshoe Inn**, 3 miles north of Bandera on Texas 173 (doubles, $35–$45; 800-364-3833), or the **River Front Motel** in Bandera, with eleven cottages suitable for families alongside a river where you can swim, fish, and canoe (doubles, $48, plus $3–$5 per child; minimum 2 nights; 210-460-3690). For more information, call the **Bandera Convention and Visitors Bureau** at 800-364-3833 or 210-796-3045.

—James Rodewald

THE ROCKIES

Sawtooth Mountains
Idaho

If planning a weeklong camping trip seems daunting, Backroads may have the answer. One of the few bicycle-touring companies that offers trips geared toward families, Backroads runs a 5-day loop through the Sawtooth National Forest in central Idaho that's fully supported and extremely flexible. The trip starts at Boulder View campground, near Ketchum (about 155 miles east of Boise). Average mileage is 149, ranging from 8 to 50 miles per day. There are three options: low-, average-, and high-mileage trips. If your family is divided into yearners for huge uphills and those preferring an easier day, there's always a short option with a van shuttle available. The routes wind through mountainous terrain and evergreen forest, with most on dirt roads rather than white-knuckle single-track.

Though kids as young as 8 have done the trip, such precociousness is the exception. A better starting age is 10 or 11. Two or three trips run each summer. The cost is $750 per person, including meals, and there's a 20 percent discount for ages 7 to 12, 10 percent for ages 13 to 16. Call 800-462-2848.

—James Rodewald

THE HYSTERICAL PARENT

Is There a Doctor in the Woods?!

You would be a fool to venture into the wilderness without someone in your party being certified in first aid. Call your pediatrician or hospital for information on when and where classes are offered so you can learn to set broken bones and deal with cuts, bites, blisters, poisonous plants, and hypothermia (yes, even in summer). From there, Murphy's Law applies. If you have the training, you won't need it; if you don't, all hell will probably break loose.

What If We Get a Flat in the Middle of Nowhere?

Every mountain biker should know how to fix a flat tire. Call your bike shop and ask about repair kits and a crash course on how to use them. And don't feel foolish asking for help. Bikers are generous when it comes to offering aid to neophytes.

What's in the Water?

You don't want to know. That cascading mountain stream may look pristine, but one sip and you're gut-wrenchingly sick for weeks. The problem is the *giardia* parasite, and it's everywhere. That's why a water filter is essential backcountry gear, and it's no more complicated to use than a tea strainer. Otherwise, a vigorous 5-minute boil will kill off all waterborne microbes.

—*Lisa Twyman Bessone*

Crested Butte
Colorado

A week of mountain biking in Crested Butte is great under any circumstance. Because the trail system is shaped like a wheel, you can head out in any direction on dirt roads or single-track—and those trails traverse the mountain, which means that neither climbs nor descents are particularly brutal. That said, there is a best time to be there: Crested Butte's **Fat Tire Bike Week**, the granddaddy of mountain-bike festivals, celebrates its sixteenth anniversary on June 25–29, 1997.

The week's activities include special programs for kids ages 7 to 13: group rides, two clinics covering single-track riding and how to maneuver over rocks and sticks, an obstacle course, and a bicycle rodeo (bike limbo, anyone?). For adults there are clinics covering everything from proper breathing technique (which is crucial at this high altitude) to racing strategies, official bicycle polo, and several races. All activities, plus admission to the Saturday barbecue, are included in the $30 kids registration fee (adults pay $60, or $100 if they plan to race; call 802-484-5737 for information and registration).

For a good family ride, try Slate River Road, a relatively flat, 10- to 15-mile route that winds through fields of wildflowers en route to Paradise Divide and its stunning mountain vistas. In town, stop by the **Mountain Bike Hall of**

Fame (970-349-6817), which displays prototypes of early mountain bikes and the history of bike racing.

Though most nearby campgrounds don't open until July, **Cement Creek Campground,** 5 miles south of Crested Butte, opens in June (first-come, first-served; no reservations). Several condo facilities work well for families: Try the **Three Seasons,** with a pool and hot tub; **Eagle's Nest** town houses, with three levels and great views; or **The Chateau,** which has a clubhouse, outdoor pool, and hot tub. Rates at all three run $105–$146 per night for two- to four-bedroom units (1 night is free with a 7-night stay). Call 800-821-3718 or 970-349-2448.   —JAMES RODEWALD

THE MID-ATLANTIC

Greenbrier River
West Virginia

In the first part of the century, this region of the Alleghenies in southern West Virginia served as a lumber hub and route stop for the Chesapeake and Ohio railroad. Today, its low altitude and fairly flat terrain make family mountain biking a breeze. Easily accessible from U.S. 219 is the Greenbrier River and its neighboring towns, providers of all you'll need for a hassle-free weekend.

Any family can easily pedal along the Greenbrier River Trail, a 75-mile stretch of single- and double-track along the river. But best suited for families is the 10.3-mile section between the tiny towns of Seebert and Marlinton. Start in **Watoga State Park** (304-799-4087), 1 mile from Seebert at trail marker 45.8, where there's a riverside campground with fifty sites, showers, a swimming pool, and a diner. From the 15-mile trail system within the park, riders connect with the groomed railroad line, rarely straying more than 100 yards from the river and never gaining more than a few hundred feet in elevation. Around mile 2, the 287-foot Watoga Bridge spits riders across the river into the old town of Watoga. Along the way, watch for wild turkeys, black bears, deer, and ruffed grouse. As you continue north, stop for a dip in the river or try your hand at bass fishing. By early afternoon, you'll arrive in Marlinton, the first settlement west of the Alleghenies.

Families who want to log a few extra miles can continue north, stopping 8 miles up the trail at Sharp's Tunnel, a now-defunct railroad passage. Or try the 25-mile ride from Marlinton to Cass. (Flooding caused some washout last season, so call ahead for trail conditions.) If you don't want to retrace your route, several shuttle options are available. **Appalachian Sport** in Marlinton (304-799-4050) rents bikes for $15 per day and offers custom shuttle service, as does **Jack Horner's Corner** (304-653-4515) in Seebert. Noncampers should bed down at the **Current** (doubles, $55; 304-653-4722), a B&B in Seebert, or the **Gasthaus** (doubles, $45; 304-799-6711) in Marlinton.   —MICHAEL KESSLER

THE NORTHEAST

Mount Snow
Vermont

Home of the oldest mountain-biking school in the country and smack in southern Vermont, Mount Snow offers some 140 miles of trails—from dirt roads to single-track—for every riding level. The routes traverse open valleys and hilly forests of evergreen, maple, and oak; a series of trails at the mountain's base lets riders get their tires dirty without long uphill grinds. Mount Snow's chairlifts are open from Memorial Day to Columbus Day, weather permitting; full-day lift access with your bike costs $28 and includes the $9 trail fee.

The mountain-biking school, founded ten years ago, will have two family sessions in 1997 ($165 per person with bike rental, $149 without; daily lunch included; call ahead for dates). These family weekends consist of two half-day instructional sessions on how to ride uphill and downhill safely, turn on bumpy terrain, maneuver in and out of trees, and more. Families can either ride together or join groups commensurate with their skill level. If you can't be here for one of the specifically family-oriented weekends, the school will put together custom-tailored sessions anytime.

Gary Fisher bikes—both adult- and kid-sized—are available for rent (about $30 per day). There's a full repair shop at the **Mount Snow Mountain Bike Center,** where you can also pick up trail maps. Call 800-245-7669.

When you're not taking a class, try **Crosstown,** a good family trail that's relatively flat. The 20-mile route covers a jeep trail through a valley—with a bit of single-track mixed in as well.

The favorite campground for mountain bikers is **Bald Mountain Campground,** 20 minutes from Mount Snow off Vermont 30. Set in a mountain-ringed river valley, it has showers, water at every site, and beautiful views (campsites, $15–$18; call 802-365-7510). Noncampers can try the **Cooper Hill Inn,** a 200-year-old farmhouse just 12 minutes from Mount Snow with rooms and two-room family suites (2-night stay with breakfast, $160 for two; ages 12 and under pay an additional $15 per night; 800-783-3229 or 802-348-6333). —JAMES RODEWALD

Randolph
Vermont

For years, Vermont's most cherished mountain-bike trails were off-limits to out-of-towners. If you were fortunate enough to know the farmer next door, you could ride on the sinuous single-track that cut through his cornfields, but everyone else was forced to bike with the crowds at downhill or cross-country ski centers. That all changed in 1994 when Paul Rea opened up Slab City Bike & Sports in Randolph and created the White River Valley Trails Association.

The tenacious Rea knocked on landowners' doors, asking (sometimes begging) permission to link together a network of trails in this rural county. Remarkably, everyone agreed, and the result is a 240-mile system of mapped trails open to all. The terrain varies from dirt roads to technical single-track, but the majority of the riding is on grassy double-track that's now closed to all vehicles except two-wheelers. The trails are ideal for children; for the past 2 years Randolph has been the home of the **New England Mountain Biking Festival,** a 3-day noncompetitive event with guided rides for all levels (the 1997 festival is September 26–28; call 802-484-5737 for information).

One particularly good route is the 12-mile Mud Pond Loop. From Slab City in Randolph, the ride climbs steeply up a hill through farmland. You'll ride past cows, rows of corn, and the quintessential white Vermont steeple before ducking into a forest of pines to hidden Mud Pond. For an encore, hard-core families can try the 44.9-mile double-track Circus Ride, which was used decades ago to bring the circus into town.

Rental bikes ($20 per day) and detailed maps are available from **Slab City Bike & Sports** (802-728-5747). Campers should stay in **Silver Lake State Park** in nearby Barnard (campsites, $12–$16; call 802-234-9451). Or stay at the **Three Stallion Inn**, about 1 mile from Randolph. Located on the Green Mountain Stock Farm, the Three Stallion (doubles, $99; 800-424-5575) has about 33 miles of single-track where you'll rarely see another biker.

—Stephen Jermanok

5

Road Biking

Spin Control

Can your kids handle a bike tour? In cycling—as in life—different kids are up to different challenges. However, a rule of thumb is that fit 10-year-olds can usually ride 30 miles of relatively flat roads in a day, while energetic 12-year-olds can handle 40. But be conservative with each day's mileage. A 50-mile Saturday spin followed by a lazy Sunday is one thing; it's something else to ride 40 miles, then do it all over again for 3 more days. Let the youngest or weakest rider set the pace, then plan for lots of contingencies—nearby roads will lead to civilized pleasures like ice cream, dry socks, and Big Macs. Let the stronger cyclists splinter off on side trips to burn a little tread. For the younger kids, hitch a trailer to your bike, scatter its floor with books and toys, and take off for hours.

The trips we cite let you either go it alone or enlist some help. If you're worried that your 10-year-old might suffer midtrip meltdown, hire an outfitter. It's more expensive, but they'll map out the route and supply a support van, which picks up tired riders (don't kid yourself—that rider may be you).

—LAURA HILGERS

THE WEST COAST

The San Juan Islands
Washington

The Big Picture: Just 100 miles northwest of Seattle, the San Juan Islands make a great starter trip for a family bicycling vacation. This 4-day route past rocky beaches and stands of Douglas fir offers minimal car traffic, relatively flat riding, and frequent ferry rides from one island to the next—a real kid-pleaser.

Route: Because the islands' few roads are generally quiet, you can cycle off in any direction without fear of hitting much traffic and still carve out 15- to 30-mile loops. Begin the trip by taking the 1-hour-and-20-minute ferry ride from Anacortes, Washington, to Orcas Island. Spend your first day on Orcas, the largest and hilliest of the islands, riding north and then east from the ferry to Cascade Lake at Moran State Park, about 13 miles, for swimming and a picnic. Then cycle south 2 miles to the town of Olga to visit Olga Café and Artworks, where you can see the work of local artists. Stay the night either at a campsite in Moran State Park, or 6 miles northwest in Eastsound, the island's largest town.

The next day, take the 40-minute ferry ride to Lopez Island, the flattest of the San Juans. Lopez is primarily agricultural and a bit of a cycling snore, but it's great terrain for younger riders. Ride south from the ferry, past stretches of farmland, to Hummel Lake for swimming and to Shark Reef for an eyeful of sunbathing seals. Then loop north to settle for the night in Lopez Village.

Take the ferry the following morning from Lopez to San Juan Island, whose shops, galleries, and restaurants will probably seem like downtown Manhattan after sleepy Lopez. From the ferry at Friday Harbor, ride 4.5 miles north to Lakedale Resort, where the kids can swim in the lake, and either camp overnight there or head back to Friday Harbor.

On the fourth day, make a loop around San Juan Island, stopping at British Camp, part of the San Juan National Historical Park, to learn about the island's history. At the lighthouse in Lime Kiln State Park, you can watch the killer whales before heading back to Friday Harbor and taking the ferry back to Anacortes.

Local Wisdom: To avoid getting caught in traffic, wait 15 or 20 minutes after a ferry docks before cycling out of town.

Side Trip Not to Miss: At Moran State Park on Orcas, bike the 5 steep miles up Mount Constitution for some heart-stopping views of Puget Sound, Mount Baker, and Mount Rainier.

Eating and Sleeping: Camp at the **Moran State Park** campground; it has showers and is near Cascade Lake ($11 per night, with a $6 reservations fee; reservations, 800-452-5687). On San Juan, stay at the **Inn at Friday Harbor Suites**, which has a restaurant and suites with kitchenettes (suites, $123; 800-752-5752). For family-style Italian food on Orcas, check out **La Famiglia Ristorante**; on Lopez, visit **Holly B's Bakery**.

Information: Your best source on the San Juans proper is *The San Juan Islands: Afoot and Afloat*, by Marge and Ted Mueller (published by The Mountaineers, Seattle), which also includes cycling info. For a broader survey of where to get outside in the San Juans and elsewhere in the Northwest, pick up Karl Samson's *Outside Magazine's Adventure Guide to the Pacific Northwest* (Macmillan Travel). For ferry information, call 206-464-6400. For additional help, you can call the **San Juan Islands Visitor Information Service**, 360-468-3663.

Hired Help: Backroads (800-462-2848) offers 6-day camping trips (there are six departures between early July and late August) geared specifically to families

($749 per person; discounts for children, depending on age—the younger the child, the larger the discount).

THE ROCKIES

Banff to Jasper
The Canadian Rockies

The Big Picture: This vigorous 5-day trip covering 175 miles takes you past the glaciers, emerald-green lakes, and jutting peaks of Banff and Jasper National Parks, providing glimpses of elk, moose, and bighorn sheep. The bulk of the route runs along the Icefields Parkway, which has generous passing lanes.

Route: Leave Banff heading north via the Bow Valley Parkway (Highway 1A), which follows the Bow River for 41 miles to Lake Louise. About 16 miles into the ride, stop at Johnston Canyon, where a steep, 1.7-mile hike leads to a catwalk overlooking two waterfalls.

Stay the night at Lake Louise, then head out along the Icefields Parkway, riding over the 6,787-foot Bow Pass, then stop for a picnic at green-hued Peyto Lake. At 36 miles is the no-frills Waterfowl Lake Campground, where you can spend the night.

The third day—a 40-mile ride—takes you on a 9-mile, 6,675-foot climb up Sunwapta Pass. Finish up at Athabasca Glacier, where there's a hostel, hotel, and campgrounds—and where a short hike up Parker Ridge pays off in sweeping views of the Saskatchewan Glacier.

On day 4, take a leisurely 28-mile ride, mostly downhill, through the Sunwapta River Valley, which is ringed by the towering Endless Chain Ridge. Spend the night at Sunwapta Falls Resort.

Your final day, take the parkway along the Athabasca River for about 15 miles, then turn at Athabasca Falls onto Highway 93A for a 20-mile ride into Jasper.

Local Wisdom: If you must hike the tourist-clogged trails at Lake Louise, do it in the early morning or late afternoon. All other times, the hard-soled crowd runs rampant.

Side Trip Not to Miss: With an extra day in Lake Louise, you can take a day trip to Moraine Lake—a 9-mile uphill ride. The 3.5-mile hike from there to Sentinel Pass offers astounding views of glaciers, lakes, and peaks.

Eating and Sleeping: Try the **Lake Louise Campground** (C$10 per night) near town, which sits along the Bow River and has hot running water, and head to **Lake Louise Station Restaurant** at the train station for dinner. On your way to Jasper, stop at the **Sunwapta Falls Resort**, which has rustic cabins, a primitive cafeteria, and hot showers (doubles, C$128; 403-852-4852).

Information: Check out the pamphlet *A Cyclist's Guidebook to the Canadian Rockies,* or *The Parkways of the Canadian Rockies: A Road Guide,* by Brian Patton (Summerthought Books, Banff), both available at the **Banff Book and Art Den** (403-762-3919). For further information, call **Banff National Park** (403-762-1550) and **Jasper National Park** (403-852-6161).

Hired Help: **Backroads** (800-462-2848) offers eight 5-day camping trips geared for families (departures weekly from late June through late August; C$749 per person with discounts for children; open to all ages).

THE MID-ATLANTIC

Pennsylvania Dutch Country
Lancaster County, Pennsylvania

The Big Picture: Here's your chance to show the kids a way of life without cars, electricity, or Power Rangers. On this 5-day trip, you'll ride through the lush rolling hills of Amish and Mennonite farm country, competing for road space mostly with the horse-and-buggy crowd.

Route: Take day trips (of approximately 30 miles each) along Lancaster County's back roads, staying 2 nights in Ephrata and 3 in Mount Joy. Bring a detailed local map; you'll probably ride on a total of 20 to 40 different roads (whenever possible, avoid busy Pennsylvania 772 and 23).

Start in Ephrata, taking a 29-mile loop the first day to the town of New Holland, 13 miles away. From Ephrata, ride east to Reamstown, south to New Holland, and west to West Earl Township, then return to Ephrata for the night. Along the way, you'll meander past small farms where horse-drawn plows work the land. On your second day, ride 12 miles south to Intercourse, where Amish crafts like quilts and wooden rocking chairs are sold. Then head 6 miles west to the town of Bird-In-The-Hand for a visit to the farmers' market before turning north back to Ephrata (another 20 miles or so).

The next day, ride west about 28 miles to Mount Joy, stopping after 7 miles at the town of Lititz to visit the Sturgis Pretzel House—the oldest pretzel bakery in America. From there, head west 21 miles to Mount Joy, where you'll overnight.

Continue west for 9 miles the next morning to the Nissley Winery for a picnic, then return south via Maytown (5 miles) and head north along Pinkerton Road back to Mount Joy, another 13 miles. After another night in Mount Joy, take the 28-mile ride east back to Ephrata.

Local Wisdom: Leave the camera at home or shoot only scenics; the Amish are offended by picture-taking.

Side Trip Not to Miss: Stay a night at the **Jonde Lane Farm** in Manheim (about 5 miles from Mount Joy). Run by the Nissleys, a Mennonite family of six, it's a working dairy and poultry farm where guests can help milk the cows and gather eggs (room with shared bath, $45 for two adults; $7.50 per child; 717-665-4231).

Eating and Sleeping: In Ephrata, stay at the **Inn at Doneckers** (doubles, $69–$185; 717-738-9502), an elegant country inn attached to Artworks at Doneckers, where artisans make and sell Amish crafts. In Mount Joy, stop at **Alois Bube's Brewery and Catacombs Restaurant**, or **Groff's Farm Restaurant**, a three-star restaurant specializing in Pennsylvania Dutch food.

Inside Skinny

Ride Smart; Assume Drivers Aren't

Pearl Izumi, in cooperation with The Bicycle Federation of America, is sponsoring a bicycle advocacy kit that includes these stats: Fifty percent of bike-related fatalities involve cyclists who were riding without lights at night. And riding against traffic accounts for about 20 percent of all car-bike crashes. To order the **Bicycle Advocate's Action Kit,** call 800-877-7080.

Laundry, C.O.D.

Here's a tip several road warriors shared with us: Mail a stash of clean duds to yourself at various stops you intend to make throughout your trip. The likely recipient is an inn (or two), where you might also plan a shower and hot meal after several days of camping. Include a generously sized envelope, complete with the return postage, so you can send home the stuff you no longer care to haul around.

Saddle Sore

"The reason that the saddle design hasn't changed throughout history is that the original design works so well," says Georgena Terry, owner of Terry Precision Bikes. But there have been some memorable attempts at improvement. Who can forget the hammock sling seat—or the one with individual seats for each cheek? Today's innovations are more practical, such as seats just for women—they're wider and squatter than a traditional saddle to better accommodate a woman's wider pelvic structure. But the best advice for a comfy long ride: Get used to sitting on a seat for extended periods of time.

Information: A local map with good detail is Patton Maps' (215-345-0700) "Lancaster, Pennsylvania Street and Road Map." For local color, get *Scenic Tours of Lancaster County* (send $9.95 plus $2 handling to the Lancaster

Bicycle Club, P.O. Box 535, Lancaster, PA 17608-0535). For more information, call the **Pennsylvania Dutch Convention and Visitors Bureau,** 717-299-8901.

Hired Help: **Vermont Bicycle Touring** (802-453-4811) offers four 5-day, inn-to-inn trips during the summer and fall ($995 per person; discounts for kids under 17; open to ages 10 and up).

THE NORTHEAST

Middlebury and Lake Champlain
Vermont's Champlain Valley

The Big Picture: You'll travel a 5-day route through the verdant hills of the Champlain Valley, with Lake Champlain to the west, the Green Mountains to the east, and the college town of Middlebury in between. Kids especially enjoy riding from town to town (plenty of ice cream opportunities) and stopping at lakes and rivers to swim. You'll hit some hills, but traffic along the back roads is light and cyclist-friendly.

Route: Settle in Middlebury for a few days and take day trips from there to surrounding points of interest. For swimming and picnicking, go just beyond the town of Bristol to Bartlett's Falls at the edge of the Green Mountain National Forest (30 miles round-trip; follow Munger Street to Vermont 116 and then Vermont 17).

The next day, ride 20 miles along Weybridge Street and Vermont 17 to Lake Champlain and Chimney Point State Historic Site—the site, at different times, of former American Indian and French settlements. Then cycle 20 miles to Shoreham along Vermont 125 and 74, settling in at the Shoreham Inn and Country Store, an old stagecoach stop from the 1790s.

On day 3, cycle 30 miles from Shoreham to Brandon along Vermont 73, which takes you through the heart of apple country and along scenic Otter Creek. From Brandon, make a 28-mile round-trip to Proctor along Florence Road to visit the Vermont Marble Exhibit, where you can watch demonstrations by craftspeople. On your final day, meander the 24 miles back to Middlebury along Vermont 73, Route 53, and Vermont 116, stopping at Lake Dunmore, one of Vermont's most spectacular lakes, for a swim.

Local Wisdom: Stay off Vermont 7 and 22A, which have considerable car traffic.

Side Trip Not to Miss: If you stay an extra night in Shoreham, consider a day trip to **Fort Ticonderoga,** which played a major role in the Revolutionary War, where you can watch reenactments of life from that era. Cycle from Shoreham to Larrabee's Point (5 miles), then ferry across Lake Champlain to the fort.

Eating and Sleeping: In Middlebury, stay at the **Swift House Inn,** the former mansion of Governor John W.

Stewart (doubles, $95–$175; 802-388-9925). Check out **Calvi's Old Fashioned Soda Fountain** in Middlebury for a float or sundae, then cab it (the roads are too busy for cycling) to the **Dog Team Tavern**, which serves up traditional New England fare. In Shoreham, stay at the **Shoreham Inn and Country Store**, which has a good restaurant (double with shared bath, $85; 802-897-5081).

Information: Call the **Addison County Chamber of Commerce** (800-733-8376) for maps and information, and check out *Vermont: An Explorer's Guide*, by Christina Tree and Peter Jennison (Countryman Press, Woodstock, Vermont).

Hired Help: **Bike Vermont Inc.** (800-257-2226) offers fourteen 5-day, inn-to-inn trips in summer and fall ($735 per person; open to ages 10 and up).

The Blue Heron Loop
Prince Edward Island, Canada

The Big Picture: Only 40 miles wide at its broadest point, Prince Edward Island, off the coast of Nova Scotia, is ringed by sandy beaches that plunge into surprisingly warm water. Along the south shore you'll hunt for clams, snails, and seaweed; the north shore is great for hikes along beaches bordered by white sand dunes. With the island's gently rolling hills and light traffic, this 5-day trip is especially good for families.

Route: From Charlottetown, the capital, take a day trip (15 miles one-way) to Brackley Beach—part of the Prince

Edward Island National Park—by following Highways 223 and 6. Start your trip the next day on Blue Heron Drive, a scenic route that follows a number of rural roads around the coastline of the island's midsection. Ride 43 miles to the town of Victoria, where you'll spend the night. At 31 miles, stop at the Argyle Shore Provincial Park, where you can dig for clams and swim.

The next day, ride 30 miles—continuing on the Blue Heron Drive along the south shore—to Summerside, a charming seaside town that hosts a summer lobster carnival the third week in July.

On day 4 cycle the Blue Heron 36 miles up to Cavendish, a community obsessed with Lucy Maud Montgomery, author of *Anne of Green Gables:* The town is swarming with Gable-related activities.

On your final day, leave Cavendish along the Blue Heron Drive; at about 16 miles, take Highway 233, then Highway 236, for the 15 miles back to Charlottetown.

Local Wisdom: For swimming, stick to the warmer waters of the south shore.

Side Trip Not to Miss: If you overnight in Summerside, consider a visit to the **Acadian Pioneer Village** in Mont-Carmel, a museum with reproductions of French Acadian life in the 1820s. To get there, make a loop along Highways 11 and 124 (15 miles), then return on Highway 2 (about 25 miles).

Eating and Sleeping: In Charlottetown, stay downtown at **The Charlottetown-Rodd Classic Hotel,** a lovely, Victorian-style hotel (doubles, C$119 and up; 800-565-7633). Walk to Peake's Wharf for dinner at **Lobster on the Wharf**. In Victoria, stay at the **Orient Hotel**, a turn-of-the-century inn (doubles, C$75–C$115; C$15 each additional person; 800-565-ORIENT or 902-658-2503). At the Acadian Pioneer Village in Mont-Carmel, be sure to try **Étoile de Mer** for Acadian specialties like *rapure* (a rustic potato dish).

Information: For flights into Charlottetown, call **Canadian Airlines/Air Atlantic** (800-426-7000) or **Air Canada/ Air Nova** (800-776-3000). For a highway map, call **Prince Edward Island Visitor Services**, 800-463-4734.

Hired Help: **Classic Adventures** (800-777-8090) leads two 6-night trips along Blue Heron Drive (in late July and early August; C$1,149 per person, ages 12 and up).

6

For the past 16 years (my entire life), I've lived with my parents and my 14-year-old sister, Carolyn, on the 47-foot *Chez Nous*. We spend summers sailing the east coast and making our way to the Bahamas, where we winter. (We're home-schooled.) Each spring, we return north.

The thing to remember about sailing is that you're not stuck on the boat. Actually, we spend a lot of our time in the water: We go snorkeling, boardsailing, and bodysurfing, or explore inlets and coves in a dinghy. If it's raining or we're on the move, we read, draw, and listen to music. The VHF radio is always on, which is the primary way we keep up with the world.

People wonder what happens if we get mad at our parents or each other. One option is going to our side of the bedroom and closing a curtain around the bed, then putting on headphones

Sailing Windward Ho!

and cranking up The Smashing Pumpkins. If we really need to be alone, we'll hang out in the head, the only totally private place on board. But those are temporary solutions. Basically, we've all just learned to get along. Luckily, there are usually other cruising kids around, which makes family life less intense. We've made lots of friends and write to people all over the world.

For the most part, we go ashore only when we have to; it actually feels a bit unnatural to be on solid land. Although we don't get "land-sick," we do find that we have trouble balancing and that it's hard to sleep in a nonrocking bed. We usually can't wait to get back aboard the *Chez Nous.* Kevin Costner, in his line from *Waterworld,* put it best: "Land just doesn't move right."

—MELANIE AND CAROLYN NEALE

THE WEST COAST

San Diego to Santa Catalina Island

The Big Picture: This sunny, easy cruising route will give your family an overview of California beach culture—from big-league urban attractions like San Diego's zoo and museums to the more traditional oceanside pleasures of

snorkeling, swimming, boardsailing, and bodysurfing. Santa Catalina Island, 22 miles offshore, adds another dimension. Despite its popularity with day-trippers who arrive by ferry, the rugged, mountainous island is quite wild. Buffalo, boar, goats, eagles, and seals populate the 21-mile-long island, most of which is maintained as a conservancy. Comfortable temperatures, calm waters, and reliable 10- to 15-knot winds make midsummer an ideal time to sail here. By late summer and early fall, powerful Santa Ana winds sometimes make the crossing difficult or impossible for boats smaller than about 25 feet.

Plotting a Course: From San Diego Harbor, head north to Mission Bay, 4 to 6 hours away. Overnight in the big marina or anchor in adjacent Mariner's Basin, just off a sandy beach. After spending a night or two, sail about 6 hours north to Oceanside Harbor, where guest slips are always available. Start at dawn for Catalina, 22 miles across the San Pedro Channel. You'll arrive in Avalon, the island's pretty, Mediterranean-style resort town, by early afternoon. Divide your time between Avalon and Two Harbors, 2 hours away on the undeveloped northwest end of the island. It's a 10- to 12-hour broad reach back to San Diego, but schools of tagalong dolphins make the trip go faster for restless kids.

Best Reasons to Anchor: Before you leave San Diego Bay, spend at least half a day at the **San Diego Zoo** (619-234-3153). In Mission Bay Park, take your dinghy under the bridge into the huge aquatic playground with designated sport-specific areas for activities

THE HYSTERICAL PARENT

hat if I go to all the trouble and expense of planning a sailing vacation and then discover that a member of my family gets seasick?

For the record, seasickness has very little to do with the sea. What's going on is sensory conflict. Your inner ear, nerves, and muscles might be sensing motion while your eyes see stability. That's why Lawrence of Arabia got sick riding camels across the desert and a pope became queasy when carried on people's shoulders in his ceremonial chair. You don't hear about it much, but some astronauts have a terrible problem with motion sickness.

If you do feel ill on a boat, stay on deck, breathe in fresh air, and keep your mind occupied. Just as drivers rarely get carsick, sailors busy with prescribed tasks are less likely to get seasick. Some people suck lemons; others eat a roll they've poked with a finger and filled with Worcestershire sauce. I have a friend who swears by acupressure wristbands, but I wear them and still get sick. Another friend, a captain in the Coast Guard, says his trick is a handful of salted peanuts every day before breakfast. While seasickness is a physical malady, there's also a strong psychological component: A placebo dispensed with authority, such as a swig of Coke or a piece of dry toast, can be quite effective.

If that doesn't work, there are a number of over-the-counter drugs, most of which contain one of three active ingredients—cyclizin, dimenhydrate, or meclizine hydrochloride. It's a wise idea to have a pretrip chat with your doctor, as well as a trial dose of the medication (to test for side effects). I once took a drug that prevented seasickness but also left me unconscious for 24 hours

—Charlie Mazel is the author of
Heave Ho! My Little Green Book of Seasickness *(Bernel Books).*

such as boardsailing, kayaking, fishing, and water-skiing. Rental gear and instruction are available at **Mission Bay Sportcenter** (619-488-1004). **Sea World of California** (619-222-6363) and the Giant Dipper, a restored wooden roller coaster, are also nearby. On Catalina, there are several wildlife-viewing bus and boat tours; one of the best is **Catalina Adventure Tours's** (310-510-2888) glass-bottom boat trip over giant kelp beds (adults, $8; chil-

dren, $4.25). The beaches near Avalon are crowded; those at Two Harbors are nearly empty. There's good snorkeling at both ends of the island, where you can see California garibaldi, rock bass, and blue and button perch. **Catalina Stables** (310-510-0478) offers guided horseback trips for $20 per one-half hour and $35 for 1 hour and 15 minutes (prices don't include tax); mountain bikes can be rented at **Brown's Bikes** ($9 per hour, $20 per day; 310-510-0986). For information about hiking, horse-back riding, or mountain biking, contact the **Catalina Island Chamber of Commerce and Visitors Bureau** (310-510-1520).

Local Wisdom: If you moor in Avalon Harbor, remember to leave your trash out on your swim step before you go to bed. A garbage boat collects trash each morning from visiting boats.

Getting Underway: San Diego Yacht **Charters** (800-456-0222; 619-297-4555) offers bareboat and crewed yachts, and arranges flotillas. Bareboat rates range from $160 per day for a 28-foot boat up to $395 per day for a 42-foot boat. A Catalina 400 rents for $395 on weekdays and $425 on weekends and holidays. **Marina Sailing** (800-600-7245), in San Diego, offers bare, crewed, and flotilla charters from 28 feet to 42 feet for $1,390–$2,990 per week.

THE MIDWEST

Northern Lake Michigan

The Big Picture: A week on these waters is a cruise through quintessential American freshwater summer, from the Cherry Festival in Traverse City to the stone-skipping contest on tiny Mackinac Island. Along the way, you'll make stops to swim off clean, sandy beaches, hike wooded trails, visit historic forts, and walk through the prim resort towns with their fudge shops and whitewashed inns. Summer sailing conditions are ideal, with temperatures in the 80s and moderate winds.

Say yes to Michigan!

Storms are capable of whipping up big waves in the open-water portion of the trip. When that happens, simply buy a box of fudge and hole up in port till the weather gets better.

Plotting a Course: From Traverse City, sail 4 hours to Northport and get a slip for the night. Leave Northport in the morning and arrive on Beaver Island, 30 miles offshore, about 6 hours later. The next day, plan on sailing for 6½ hours from Beaver Island to Mackinac Island. Spend 2 days on the island, then work your way back to Traverse City, overnighting in Charlevoix, about 8 hours from Mackinac, after making a stop in Harbor Springs.

Best Reasons to Anchor: In Traverse City, visit the **Madeline** (616-946-2647), a full-scale replica of an 1850 Great Lakes schooner. The Cherry Festival, with pageants, concerts, and parades, takes place the second week in July. On tiny, walkable Beaver Island, stop in at the St. James Boat Shop, where canoes, dinghies, and boat models are made, and the Beaver Island Toy Museum. Rent bicycles (**Iroquois Bikes,** about $5 per hour; 906-847-3221) or horses (**Chambers' Riding Stables,** $20 per hour; 906-847-6112) and ride some of the 144 trails of Mackinac Island, most of which is a state park (906-847-3328). Fort Mackinac, also in the park, is a restored eighteenth-century landmark high on a bluff above the town docks. Harbor Springs is a pretty resort town with lots of manicured waterfront estates, sidewalk cafes, and galleries. The best beach in Charlevoix is Mount McSauba, which has an 8-mile network of woodland trails behind its dunes.

Local Wisdom: In mid-to-late July, two long-distance regattas, one from Port Huron and the other from Chicago, terminate on Mackinac Island. Most of the marina is reserved for race participants; cruising sailors should arrive early to lay claim to a first-come, first-served mooring.

Getting Underway: Bay Breeze Yacht Charters in Traverse City (616-941-0535) has bareboats from 24 to 44 feet for $700 to $3,360 per week. With a captain, add $125 per day.

THE MID-ATLANTIC

Chesapeake Bay

The Big Picture: You could spend weeks poking along the gentle shoreline of 200-mile-long Chesapeake Bay, living on crab cakes, and holing up in hidden coves. Along the way, your kids would be soaking up the unique history and culture of the bay—the 300-year-old port towns, the seaside museums, and the parade of boat traffic that features everything from schooners to skipjacks, crabbers' boats, and container ships. Although midsummer—with its threat of frequent thunderstorms, light winds, and high heat—is not the Chesapeake's prime cruising time (spring and early fall are considered ideal), many charterers, relishing the season's slower pace, scale down their itineraries to fit the conditions.

Plotting a Course: Spend 2 days exploring Annapolis, then sail for St. Michaels on the eastern shore, a 5- to 8-hour trip. After 2 nights in St. Michaels,

Inside Skinny

Talk the Talk

Salts have a language all their own. Everyone knows that on a boat you call the toilet the head, the right side starboard, and the left side port. But do you know why? Centuries ago the lavatory was always located at the front of the boat, or the head. Starboard derives its name from the steering board, used to steer boats back in the days of the British admiralty. This device hung off the ship's right side. Back then, the left side was called the larboard, far too difficult to distinguish from starboard. Some unknown simply changed this to port, which was logical: At dock, the boats had to be tied on the opposite side of the steering board. Other translations: kitchen is galley, map is chart, rope is line. Our pals at the Museum of Yachting in Newport, Rhode Island, couldn't come up with the origins of these terms.

The Long Leash

Worried about your toddler toddling right off the side of the boat? No need: Ask your charter company to provide you with a tether or bring your own. These are simple leashes that attach at one end to your child's life jacket and at the other to, say, the cabin. Another option is protective netting that attaches to the lifeline around the boat's perimeter. Once in place, the boat is entirely enclosed, sort of like a floating playpen. When you're underway after dark, adults on deck should also clip in—with a chest harness, steel carabiner, and tether. Contact **Lirakis Safety Harness**, which manufactures gear for both adults and children (401-846-5356).

head south to Oxford on the Tred Avon River, where you will overnight. Plan on a half-day to get to Solomons, on the tip of the peninsula where the Patuxent River empties into the Chesapeake. On your final day, turn your boat north for the daylong cruise back to Annapolis.

Best Reasons to Anchor: In Annapolis, tour the visitor center and museum at the **United States Naval Academy** (410-263-6933). The Naval Academy band performs Tuesday evenings on the Annapolis City Dock, Thursday evenings on the academy grounds, from mid-July to mid-August. In St. Michaels, a yachting center on the Miles River, visit the **Chesapeake Bay Maritime Museum** (410-745-2916), which has a boat-building workshop and small-craft displays. Rent bicycles and power boats at **St. Michaels Town Dock Marina** (410-745-2400). The town of Solomons has a quiet harborfront lined with shops and restaurants and the **Calvert Marine Museum** (410-326-2042), with special hands-on children's exhibits. Kids love Solomons Crab House, a converted firehouse where diners open hard-shell crabs with wooden mallets.

Local Wisdom: Sea nettles sometimes inundate the bay. Some charter companies rent "boat pools," large inflatable tubes from which nets are suspended, allowing you to swim safely out of jellyfish-reach. If you do get stung, Adolph's meat tenderizer takes the sting away.

Two Family-Oriented New England Windjammer Trips

Although sailing trips usually aim to induce a euphoric torpor among adults, the windjammer *Isaac H. Evans*, out of Rockland, Maine, now offers 3-day trips geared to the kinetics of kids. As the historic 20-passenger, 105-foot schooner navigates the island-specked waters of Penobscot Bay, Captain Ed Glaser puts kids to work furling mains, coiling lines, and practicing other nautical techniques and terminology (minus the singing, which kids find dorky). Glaser also introduces them to the local seals, porpoises, eagles, osprey, and the rare whale, and takes them ashore to investigate tide pools. Kids can also learn to row and sail small boats. All trips include an island lobster bake, but the trip to book is the July 10 departure, which coincides with Rockland Schooner Days: Historic ships will pass in the daylight, and fireworks will boom at night. All cabins (though snug, have a window that actually opens and a sink) are doubles, and Glaser will pair up spare kids if necessary. **Ages:** 8 and up. **Family trip dates:** July 10, 21, 28, and August 11. **Cost:** $390 per person. **Phone:** 800-648-4544.

As an alternative, sign on with the *Edna*, a 22-passenger, 80-foot staysail schooner that makes 7-day trips out of Boston and Newport under the auspices of the Boston Nautical Heritage Group. Education is the watchword here, and kids will find themselves navigating, steering, climbing the rigging, and standing watch. **Ages:** 10 and up. **Trip dates:** Weekly Sunday to Saturday cruises throughout July and August. **Cost:** $895 per adult; $695 for kids 16 and under. **Phone:** 617-344-1749.

—HANNAH HOLMES

STAYING SAFE: CHOOSING A CHARTER

There are three sailboat-chartering options for families. To decide which is best for yours, evaluate your sailing ability and your willingness to shoulder the responsibility for your brood's safety at sea.

Bareboats: Experienced sailors can charter boats without a professional skipper or crew aboard; this gives you the most freedom and privacy but also requires greater skill and responsibility. Before booking your boat, charter companies will require documentation (licenses or sailing resumes) of your boat-handling skills. Upon arrival, you'll be thoroughly briefed and checked out before being given the helm. It's always desirable—and sometimes necessary—to have more than one able sailor aboard.

Crewed Charters: Your boat comes with a paid skipper (and possibly a mate), who will be in charge of sailing the boat, keeping it clean, overseeing provisions, and, in some cases, preparing meals. This is the most expensive, least stressful way to sail; you can pitch in as much or as little as you wish. Be sure to request a crew that enjoys sailing with kids, specifying your children's ages.

Flotilla Charters: For those who can't quite stomach the price tag of a crewed charter, there's flotilla sailing: A group of boats follows a lead boat manned by a skipper and a bos'n. Cabins on the lead boat are considerably discounted from the cost of a personal charter, and families usually find the camaraderie among fellow charterers to be well worth the loss of freedom.　—*M.L.N.*

Getting Underway: Hartge Chesapeake Charters (410-867-7240) in Galesville, Maryland, has bareboats from 28 feet to 44 feet; 7-day charters range from $730 to $1,750. **Tred Avon Yacht Sales & Charters** (410-226-5000) has 30- to 45-foot boats, bare and captained, for $1,100 to $2,100 a week. **Annapolis Bay Charters** (800-292-1119) organizes flotillas and charters bareboats from 29 to 51 feet for $960 to $3,250 per week. For a captain, add $150 the first day, $110 each additional day.

THE NORTHEAST

Cape Cod and the Islands

The Big Picture: They may share a similar topography and climate, but the Elizabeth Islands, Martha's Vineyard, and Nantucket are anything but homogenous—that's what makes cruising these waters so appealing. One day you're anchored off a grassy, uninhabited island watching deer graze along the shoreline, the next you're

The Annapolis Sailing School

A family working together like a well-oiled machine. Teenage kids willingly following orders, performing their assigned chores with enthusiasm. Fantasy? Maybe not—for 1 week, at least.

Annapolis Sailing School's Become a Sailing Family course, for groups of three to six, starts with a weekend of introductory sailing lessons in Chesapeake Bay. Parents and kids 12 and older learn aboard a 24-foot Rainbow sloop, while kids under 12 participate in the KidShip program, which teaches the basics in small centerboard dinghies. Next, the family reunites and, accompanied by an instructor, you'll embark on a 5-day cruise aboard a Newport 30, part of the school's flotilla of vessels. Bunks are ashore in a hotel the first 3 nights. Then, anchoring in coves or marinas, your family will sleep aboard while your instructor disembarks at night. By the end of the week, you'll be a competent, well-coordinated sailing crew. Cost is $2,650–$3,655, depending on your group's size.

In lieu of taking the family course, you can coordinate 2-, 3-, and 5-day adult beginner courses, also on the Rainbow 24, with KidShip Sailing School classes. The 2-day course is $225 for a single adult, $430 for a couple. Three-day courses are $340 for a single adult, $650 for two. Prices for the 5-day trip are $495 and $945 for an adult or couple. The 2-day KidShip program runs $180 for one kid, $340 for two; the 3-day program is $275 for one child, $525 for two; the 5-day program is $325 for one child, $600 for two. For additional information, call 800-638-9192.

—David Noland

docked near million-dollar homes and trendy restaurants. But your kids probably won't really notice the vast gulf in economies and wealth on these shores; they'll be too busy swimming in the Gulf Stream–warmed waters, picking blueberries, fishing for striped bass and bluefish, biking through scrubby moors, and watching the big ferries come and go. Midsummer brings prevailing southwesterly winds and relief from the morning and evening fog typical of spring and early summer.

Plotting a Course: From Mattapoisett, just north of Cape Cod, sail about 3 hours across Buzzards Bay to Hadley Harbor off Naushon Island. Spend the night, then head to tiny, uninhabited Weepecket for lunch. It's another 2½ hours to Cuttyhunk Island, where you'll anchor for the night. In the morning, sail through Quick's Hole, stop at Tarpaulin Cove for lunch, then make the 3-hour crossing to Edgartown. Spend the next 2 days exploring Martha's Vineyard, then sail for Nantucket, a 3- to 4-hour trip. You can anchor, moor, or dock at the boat basin. After 2 days on Nantucket, head across Nantucket Sound to Quissett Harbor on Cape Cod, about a 6-hour journey. The next morning, make the 3-hour trip back to Mattapoisett.

Best Reasons to Anchor: Hadley Harbor and Tarpaulin Cove, both off Naushon Island (owned by the Forbes family), offer great swimming and sandy beaches. On Martha's Vineyard, bicycles are the best way to get around. Rent them at **Wheel Happy** (508-627-5928) or **R.W. Cutler** (508-627-4052) for $10–$15 per day. In Oak Bluffs, stop by the **Flying Horses carousel,** the oldest in the country, and the Victorian cottage community known as Oak Bluffs Campmeeting Association. For big surf, head to 3-mile-long Katama Beach; for calmer waters, try Joseph A. Sylvia State Beach, between Oak Bluffs and Edgartown. In Menemsha, a working fishing village, the catch of the day can be viewed and bought from markets along Dutcher's Dock. Rent surfboards, Boogie boards, sea kayaks, sailboards, and small sailboats at **Wind's Up!** (508-693-4252). On Nantucket, rent bicycles at **Young's Bicycle Shop** (about $20 per day; 508-228-1151) or in-line skates at **Sports Locker on Wheels** ($16.95 per half-day; half-price for kids; 508-228-6610) and hit the 37 miles of paved bike paths that traverse the island. In Nantucket Town, visit the excellent **Nantucket Whaling Museum** (508-228-1894). Tiny Children's Beach, a short walk from the harbor, and the much larger Jetties Beach, are an easy bike ride from town and are the best bets for families with small children. Strong surf can be found at Surfside and Madaket beaches, both on the bike paths.

Local Wisdom: These islands are infested with Lyme disease–carrying ticks. If you venture off the beaches into grasslands or woods, wear long pants tucked into socks and check for ticks daily.

Getting Underway: If you have your own boat, just check in with the Mattapoisett marina (508-993-3100). To charter a boat you'll need to range afield a bit; try **Fiddler's Cove Yacht Charters** in North Falmouth (508-564-6327), which charters 38-foot bareboats ($2,200 per week). Another option would be to set sail from Portsmouth, Rhode Island; both **East Passage Sailing** (401-683-5930) and **Freedom Yacht Charters** (800-999-2909) have bareboat and crewed/skippered charters, beginning at around $1,800 a week.

THE CARIBBEAN

The British Virgin Islands

The Big Picture: Warm, Windex-clear water, pristine beaches and reefs, short distances between anchorages, and steady tropical trade winds make this 35-mile chain of hilly islands one of the world's premier winter charter destinations. Few people know, though, that summer may be an even better time to sail here, especially for families who don't want to be in competition with other charterers for prime moorings, dinner reservations, or kicking room in the choice snorkeling spots. But summer does carry the risk of hurricanes, particularly as the season wears on. So to be safe, plan on completing your trip by mid-August.

Plotting a Course: Because the islands are so close together, you can design your route as you go, backtracking several times if you wish. On a 7-day cruise, you might depart from Road Town on Tortola and sail for Norman Island, about 2 hours away.

After overnighting there, sail 3 hours to Cooper Island. The following day, make the 2½-hour crossing to Marina Cay and moor for the night. In the morning, sail for Virgin Gorda, about 2 hours away (you'll want to give yourself 2 days to explore here). Then, making the 3-hour passage to Guana Island for lunch, push on for another 3 hours to Cane Garden Bay on Tortola. The last day, sail to Sandy Cay or Jost Van Dyke, 1½ hours away, then return to Road Town.

Best Reasons to Dock: The Bight on Norman Island has great snorkeling, and if you motor around the corner to Treasure Point, you'll find shoreline caves that once held pirate treasure and are said to have been the inspiration for Robert Louis Stevenson's *Treasure Island*. The **Cooper Island Beach Club** (800-542-4624), on a protected bay, rents small sailboats ($15 per half-day), sailboards ($35 per day), sea kayaks, and snorkeling gear, and its restaurant serves mahimahi and conch fritters—plus tunes by local reggae bands. On Virgin Gorda, you'll undoubtedly visit The Baths, a jumble of boulders and hidden grottoes that's become the Wal-Mart of the Caribbean—nobody sails by without stopping. Near the north-

east end of Virgin Gorda, the **Bitter End Yacht Club** (800-872-2392) has moorings for transients, a shark pen, a good restaurant, and free movies at the outdoor Sand Palace. Snorkeling is best just off nearby Prickly Pear Island, where you'll see multicolored sponges, coral polyps, parrotfish, and barracuda. Back on Tortola, in tranquil Cane Garden Bay, **Stanley's Welcome Bar & Restaurant** will serve you a cool drink while your kids frolic on the beachfront tire swing.

Local Wisdom: Make sure everyone in your party wears reef shoes. A coral cut, which is highly susceptible to infection, can keep you out of the water for the rest of the trip.

Getting Underway: The Moorings (800-535-7289) has customized bareboats out of Road Town from 31 to 51 feet for $1,330 to $3,850 per week in the summer. With a skipper, add $109 per day; with a cook, add $89 per day. **Caribbean Yacht Charters Inc.** (800-225-2520) charters boats from 36 to 51 feet for $1,995 to $3,320 a week from June to October. Their charters originate in St. Thomas, and itineraries usually include St. John.

—MEG LUKENS NOONAN

7

The basic sea kayak design, 4,000 years old, still offers a reassuring body-hug. These boats are faster, more stable, and easier to paddle than canoes, and you can cram an awful lot of stuff into the bow and stern. More than one first-time sea kayaker has wondered why anybody would ever again shoulder a load that floats so easily on the water.

Sea Kayaking
Be Amphibious

Until your child is 14 or so, he or she won't provide much in the way of paddling power, so for younger kids you'll have to make some adjustments. While covering 8 miles before lunch at full steam without rest stops may be your objective, such rigidity won't appeal to your kids. They're interested in the here and now and would much rather stop to watch a nearby turtle sun itself than meet an arbitrary deadline.

Give each child a responsibility, even if you have to make one up. It makes them feel important and included, which then makes them more agreeable. (My girlfriend and I provide her 9-year-old with a compass-on-a-necklace and our heading. If we get more than 15 degrees off course, Molly issues corrections.) Likewise, everybody gets a paddle, even if it's plastic and only 18 inches long. In addition to having the obvious things instantly accessible (snacks, drinks, sunscreen, a broad-brimmed hat, insect repellent, extra layers, and raingear), it's a good idea to bring surprises (a string to tow their own personal ocean liner behind the boat, tiny plastic action figures, a toy compass).

The following routes will maximize your time close to shore, which is not only safer but also more interesting (novices should sign on with an outfitted trip). And remember the answer to 90 percent of the paddling questions posed by children between 7 and 12: "In about 20 minutes."

THE WEST COAST

Queen Charlotte Islands
British Columbia

The 150 islands known as the Queen Charlottes have achieved near-mythic status among paddlers. They're well off the mainstream kayaking routes along the Northwest coast, and you don't end up in this green and misty wilderness by accident (six ferries a week in summer make the half-day trip from Prince Rupert to Skidegate across the turbulent Hecate Strait). Dubbed the Canadian Galápagos for the relic species that survived when the last ice age bypassed the area, the Charlottes play host to the world's largest black bears—as well as to unique subspecies of pine-marten, saw-whet owl, and hairy woodpecker. There are spruce trees 200 feet tall, and red cedars dip their lower branches into the sea during the 20-foot high tides.

Critter Factor: Family harmony requires multiple sets

THE HYSTERICAL PARENT

hat if my kid capsizes in icy water, and hypothermia sets in before I'm able to pull him out?

If a sea kayak does flip, it's usually because the paddler is inexperienced. Sea kayaks are infinitely more stable than whitewater kayaks, and all doubles have a rudder, which, combined with their length (some 19 feet), makes them easier to steer and therefore helps keep them upright even amid big rollers. But no reputable outfitter would ever take a family out in high-wave conditions—and no parent, paddling unguided, should either. But what if you and your child do wind up in the water? In 50- to 65-degree water, like that of the Northwest and Northeast, it's an emergency situation. If you're paddling on your own, and you haven't mastered the delicate balancing act known as a self-rescue, you have no business kayaking—much less taking a child out—without a reputable guide or experienced paddler.

In a fleet of several boats, we practice what's called an assisted rescue: The other kayaks gather around the flipped boat to form a pontoon-like raft, then we immediately work to right the boat, pull the paddlers out of the water, and get them to shore quickly.

—Constance Page, mother of two, takes her kids on the water when she's not guiding for Anadyr Adventures in Valdez, Alaska.

---

of binocs for the seals, salmon, sea lions, orcas, otters, the highest density of nesting bald eagles in western Canada, and the world's largest population of Peale's peregrine falcons.

Route: To minimize commuting time into the best areas, hire an outfitter to take you 40 miles south into Gwaii Haanas National Park Reserve and the fine gravel beach on Kunga Island, where you can camp. A 10-minute paddle away is Tanu Island, site of an overgrown former Haida Indian village. Spend a couple of days working your way down the sound between Moresby and Lyell islands, camping at

Lockeport, an abandoned copper-mining town. Head east the next day to Murchison Island, a 10-minute paddle from Hotspring Island, where you can bathe in the natural hot spring pools. Reverse the route and meet your outfitter back on Kunga Island.

Hired Help: Moresby Explorers Ltd. (800-806-7633) rents kayaks for C$145 per week; **Pacific Rim Paddling** (604-384-6103) offers 1-week trips for C$855–C$995 per person (2-week trips cost C$1,580); **Ecosummer Expeditions** (800-465-8884) runs 1-week trips for C$1,155 per person (2 weeks for C$1,875).

Gulf Islands
British Columbia

A mere few miles northwest of the San Juan Islands lies a better bet for the family. The Gulf Islands get the same 250 days of sunshine a year—but have much gentler currents, a fraction of the population, and miles of undeveloped shoreline. The 200 islands scattered between Vancouver Island and the mainland form a natural basin that traps and slows water: You don't have to schedule every move around the tides. It's easy to plan a trip that minimizes open-water crossings in favor of hugging the southwestern shore of the islands, uplifted sedimentary layers where honeycombed sandstone cliffs rise up to 200 feet. Their beauty is also functional, absorbing the sun's heat, shielding you from the prevailing winds, and keeping the kids busy playing Find the Monster in the Rock.

Critter Factor: Look down and see starfish; look up and see bald eagles. You'll also find river otters, sea lions, and kingfishers, mink scavenging the shore, and seals and orcas cruising the waters.

Route: Take the ferry from Tsawwassen on the mainland, or from Vancouver Island, to 18-mile-long Galiano Island (population 700), then drive to Montague Harbor Provincial Park. Camp here for the night, then paddle up the coast of Galiano and west to Wallace Island. It's a 5-mile paddle, only the last mile of which is over open water. The 2-mile-long island, with no permanent inhabitants, is the site of a provincial park and plenty of flat, grassy areas to camp. Base yourself here for 3 nights, sparing yourself the daily chore of loading the boat. Take day paddles around Wallace and nearby islands. Walker Hook, southwest of Wallace, has a sandy beach, and Thetis Island, a 5-mile paddle west along the chain of islands, has a pub where you can stop in for a hot meal and a shower.

Hired Help: Gulf Island Kayaking (250-539-2442); SaltSpring Kayaking (250-653-4222) rents kayaks for C$45–C$70 per day and runs 4-day trips for C$350 per person; Sea Otter Kayaking (250-537-5678) runs 4-day trips for C$425 (20 percent discount for kids) and rents kayaks for C$15–C$30 per day.

Resources: B.C. Ferries sails from near Vancouver or Victoria to five of the Gulf Islands, including Galiano; call 604-386-3431. Contact the Supernatural British Columbia Reservation and Information Service at 800-663-6000.

THE SOUTH

The Outer Banks
North Carolina

The ever-shifting ribbon of barrier islands along the coast of North Carolina pulls in a lot of East Coast vacationers in the summer; since most never lose sight of their cars, it's easy to put the crowds behind you. On one side of you are 125 miles of prime Atlantic beach; on the other are the more protected waters of Albemarle and Pamlico sounds, a vast nursery for finfish and blue crabs, where herons and egrets stalk the shallows. The lack of legal places to camp within easy paddling distance of each other anywhere on the Outer Banks means you'll be doing mostly day trips.

Critter Factor: You'll see osprey, terns, kingfishers, gulls, hermit crabs, and horseshoe crabs. Alligator River has otters, mink, and red wolves.

Route: Camp for 2 nights at the Colington Island Campground on Colington Island, a fishing community, and buy some fresh tuna at nearly world-famous Billy's Seafood. You can do a day paddle around the islands up and down Albemarle Sound and Kitty Hawk Bay, which surround Colington. The next day, stop at Roanoke Island for lunch and visit the North Carolina Aquarium, a sleeper attraction with great hands-on exhibits for kids. Stop by the U.S. Fish and Wildlife office in Manteo for maps of Alligator River and continue 12 miles on North Carolina 64, then 3 miles to the end of Buffalo City Road. Put in here, and explore the 15 miles of paddling trails at the refuge. In the morning you can move camp to the National Park Service campground, 20 miles southeast at Oregon Inlet, where you can do day paddles out to Duck Island, 2 or 3 miles out in Pamlico Sound, and see the 1,142-pound world-record Atlantic blue marlin on 24-hour display outside the Oregon Inlet Fishing Center.

Hired Help: Kitty Hawk Sports (800-948-0759) rents out sea kayaks ($28–$52 per day) and runs overnight trips ($199 per person for 2 days and 1 night; includes guide, kayak, camping gear, food, and transportation).

Inside Skinny

Popeye Arms

Bulging biceps are not required for sea kayaking, so if your arms are completely trashed at the end of the day, you're probably not paddling correctly. The muscles doing the bulk of the work should be the abdominals; your arms do little more than facilitate the transfer of power from these big muscle groups to the paddle. To paddle most efficiently, remember the mechanics of a cyclist with toeclips: The downstroke leg pushes, while the opposite leg pulls up. The same is true in kayaking: The ideal stroke is a simultaneous pushing and pulling.

Sciatic Aid

Wad your jacket or shell and cram it under your thighs: Now your jacket is not only accessible, it also supports the hamstring muscles (the kayak bench you sit on is only 6 inches wide at best). This relieves pressure on the lower back and sciatic nerve, which improves your posture and, therefore, your paddling technique. To further help the lower back, get a Therm-a-Rest to pad your back from the cockpit's wall.

Kid Expectations

So how long can you reasonably expect your child to paddle? Ben Miltner, owner and operator of Gulf Island Kayaking in British Columbia, says it's best to stop at least every hour to hike and run around on the beach. He says that kids younger than age 14 need an occasional diversion, though they'll be fine in a kayak once it's made clear they won't be there for hours. As for paddling enthusiasm, they're "usually good for 15-minute bursts but then inevitably give up," says Miltner. Which isn't a problem if you aren't planning to cover significant mileage. In fact, it's well documented that kids frequently pull in their paddles, wiggle down into the cockpit until their life vests are positioned as neck-supporting pillows, and suddenly doze off.

Resources: Colington Park Campground, 919-441-6128; **Alligator River National Wildlife Refuge**, 919-473-1131. For information on Oregon Inlet campground, call the **Cape Hatteras National Seashore** (919-473-2111).

THE NORTHEAST

Stonington to Isle au Haut
Penobscot Bay, Maine

When a Mainer announces "I'll a hoe," he's not offering to help you garden—he's letting you in on a little secret. Millions of tourists swarm over the 54 square miles of Acadia National Park on Mount Desert Island to the east, but few ever make it down to the lesser known part of the park on Isle au Haut. While much of the Maine coast is disconcertingly exposed, the numerous islands in eastern Penobscot Bay between Stonington, a working fishing village, and Isle au Haut (just 6 miles away) offer protected paddling. The dome-shaped granitic islands pastured with evergreens and inset with crushed shell beaches make this one of the most beautiful sections of Maine's 3,600-mile coast. Most of the islands are private, but you're rarely more than a quarter mile from one should you need to make an emergency landing. June is a great time to go, when the days are long and the crowds have yet to arrive.

Critter Factor: Harbor porpoises, harbor seals, ospreys, auks, endangered roseate terns, and eider ducks can be seen, as well as mink, raccoon, and deer on some islands.

Route: Put in at Stonington and head southeast toward Russ Island, 1 mile away. From here, head east to Camp Island, then southeast to Devil Island, a paddle of about 1 hour. Just on the northwest side of Devil is Hell's Half Acre, a flat, secluded island with pine trees and good camping. In the morning, you've got an easy 3-mile paddle as you weave south between Buckle and Coombes islands, past Wreck Island, and on to Harbor Island. The western point of Harbor has a big, open field and, in season, loads of raspberries. To keep a low profile, make camp up in the woods. It's 1 hour's paddle the next day to the town of Isle au Haut on the northwest part of the island, where you can pick up basic provisions at the store (closed Sundays). The island is heavily wooded, with 18 miles of trails. Pack a picnic lunch and hike down along the coves and inlets of the west side as far as your legs feel like carrying you. From Harbor Island back to Stonington, it's an easy 3-mile paddle.

Hired Help: Maine Island Kayak Company (800-796-2373) charges $450 for a 3-day trip to Isle au Haut. **Maine Sport Outfitters** (800-722-0826) offers a 4-day camping trip for $470 per person, 6 days for $700, and also rents kayaks ($35–$50 per day).

Resources: The **Maine Island Trail Association**, 207-594-9209; the **Bureau of**

Parks and Lands, 207-287-3061 (ask for their brochure, *Your Islands on the Coast*); **Acadia National Park**, 207-288-3338.

THE CARIBBEAN

Virgin Islands

Air-conditioned by trade winds that keep temperatures in the 70s and 80s year-round, and blessed with lower humidity than most parts of the Caribbean, the Virgin Islands can be forgiven for sometimes confusing winter and summer. By mid-April the tourists have split, and the locals reclaim the palm trees, coral reefs, and crescent bays inset with white sand beaches. And summer seas are generally calmer, so it's a great time to bring the family down for low-intensity paddling. The 100 or so islands owned by the U.S. and Britain are virtually all within 1 mile of each other and have superior campgrounds and public beaches. Two-thirds of St. John is covered by the pristine 12,500-acre U.S. Virgin Islands National Park, with 20 miles of hiking trails. A third of the park lies underwater, including a 225-yard interpretive trail.

Critter Factor: Parrot fish, yellowtail snappers, sergeant majors, and occasional green and hawksbill turtles are below water. Brown pelicans, herons, and Caribbean martins hang out above.

Route: Fly directly to Tortola—or ferry over from St. John (a 30-minute trip)—and set up at the **Brewers Bay campground** (809-494-3463), on the island's north side, for a 6-day trip. Spend a couple of days here for the excellent snorkeling and day paddles out to uninhabited Sandy Cay (take the botanical walking tour) and Sandy Spit. Half an hour's paddle south along the coast is Cane Garden Bay, where there's a gorgeous beach with snorkeling in the coral gardens and along a drop-off wall. When you're ready, pack up and head west, with the wind at your back, to Jost Van Dyke, 5 miles away. Spend 2 nights on Jost, a rugged little island with a good beach at White Bay. Your next move is a 2½-hour paddle south to St. John, where you'll stay for 2 nights at **Maho Bay Camps,** an ecological showplace with 114 tent cottages on platforms (December 15–April 30 $95 per night per couple, $15 extra per child; off-season rates $60 per night per couple; $10–$12 extra per kid; 809-776-6226). Snorkel and hike the park, then paddle to nearby Trunk Bay and take the **Frett Shuttle bus** ($4) into St. John's main town, Cruz Bay. Morgan's Mango restaurant serves a great "voodoo snapper" (blackened fish smothered with fruit salsa).

Hired Help: Arawak Expeditions (800-238-8687) runs trips year-round (5 days, $750–$850; 7 days, $925–$1,025).

Resources: Virgin Islands National Park, 809-776-6201; British Virgin Islands Tourist Board, 800-835-8530.

—Bill Heavey

8

Going down the river with the family is like playing house: Cooking, cleaning, bedding down, and packing up—even plumbing—become playlike in a house with no ceilings and no clocks, just sandstone walls. The family, swept along by the flow of days, becomes a more attentive and imaginative version of itself.

Wet As You Wanna Be

Whitewater Rafting

The sun blazes down on the desert rivers near where we live: the San Juan, the Dolores, the Colorado. We insist that the girls wear light cotton pants and long-sleeved shirts and white, floppy hats. We slather them with sunscreen, and only then, like skiers ready for a storm, do we put in.

We also insist that the girls understand the importance of wearing their life jackets whenever they're in the raft, and even on shore when they're near the water. "What are the rules?" we chant. "Remember the rules."

Mostly, the rules are simple. One: Everybody helps. Loading and unloading the raft, setting up tents, pumping drinking water, preparing meals, and washing up. The kids love the responsibility of finding the most beautiful spot for "the groover," the self-contained toilet; it might be up a sandy draw, or under a mineral-streaked overhang. They've embraced with childlike fanaticism the notion of leaving no trace, not even a burrito crumb that might lure ants to the beach.

Rule number two: Everybody plays. Make drip sand castles. Carve your own cliff dwellings into sandbanks. Hunt for scorpions and pot shards. Dream about being an Anasazi living off the land. Paddle the kayak all by yourself in the big, safe, horseshoe eddy beside the camp.

When the water is flat, sometimes the girls drift behind the raft in inner tubes. When the water runs wild, we like to have them with us in the boat. I've watched them progress from trepidation at the approach of roaring whitewater to pure eagerness, the two of them in the bow, riding the haystacks like cowboys on a saddle bronc. At the take-out, nobody wants to leave. We've adjusted to the river's pace, grown simple ourselves

in response to the game's few ineluctable demands. —PETER SHELTON

THE WEST COAST

Tatshenshini River, Yukon/British Columbia/ Alaska
Class III+

A trip down the Tatshenshini is a journey to a more perfect past, where water can still be drunk, clear and cold, right from the stream, and where the abundant Alaskan brown bears are still wild. It takes 10 or 11 days to run the most popular 140 miles: from Dalton Post in the Yukon to Dry Bay on Alaska's southern panhandle, through the largest nonpolar ice fields in the world and forests and valleys dense with bears, moose, and mountain goats. The sight of a bald eagle soaring over the river to land in postage-stamp profile becomes almost commonplace. To let you absorb this scenic overload at your leisure, most outfitters incorporate 3 or 4 layover days into the itinerary. Your family will get to tramp around on 10,000-year-old glaciers and kayak in Alsek Bay through a floating sculpture garden of chlorine-blue icebergs.

Even though the rapids rarely roar above a Class III level and subside somewhat after the first day's run

Bringing Up Grandpa

We pushed the family-vacation envelope last summer when we took a multigenerational clan rafting on Idaho's North Fork of the Salmon. There were twenty-one of us in all, ranging from my 6-year-old son to my 75-year-old father. My 33-year-old brother, who happens to be an expert whitewater guide, took on the role of fearless leader.

To keep things sane, we camped in one spot for the 4 days, putting in above different stretches of river each day. Rafting bonded both ends of the generational spectrum: The younger kids and older adults preferred the mellower whitewater and, after a morning float, were happy to spend afternoons in camp—hiking, fishing, exploring, skipping rocks, and playing with the dogs. That left time for us

hard-core rafters to try some rough stuff. Although my father sometimes drove the kids to an overlook so they could watch us take on a particularly feisty wave, they missed seeing my cousin flip his raft, spilling everyone into the drink.

The river turned out to be a great family equalizer. My father, used to being in charge, willingly submitted to my PFD checks and my brother's river-rescue drills. And all the kids hauled gear twice their size up and down the steep riverbank.

As for me, I was exhausted. I felt fully responsible for the care and safety of both my father and my kids—a prime example of what sociologists refer to as the Sandwich Generation. In the end, though, my worries were unfounded: The tribe thrived. —MICHELE MORRIS

---

through a narrow canyon, this is not a trip outfitters recommend for children under 12. Both **James Henry River Journeys** (800-786-1830) and **Rivers & Oceans** (800-360-7238) offer 11-day trips on the Tatshenshini for about $2,300 per person. Call **Glacier Bay National Park and Preserve** (907-697-2230) for more information and a complete list of outfitters.

—MARK JANNOT

Chilko, Chilcotin, Fraser River System, British Columbia
Class II–IV+

Many people consider the Chilko, Chilcotin, and Fraser River system in southwestern British Columbia to be the

most spectacular whitewater trip in North America. Starting at 4,000-foot-high Chilko Lake, a 45-minute charter flight from Vancouver, you'll begin the 130-mile, 6-day raft trip in a stunning valley ringed with forests and snowcapped peaks. But it's the narrow lava gorges of the upper Chilko River that lure adventurous, wave-hunting families; from the outset, the milky-green Chilko cuts deep into the Chilcotin Plateau, which bristles with lodgepole pines. Lava Canyon looms ahead, 14 miles of Class III–V excitement, with heart-stopping hydraulics and towering haystacks.

By the third day you'll reach the "Gap," a 20-foot-wide chute that squirts you into the Chilcotin River, an equally powerful waterway of massive wave trains that roller-coaster for miles. Interspersed with the big stuff are stretches of relaxing flatwater and smaller but still respectable rapids, perfect for running in self-bailing, inflatable "ducky" kayaks. In camp there's plenty of time to hike, fish, or scout for wildlife—grizzlies, black bears, moose, eagles, and more.

On the fifth day, a dull roar and dancing spray announce the arrival of Farwell and Big John canyons, each with their scream-yourself-silly, knockdown rapids. Then, after gradually dropping more than 3,000 vertical feet in elevation, the countryside becomes a semi-desert of sprawling grasslands, granite canyons, and towering "hoodoos" as the Chilcotin merges into the mighty volume of the Fraser River. At the confluence is the Junction Sheep Reserve, home to the world's largest population of California bighorn sheep.

Upon leaving your sandy beach camp on the Fraser River, you'll board a train for the 210-mile journey back to Vancouver, in which every turn of the tracks unveils dramatic vistas of lakes and valleys.

Rivers and Oceans Unlimited Expeditions (800-360-7238) offers eight departures in July and August. Cost is C$1,495, including airfare from Vancouver, meals, and equipment. Minimum age is 12. For kids 6 and up, the Resort and Raft trip (same price) includes a stay at a guest ranch.

—Larry Rice

Rogue River, Oregon
Class III

One of the first National Wild and Scenic rivers (designated in 1968), the

Rogue is a classic family run. As a Class III river, the minimum age for paddlers is a mere 7. However, the rapids—particularly the percolating froth that runs through Mule Creek Canyon, where the river narrows to a width of just 15 feet—are exciting enough to satisfy even the most Nintendo-saturated adolescent synapses. (If not, they can run the canyon in an inflatable kayak to heighten the terror.) Because it's a classic drop-and-pool river, the rapids dump into calmer pools, so even a capsized kayaker isn't going to get flushed too far downstream.

With its family-friendly pedigree, a Rogue trip is more likely than most to have same-age companions for your kids. Most outfitters run the 45-mile section through the Siskiyou National Forest, from Galice to Foster Bar, in 4 or 5 days. Many offer lodge-based trips, with the seductive appeal of a nightly sojourn on a real mattress. But the real family option is the camping trip, where you can sit around the campfire at night and trade Bigfoot tales. **James Henry River Journeys** (800-786-1830), **ARTA** (800-323-2782), **O.A.R.S.** (800-346-6277), and **Outdoor Adventures** (800-323-4234) all offer 4- and 5-day trips, ranging from $625–$725 for adults, $565–$660 for kids.   —Mark Jannot

The Klamath River, California
Class III–IV

The Klamath is California's biggest and longest whitewater river, with some of the best stretches for family rafting in the state.

THE HYSTERICAL PARENT

Man Overboard!

I have three kids of my own, and I started them out on easy whitewater. On family-appropriate rivers, falling in really isn't such a big deal. It's pretty hard for your kids to get into trouble if their flotation devices fit properly (and you'll make sure they wear them at all times, right?).

To ensure my children's comfort in the water, I take them to a quiet pool and let them experience the sensation of floating in the flotation device. Then I teach them the correct way to be carried downstream: on your back, with feet pointing toward the water's flow and toes visible above the water's surface (letting you push off rocks rather than ram into them). I tell them to pay attention to their breathing so they don't suck in water. Fortunately, kids usually take quite naturally to the physics of water safety.

I never put fragile cargo (kids and the elderly) in the first raft. This creates a downstream safety net to easily catch such passengers if they were to fall overboard. I also put them in an oar–paddle combination raft, piloted by one of my senior guides. With that extra oar, it only takes two good strokes to get to someone in the water. For anxious parents there are riverbank footpaths: You can walk down the stretches of river you don't want to ride down. But it's been my experience that all anxieties vanish after the first rapid.

—Marty McDonnell, owner of Sierra Mac River Trips,
has been a river guide for 31 years.

When Zeus Rages

Get off the water at the first signs of a storm. Lightning usually strikes the highest object or landmass in its path, so stay out of open areas and never take cover under an isolated tree or at the base of a cliff. You'll be least vulnerable away from the shoreline, at the bottom of a valley or among trees of uniform height. Sit on your mattress pad to keep yourself from being grounded.

—Lisa Twyman Bessone

Snakes in the Grass

Snakes don't coil undercover, eagerly awaiting the chance to leap out and strike. They avoid humans and only bite when threatened, so stay on the trail. When scrambling over rocks, don't put your hands or feet in nooks or on outcroppings that you can't see. (You might surprise a dozing herp.) Finally, if you come across a snake, give it wide berth. Don't prod it or try to pick it up.

—Lisa Twyman Bessone

The minimum age for most outfitted trips is only 7; warm water, sandy beaches, and side creeks keep the little rafters happy, and because it's a classic pool-and-drop river, even in a worst-case scenario—a flip—everyone washes out into the calm water below.

It's possible to run more than 180 miles of the Klamath, but some of the best family whitewater action happens along the 26-mile stretch of the lower Klamath between Happy Camp and Presidio Bar.

The first 3 miles below the put-in at Indian Creek in Happy Camp begin gently, on bouncy Class II water perfect for practicing your paddling before reaching the first major rapid. Scary-looking Class III Rattlesnake will get your pulse going, but there's a straight-as-an-arrow sneak route along the left that lets you avoid all the major hazards.

Below here the river narrows through a 20-foot-wide squeeze, known alternately as The Slot, The Wall, or The Trough, before opening back up into a long series of pools, side creeks, and sandy beaches. Along the way you'll get to see plenty of turtles, osprey, eagles, deer, herons, river otters, and probably even some bears.

Many more Class III rapids stretch out for miles downstream, culminating with a hair-raising ride through Class III Dragon's Tooth, named for a jagged rock in the middle of the river. (If you don't feel comfortable running it, there's an easy hiking trail around it.)

A mile and a half downstream, try the easy hike three-quarters of a mile up Ukonom Creek through a beautiful old-growth forest to the twin Ukonom Falls—a Klamath rafting tradition.

Turtle River Rafting Company (916-926-3223) out of Mt. Shasta and

Whitewater Voyages from El Sobrante (800-488-7238) run 1- to 5-day trips on the Klamath from $86 to $610 per person depending on age and the length of the trip (minimum age is 6 for Turtle River; 7 for Whitewater Voyages); most go through the steep canyon below Happy Camp. Everything is included in the price except for tents and sleeping bags.　　　　　—ANDREW RICE

Tuolumne River, California
Class IV+

This is a whitewater trip that families have to earn. "For a family that hikes, camps, maybe does some boardsailing, and feels comfortable in action adventure sports, the T would be a great first choice," says Marty McDonnell of Sierra Mac River Trips. The standard 19-mile run from Meral's Pool to Ward's Ferry, just west of Yosemite National Park, may be the most revered whitewater trip in California. It's certainly a triumph of the Wild and Scenic River system, which bestowed its protection on the river in 1984, saving it from submersion by yet another dam. McDonnell recommends that families make the trip in midsummer, when the waters have quieted a bit but are still kept well-fed by regular releases from the Hetch Hetchy Reservoir in Yosemite. Even in midseason, numerous Class IV rapids—Nemesis, Hackamack's Hole, Squeeze, Evangelist—serve as a pounding prelude to the river's main attraction, the legendary 15-foot Clavey Falls, a Class V monster with a raft-swallowing hole at the bottom. (Outfitters love to set up camp just above the falls to heighten their passengers' dread and anticipation, causing some to lose their

DON'T FORGET...
polypropylene socks
bandanna
lip balm
Paktowl
waterproof sunscreen
Ziploc bags
water filter
baseball cap

nerve—or regain their sanity—and skirt the falls on foot.)

Sierra Mac (800-457-2580), **Whitewater Voyages** (800-488-7238), **O.A.R.S.** (800-346-6277), and **Outdoor Adventures** (800-323-4234) all offer 2- and 3-day trips for $315–$460 per person. The 3-day trips leave enough time for exploring side-canyon water slides and swimming holes. Most outfitters accept kids as young as 12. Call the **Stanislaus National Forest** (209-962-7825) for information on private rafting permits and a complete list of outfitters. —MARK JANNOT

THE SOUTHWEST

Desolation Canyon, Green River, Utah
Class II–III

For 84 miles, from Sand Wash Boat Ramp near Roosevelt, Utah, to Swasey's Beach, the Green River slices southward into the broad uplift of northeastern Utah's Tavaputs Plateau. A few miles downstream of your launch site is the entrance to Desolation Canyon, the deepest canyon in Utah; in places the river lies more than 5,000 feet below the canyon rim. The ensuing run is one of Canyon Country's premier wilderness floats, with easy to moderate whitewater, superb side hikes, cushy sandbar campsites, and abundant wildlife ranging from bighorn sheep to golden eagles. There are some 60 moderate rapids and many smaller riffles on this 5- to 6-day trip suitable for kids as young as 5.

Between runs, short hikes lead you to abandoned homesteads, shadow-filled grottoes, and Fremont Indian pictographs etched on rock walls some 1,000 years ago. Longer hikes take you into stark chasms virtually untouched by civilization, or up towering mesas.

After about 60 miles, Desolation's towering red walls abruptly end, giving way to a short, open valley followed by lower cliffs of gray, brown, yellow, and white sandstone. This is Gray Canyon, which Butch Cassidy and his bunch used as their hideout around the turn of the century.

Bill Dvorak's Kayak & Rafting Expeditions, Inc. (800-824-3795) offers five trips for families. In June and July, each adult guardian signing up for the Green River 6-day trip and paying full price ($935) can bring a child under 13 for free. Minimum age for kids is 5 (the standard kid's rate is $855). For general information on running Desolation and Gray Canyons, contact the **Bureau of Land Management** at 801-637-4591. —LARRY RICE

STAYING SAFE: CHOOSING A RIVER GUIDE

Unless you're married to Meryl Streep's character in *The River Wild*, your summer whitewater trip is probably going to be with a guide. Here are some questions to help determine whether the outfitter on the other end of the telephone is the one for you. Don't offer up answers to the following questions; instead, make the outfitting company convince you of its competence.

What are your guides' average age and average length of experience? If the answer is that they're college-age, with 2 to 3 years of experience, weigh this against how old your kids are and how tough the water is. While younger guides can be exuberant and perform feats of mind-melding with your teenagers, younger children or challenging water will probably make you want someone who's a bit more wizened (a thirtysomething) and field-tested (12–15 years of experience).

What medical training do your guides have? Basic first aid is a must; advanced first aid is preferable. Now outdoor professionals can take 40-plus-hour courses in specialized wilderness first aid, which empowers guides even more to handle medical emergencies. If guides on staff are EMTs (emergency medical technicians), all the better for you. And look for guides who are trained in river rescue.

What is the ratio of guests to guides? For families with young kids (requiring more care and attention), 4- or 5-to-1 is the answer you're looking for.

How many clients do you put in a raft? Four is best, six is fine, and eight is the absolute limit for multiday trips.

Are your Personal Flotation Devices (PFDs) Coast Guard-approved? Even the most meatheaded outfit has to provide PFDs and ones that are Coast Guard approved are the industry standard. What you need to determine is whether your outfitter's PFDs will adequately protect your children. If they assure you that your child will be safe in a small adult PFD, hang up the phone. You want your child in a Youth Type 1 or 5 jacket—specifically designed for your child's body weight.

Can you provide me with the names and telephone numbers of some former clients? Ask for references. A good family outfitter will happily provide you with this information. Specify that you want to interview former clients who took kids the same age as yours on the trip.

—*Lisa Twyman Bessone*

San Juan River, Utah
Class II

Norman Nevills pioneered commercial river running on the San Juan in 1938. Setting out from Mexican Hat on a raft made of old outhouse planks, he inaugurated a river that has become perhaps the best introductory trip in the country. This classic spans 83 miles of southeastern Utah, from Sand Island to Clay Hills Crossing on Lake Powell. Running through Navajo lands, it flows past some of the best-preserved Anasazi ruins and petroglyphs in the Southwest.

The San Juan is most famous for a long stretch of meandering river, known as the Goosenecks, which is bound by 2,000-foot sandstone and limestone canyon walls. At one point the river travels 7 miles to go only 2 miles as the crow flies. The current is among the fastest in the country, particularly in the early summer; though that speed doesn't translate into churning rapids, it does account for the intermittent "sand waves" that arise out of nowhere, carrying rafts along on their roller-coaster crests. The water temperature in summer settles at 70 degrees or so—perfect for swimming, mud fights, and frolicking.

Holiday River Expeditions (800-624-6323) offers 3- and 4-day trips in May and June for $460 and $600 for adults, $360 and $500 for children. (The 3-day trip launches at Mexican Hat and misses some of the better Anasazi sites upriver.) **O.A.R.S.** (800-346-6277) runs 3-, 4-, and 6-day trips throughout the summer, from $495 to $695 for adults, $440 to $640 for kids. Both outfitters will take children as young as 5 years old.   —MARK JANNOT

Colorado River, Arizona
Class I–X on its own scale

Hundreds of rapids, including Lava Falls and Crystal—among the biggest whitewater in the world—draw seasoned river rats to the Colorado from around the globe. The Colorado's rapids are so big (though not always technically difficult) that it's the only river to be rated on a scale of I–X; kids should be at least 12 to run this one (for the section below Whitmore Wash the minimum age is 7).

But the trip also includes long stretches of serene floating between canyon walls that range in color from chocolate to violet to yellow, and that may be as old as half a billion years. Side trips take you past enormous stone amphitheaters, rock spires, and hanging gardens of columbine and cardinal monkey flower, as well as to ancient Anasazi cliff dwellings. Other highlights include splashing beneath dramatic Havasu Falls, and soaking in the warm blue Little Colorado, a tributary.

Families can run one of a handful of sections, or the entire 279 miles, on outfitted trips ranging from 5 to 19 days. And if you travel with Grand Canyon Dories, you can emulate the river's first explorers by experiencing the mother-of-all-river-trips in handcrafted boats.

Most trips begin at four major access points: Lees Ferry (mile 0, just below the Utah border in Arizona), Phantom Ranch (mile 88), Whitmore Wash (mile 188, accessible only by helicopter) and Diamond Point (mile 226); they end at Pierce Ferry (mile 280, the terminus at Lake Mead). The first section, known as Marble Canyon, features fun rapids that shouldn't frighten the adults too badly. The scariest whitewater—including Lava and Crystal, both rated as X, and a handful of others rated as high as IX—roils in the stretch below Phantom Ranch. The best time to float the Colorado is in spring or fall; summer visitors should bring along light-colored clothing, sunscreen and big hats, and drink plenty of water; temperatures can reach three digits.

Grand Canyon Dories (800-877-3679) runs seven trips from 5 to 19 days for $1,124 to $3,256 (minimum age is 12). **Outdoors Unlimited River Trips** (520-526-4546) runs 5-, 8-, and 12-day trips for $1,025, $1,575, and $2,075 (minimum age 10). Grand Canyon Dories also offers a 94-mile, 5-day lower Colorado trip suitable for children as young as 7 ($1,124 per person). Passengers beginning or ending at Phantom Ranch should be fit enough to endure the 9-mile, 5,000-foot hike in or out (that's up or down) of the Grand Canyon on the Bright Angel Trail.

—JEFF WALLACH

Rio Chama, New Mexico
Class II–III

The Chama, a National Wild and Scenic River, is an ideal shorter trip, featuring exciting easy to moderate rapids on a manageable 2- or 3-day descent from the El Vado Dam through the Chama Canyon to the Abiquiú Reservoir, spanning a high-forest terrain of Douglas firs and ponderosa pines as well as sagebrush desert. The New Mexico air is crisp and clear; in the upper canyon, peregrine falcons and golden eagles fly overhead, with wild turkeys a common sight on the banks. The last third of the run, below Christ in the Desert Monastery, features yellow, red, and green sandstone formations that pop off the canyon walls. Most of the whitewater is packed into the last few miles of the trip, sending the kids off the river thrilled and happy.

Campsites are on huge shelves among thick stands of pine. The 3-day trip especially allows for hiking time in the forests, where you can discover ancient Anasazi encampments and other archaeological sites—ask the guides to point out some less-obvious artifacts.

May and June are the best months to go, with higher river volumes and fewer rafting parties to disturb the peace. **Far Flung Adventures** (800-359-2627) runs 2- and 3-day rafting trips for $202 and $303. **Kokopelli Rafting Adventures** (800-879-9035) charges $87 per person for day trips. —MARK JANNOT

Rio Grande, Lower Canyons, Texas
Class II–III

The tremendous sense of isolation and the hugeness in these canyons along the Texas-Mexico border can be almost overpowering at times. And one-upping that sense of awe is your incredulity at stumbling upon signs of long-ago habitation, such as the mysterious ruins of old *candelilla* (wax-making) operations.

The Rio Grande is relatively calm as it winds through this landscape of cliffs and desert flats, with maybe twelve significant rapids dotting a span of 85 miles. It's thus an ideal river for learning to kayak, for taking time to appreciate the environment's majesty, and for swimming in the warm currents and bathing in the hot springs. "Kids just love to explore down there," says Bill Dvorak of Dvorak's Kayak and Rafting Expeditions. "You see lots of turtles, fish, horses, roadrunners, peregrine falcons." Parents of young children, though, might consider whether they are ready to be so isolated for 7 full days.

Summer temperatures in the canyons can become almost unbearable, so it's best to go either before or after the height of summer. Both **Dvorak's** (800-824-3795) and **Far Flung Adventures** (800-359-4138) run 7-day trips from $700–$870 per person. If you're looking for a shorter but equally dramatic trip in

the same area, Far Flung Adventures offers 1- to 5-day trips in the Colorado, Santa Elena, Mariscal, and Boquillas canyons of Big Bend National Park.

—MARK JANNOT

THE ROCKIES

Snake River, Idaho
Class III

Forming the Oregon/Idaho border, the clear, green Snake River has, over time,

Stargazing

Far away from that big city glow, backcountry camping provides the perfect opportunity for an impromptu astronomy lesson. The best time to view any astronomical light show is when the moon is a sliver, so avoid the full moons of June 20, July 19, and August 18.

Between June and August, the Big Dipper is almost directly overhead. Follow the curve of the Dipper's handle westward to the bright orange Arcturus. As the most prominent star in Bootes—the Herdsman—Arcturus forms the "foot" in this eight-star, kite-shaped constellation. In mid-June, the glowing Vega—at about 45 degrees, or halfway between the eastern horizon and directly overhead—forms the top point of Lyra or "harp," which contains five stars in the shape of a diamond. Deneb, the eighth star and tail in Cygnus or "flying swan," can be found at an 8 o'clock position be-

low Lyra, and about 25 degrees above the northeast horizon. Both constellations are nearly overhead by mid-August.

At the end of June, Venus is a striking white light in the northwest that hovers above the horizon right after sunset. The second-brightest planet is Jupiter, a yellowish sphere visible in the east during evening hours. Also look for the red planet, Mars, which is most apparent around June 12, when it is situated next to the moon.

On August 11 and 12, from 10 P.M. to sunrise, you can watch an estimated 100 meteors per hour during the Perseid Meteor Shower, which occurs annually when the earth passes through the trail of sand-grain sized debris left by Swift-Tuttle, a comet that appears every 130 years.

A star chart (available from The Nature Company for $15; 800-227-1114) and compass always come in handy.

—LORIEN WARNER

THE FUN FILE: WHAT TO DO WHEN THE WATER'S CALM

Rock Painting. Pack watercolors, brushes, and white glue (to seal your creation once completed). Smooth rocks are everywhere.

Clay Works. Dig along riverbeds or under the water to find clay. To make a coil pot, flatten and cut out a base, then roll out coils and wind these up to form the pot's walls. Dry in the sun until hard. Paint and glaze with glue.

Fossil Rubbings. Riverbeds are fossil treasure troves. Lay a piece of paper over the fossil, then color over it with a charcoal pencil or crayon.

Plant Weaving. Look for the green leaves of reeds that are easy to bend. Cut thirty into uniform lengths of 2 feet with the tops and bottoms squared off. Lay fifteen side by side. Weave the remaining fifteen into these to form a place mat. When done, secure the four corners by sewing an X with string. Air dry thoroughly.

Nature Collage. Pack sheets of cardboard, markers, and colored glue. Hunt around camp for bark, berries, stones, pinecones, feathers, acorns, leaves, etc. Arrange and glue down to create your work of art.

Make a Snorkel. Find a hollow reed and cut the ends to make a snorkel. (The mask you'll have to pack.)

Sponge Off. Pack a lowly kitchen sponge and let the little ones go nuts, dipping it in the river and washing down the raft.

Learn About Animal Tracks. Soft riverbanks are an especially good medium for paw and claw prints. Paul Rezendes's *Tracking and the Art of Seeing* (Camden House Publishing, $19.95) is full of photos and animal behavior information. Keep a log, complete with sketches of tracks you've found.

Make a Waterscope. Pack a large plastic yogurt container, some clear plastic wrap, and some rubber bands. Cut out the bottom of the container and cover with the wrap, then secure with the rubber band. Seek out shallows for the best viewing.

String Up a Rope Swing. Find a strong tree and knot the bottom of a 10-foot length of rope for swingers to stand on. If the tree hangs over the water, all the better.

—*Lisa Twyman Bessone*

carved Hells Canyon, the deepest gorge in North America. In spite of the canyon's intimidating name, the portion of the river that runs through it is exciting without being threatening, making for a heavenly 3- to 5-day family camping trip. Encompassing steep slopes covered with cheatgrass, primrose, Ponderosa pine, and prickly pear cactus, and occasionally closed in by towering black basalt cliffs, Hells Canyon epitomizes the word BIG. The river through here carries twice the volume of water as the Colorado River, though in gentler style. First visited by Lewis and Clark in 1805 and more fully explored by fur traders a few years later, the gorgeous, sometimes foreboding canyon still exudes a pure and wild feel.

Just downstream of the put-in below Hells Canyon Dam (about a 5-hour drive northwest from Boise), the Snake drops steeply into Wild Sheep Rapid. Granite, a Class IV rapid not much further along, is ranked as one of the ten biggest drops in North America (the fearful can hike around it). But following these initial challenges, the rapids calm; the water becomes perfect for swimming and piloting a two-person inflatable kayak. Side hikes to Indian petroglyphs and old homesteads, great fishing for trout and bass, such potential visitors as elk, bear, and bighorn sheep, and the mostly tranquil pace make Hells Canyon an ideal family outing.

O.A.R.S. (800-346-6277) and **Holiday Expeditions** (800-624-6323) run 3- and 5-day trips for about $630–$935 per adult, $577–$861 per child. Children should be at least 7 years old (8 for the O.A.R.S. trip); during the high water in May to early June, 12 is the suggested minimum age.

—JEFF WALLACH

Middle Fork of the Salmon River, Idaho
Class IV

The legendary Middle Fork is really two rivers, depending on when you launch and how much snowpack the winter weather has created for melting and flowing into the river from its source in the Sawtooth Mountains. In the early season—until about mid-July—it's a frigid, high-water behemoth, barreling the 100 miles from Boundary Creek to Cache Bar with intemperate haste and at temperatures as low as 42 degrees. During this period, 12 is usually the minimum age to be on the river. Later, though, the water warms and calms (a bit), and low water often forces the trip to be shortened to 75 miles; under these conditions outfitters have been known to take the occasional 6-year-old. "We've had really fun times with kids in the 9 to 12 bracket, teaching them how to fly-fish and how to handle an inflatable kayak," says Jerry Hughes of Hughes River Expeditions.

At either water level, the Class IV rapids—Velvet Falls, Pistol Creek, Powerhouse—are guaranteed to thrill. The Middle Fork drops an average of 27 feet a mile, finally tumbling into the trip-capping whitewater of Impassable Canyon. This is near where Captain Ruben Bernard came with his troops in 1879 to massacre the Sheepeater Indians. It's also the best place to spy bighorn sheep high on the canyon walls—up where Earl Parrot, "the hermit of Impassable Canyon," made his home for 27 years in the early 1900s (his cabins survive to this day).

Surprisingly enough, the rapids often come in second to other pleasures as the high point of a young rafter's vacation. When Ann Despont brought her two daughters down the river last summer, their lasting stories were of sitting around the campfire at night, of showering under the 150-foot spume of Veil Falls, and of bathing in hot springs under the moon.

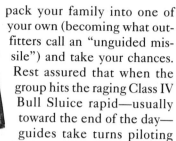

Hughes River Expeditions (208-257-3477), **O.A.R.S.** (800-346-6277), and **Hatch River Expeditions** (800-342-8243) offer 5- and 6-day trips on the Middle Fork, for about $1,300 a person. —MARK JANNOT

THE SOUTH

Chattooga River, South Carolina/Georgia
Class II–III

The Chattooga is most famous as the site of Burt Reynolds's river trip from hell in *Deliverance*, but don't cue up the dueling banjos just yet: The crazy Class V stuff showcased in the movie is on Section 4 of the Chattooga, which runs along the South Carolina–Georgia border through the Chattahoochee and Sumter National Forests. Upstream on Section 3, the rapids are more manageable and much better suited for a family day trip.

The scenery, though, is still as dramatic as it was in the movie, and the calm patches between rapids leave more time to appreciate the lush mountainsides bursting with mountain laurel and wild rhododendron in the early summer, or fall's changing leaves.

You'll have a choice in how much control you want over your own destiny—either paddle in a guided raft, or pack your family into one of your own (becoming what outfitters call an "unguided missile") and take your chances. Rest assured that when the group hits the raging Class IV Bull Sluice rapid—usually toward the end of the day—guides take turns piloting each raft to safety. On hot days the guides are likely to pull off to the side just below Bull Sluice so the kids can cool off by swimming through a Class II rapid.

Nantahala Outdoor Center (800-232-7238) and **Wildwater Limited** (800-451-9972) both offer day trips for about $60 per person. Minimum age for kids is 10. Call the **Stumphouse Ranger Station** at 864-638-9568 for more information. —MARK JANNOT

THE MID-ATLANTIC

Upper New River, West Virginia
Class I–III

The New River is actually the oldest river in North America, probably second only to the Nile in worldwide antiquity. Its source is in the Blue Ridge mountains of North Carolina; from there it flows north and west, through Virginia and West Virginia, toward the Mississippi. Because the land surrounding it never flooded during the Ice Age, it's a veritable laboratory of natural diversity, with bug and reptile species rarely seen elsewhere. The Upper New is a great beginner whitewater river: Its clear water flows over long, gentle Class I and II rapids,

IT'S TIME FOR WHITEWATER CLASS

Whitewater rafting can be one of the best ways for families to spend quality time together—the kids can't wander farther than the confines of the raft's rubber rim and there's plenty of time to joke and laugh between the spray. But be sure to pick your family's appropriate whitewater from Class I to Class V or laughter may quickly turn to tears—or terror.

—Stephanie Gregory

Class	What It Is	Appropriate Age	Scream Factor	Sample River	Outfitter
I	Calm, moving water with occasional riffles	5	Giggles	Upper Colorado	Wilderness Aware Rafting, 800-462-7238; 719-396-2112
II	Little bursts of bouncing rapids in clear, wide channels between long stretches of calm	5–7	Squeals of delight	Lower Klamath (Class II and III)	Whitewater Voyages, 800-488-7238
III	Irregular waves through narrower channels where maneuvering around rocks is required	7–12	Five out of ten on the scream scale; tonsils may be visible at times	Green River, Utah	Action Whitewater Adventures, 800-453-1482, 801-375-4111
IV	Rapids are intense, loud, and long, with complex, rocky obstacles in the way	12 and older	Level eight on the scream scale; mouth begins to hurt from extended periods of screaming	Hell's Canyon Gorge, Snake River	O.A.R.S., 800-346-6277
V	Rapids are long, loud, narrow, and violent, following one after the other without interruption	16 and older	Level ten on the scream scale; screams turn to terrifying animal sounds	Upper Gauley, West Virginia	Class VI, 800-252-7784

with the occasional III thrown in for excitement. And the stretch through the New River Gorge is among the best whitewater in the East.

Sometimes the disjunction between the roiling whitewater of the Gorge and the gentle rapids of the Upper New has a tendency to split families, with one parent taking teens downriver for an adrenaline rush while the other paddles with the younger kids on calmer stretches upstream. But to keep all family members together and happy on the Upper New, outfitters dole out all manner of river craft, from no-effort, oar-powered rafts to paddle rafts to self-bailing, inflatable "ducky" kayaks to Torrents—extremely responsive hard-shelled kayaks that older kids ride atop, making even Class II foam a thrill.

The 40-mile, pristine river that flows through Prince Canyon, Grand View Canyon, and Surprise Canyon on the Upper New gives outfitters the flexibility of tailoring a day trip to the season or stretching a longer trip over several days, for one of the only overnight raft trips in the East. **Class VI River Runners** (800-252-7784), **ACE Whitewater** (800-787-3982), and **North American River Runners** (800-950-2585) all offer day trips and overnight trips on the river. Kids as young as 5 can make the trip.

—MARK JANNOT

THE NORTHEAST

Magpie River, Québec
Class IV

Any whitewater river worth its foam will, over the years, acquire evocative names for its rapids. The Magpie's claim to fame is just the opposite—it is so remote that none of its rapids has a name. The closest road to the put-in on Magpie Lake is 100 miles away. The only way in is by a spectacular 40-minute float-plane flight from the small, French-speaking town of Sept-Îles. The only way out is the 6-day float to the St. Lawrence River.

When it isn't churning over the numerous unnamed rapids, the Magpie moves at more of a meander, winding through a northern wilderness of pine forests and foot-deep moss, past rocky driftwood-strewn shores and towering granite cliffs. Toward the end of the trip, the river plunges 80 feet off the Laurentian plateau in a dramatic crescendo of sound and spray that has, in deference to its majesty, been granted a name (albeit an unimaginative one): Magpie Falls. Helicopters carry the boats and baggage around the falls, and groups camp directly across from the roiling monster.

Because of its remoteness and Class IV rapids, the Magpie is best suited for teenagers, although no river-running experience is necessary. **Earth River Expeditions**, the only commercial outfitter to run the river, offers one trip in 1997, from August 10 to August 17, for C$1,400 per person. Call 800-643-2784 for more information.

—MARK JANNOT

9

Sometime this summer, while sweltering in a traffic jam somewhere between hell and Mammoth Hot Springs, you will pull off the road, draw in a deep breath of pure, unspoiled Winnebago effluvium, and conclude that your parents had it easy.

Of course they would be loath to admit this, prone as they are to lapsing into tales of depression (economic and marriage-related), wars (cold and hot), and general malaise. But you know it's true. Bob Dole never had to reserve a campsite.

National Parks
The Magnificent Seven

Saving the world from tyranny was one thing. Getting a spot with hookups at Old Faithful is quite another.

Unfortunately, when it comes to planning the Great National Park Campout of the 1990s, most modern parents fall victim to mental timewarp: They pack up the kids and pull out of the driveway, clicking off mental Vue-Master memories of the same trip, 1960s-style. Critical error: Abort, abort, abort! Consider the differences: Back then, all you had to do was show up and remember the bug spray. Duplicating the same, warm-memory trip today requires near Desert Storm–like strategy, equipment, and bravado. Not that you can't still trek into Yellowstone in August and have an unforgettable antelope encounter. Or drive through Glacier in July and come grill-to-snout with a moose. Or ride a mule into the Grand Canyon in June and return with major enlightenment and only minor bowleggedness. Grasping all these outdoor golden rings is exactly like it was when you were a kid—except that 4,000 times as many people are trying to do the very same thing at the very same time.

Do not let this dissuade you. The national park vacation of yesterday can still be had today; it just requires a bit more creativity—and sound advice. The following crowd-avoidance tips from seasoned national-parkers should help you with the advice part. But the leadership part is up to you. Just as it was in the 60s, the successful national-parkathon of the 90s is all in the hands of the folks in the front seat. No pressure or anything, but you're it.

—Ron C. Judd

THE WEST COAST

Yosemite National Park

Gateways: Two are on the west side: Arch Rock Entrance via California 140 and Big Oak Flat Entrance on California 120. California 41 enters the park at the South Entrance. From the northeast, Highway 120 climbs to the Tioga Pass Entrance.

Annual Visitors: 4.1 million

Annual Overnight Visitors: 2 million

Claim to Fame: For many, Yosemite is the apotheosis of the national park system. Situated in eastern California at the midpoint of the Sierra Nevada and stretching from an altitude of 2,000 to 13,000 feet, most of the park is a high-country wilderness of evergreen forests, alpine meadows, ponds and lakes, deep canyons, alabaster summits, and barren granite domes. Three groves of giant sequoias, the world's largest living trees, flank the western side of the park. Most of Yosemite's icons—El Capitan, Yosemite Falls, Bridalveil Falls, and Half Dome—line Yosemite Valley in the southwestern section.

Where Everyone Goes: This Rhode Island–size park contains wilderness on an operatic scale, so it's only natural that the crowds are epic, especially in mile-wide **Yosemite Valley.** But first-timers shouldn't miss out on exploring the 7-mile-long valley; beat the traffic on a daybreak drive around the steep-walled granite corridor to see El Capitan and other national treasures. At Yosemite Falls, buses disgorge polyglot herds that dutifully shuffle to the base of the cataract. But you could also take a bus (departing twice daily from all hotels in the valley) to Glacier Point, 3,200 feet above the valley floor, then hike 8 miles back down on the Panorama Trail past seldom-seen 370-foot Illilouette Falls. Another front-country must-see: the Mariposa Grove of giant sequoias, south of Yosemite Valley.

Out There: Head northwest to Crane Flat and the **Yosemite Institute,** a nonprofit extension of the Park Service that focuses on education. Groups of twelve or more can stay in their simple but comfortable dorms (about $55 per person per night) and eat family-style breakfast and dinner in the dining hall. Naturalists lead your group on wildflower walks in Tuolumne Meadows, sequoia strolls in the Tuolumne Grove, and short hikes from Glacier Point Road to the cliff's edge at Taft Point, where you can peer down into the valley 3,000 feet below. The institute also customizes backpack itineraries, obtains permits, and provides drop-offs and pickups. One family-friendly 3-day outing: Hike from Tuolumne Meadows up Lyell Canyon, set up a base camp near Ireland Creek, and hike up to Ireland Lake.

The park is a good place to introduce your kids to the joys of granite grappling. The **Yosemite Mountaineering School** has two locations; the Tuolumne Meadows setup is less crowded and cooler (as in temperature, not social acceptability) than the one in Yosemite Valley. Kids 12 and up can climb if accompanied by a lesson-taking parent; otherwise, the minimum age is 14. By the end of the first class, even tyros tackle 60-foot climbs. Full-day lessons for groups of three or more are $65 per person for beginners, $80 per person for intermediates.

For backcountry luxury, stay at the five **High Sierra Camps** pitched 8 to 10 miles apart along a roughly circular 50-mile trail (about $90 per person per day; minimum age is 7). Each camp has ten to twenty-four tent cabins with four beds and wood-burning stoves. The cabins are same-sex, so families may not be able to bunk together. Breakfast and dinner are served in the dining hall, where trail lunches are also prepared. Beds are reserved by lottery, so improve your odds by being flexible about dates. You could also pitch your tent near a camp and drop by for breakfast and dinner ($26.28 a day for two meals).

You can ride from camp to camp with **horsepack outfitters** (minimum age 7; 4-day trips, $562 per person; 6 days, $886). Try the 4-day, 35-mile North Loop (see spectacular White Cascade and Waterwheel Falls) or the South Loop (36 miles) to see rock formations.

Resources: For general information, call 209-372-0264.

Call 209-252-4848 for reservations at the park's roofed facilities. For campground reservations, call **Destinet** at 800-436-7275. Call **Yosemite Institute** at 209-379-9511. To reach the **Yosemite Mountaineering School,** call 209-372-8344. Call the **High Sierra Camps** (209-253-5674) from October 15 to November 30; the lottery is usually held in January, and camp reservations are due by the first week of December.

—DAVID DUNBAR

THE SOUTHWEST

Grand Canyon National Park

Gateways: South Rim: U.S. 180, 78 miles north from Flagstaff; or Arizona 64, 57 miles west from the junction with U.S. 89. North Rim: Arizona 67, 42 miles south from Jacob Lake.

Annual Visitors: 4.9 million

Annual Overnight Visitors: About 1.1 million

Claim to Fame: Despite hordes of camera-wielding tourists, air pollution, and the incessant buzz of sight-seeing planes, the Grand Canyon continues to live up to its role as America's icon of outdoor tourism. Even the most jaded teenager will find it difficult not to gasp in slack-jawed astonishment when looking out over the canyon rim.

Where Everyone Goes: Ninety percent head for **Grand Canyon Village,** the mini-metropolis on the South Rim. Sedentary folks ride the shuttle bus along **West Rim Drive** to the eight orthodox viewpoints, then retire to the air-conditioned **IMAX Theatre** just outside the park border where, for $7.50 a pop ($4.50 for kids 4 to 11), they tour the inner canyon for 30 minutes without that annoying heat, dust, and sweat. For the moderately ambulatory, there's the stroll along the 2.7-mile paved section of the **Rim Trail,** or even a day hike part of the way down into the canyon along the well-maintained **South Kaibab** and **Bright Angel** trails. The hike to the canyon floor is 13.8 miles round-trip via the South Kaibab, 19.6 miles via the Bright Angel—out of the question for the vast majority of canyon visitors. Mule rides below the rim are a Grand Canyon tradition; there's no minimum age, but riders must be at least 4'7".

Out There: Your best strategy is to head either up there—to the North Rim—or way down there, into the depths of the canyon itself. The higher, cooler North Rim usually is buried in snow through April, while the canyon floor is insufferably—even dangerously—hot in July and August.

The **North Rim,** site of the rustic Grand Canyon Lodge and a large campground, still has the feel of a remote deadend outpost, which it is. The Widforss Trail, which winds 5 miles through pine forest to a spectacular overlook, is a fine all-day hike for active kids age 10 and up. Teenagers may want to try the more challenging 9.4-mile round-trip hike down the North Kaibab Trail where the halfway point is the waterfall at Roaring Springs.

Overnighting **below the rim** requires meticulous planning done well in advance. The limited number of backcountry permits and campsites—

as well as rooms and meals at Phantom Ranch on the canyon floor—are typically booked up months ahead. An alternative is the Grand Canyon Field Institute, which offers a number of guided overnight trips below the rim. A 6-day backpack trip (September 7–12, for kids 14 and up) into phantasmagoric Havasu Canyon ($295 per person, BYO food) includes visits with the Havasupai Indians. GCFI also customizes backpacking trips and llama treks for groups of six or more.

Resources: Call **Park Headquarters** at 520-638-7888. Call the **Backcountry Office** (camping permits, $20, plus $4 per person per night) at 520-638-7875, 1–5 P.M. MST only. Call the **River Permits Office** at 520-638-7843. To make campground reservations, call 800-365-2267. Call **AmFac Parks and Resorts, Inc.** to book reservations for rim lodges and Phantom Ranch, mule rides, and smooth-water rafting trips at 303-297-2757. Reach the **Field Institute** at 520-638-2485. **Outdoors Unlimited** (800-637-7238) runs raft trips on the Colorado River; call 520-638-7843 for permits. Pick up a copy of the *Official Hiking Guide to the Grand Canyon*, published by the **Grand Canyon Association** (800-858-2808).—DAVID NOLAND

THE ROCKIES

Banff/Jasper National Parks

Gateway: Calgary, Alberta, 80 miles east of Banff.

Annual Visitors: 5 million

Annual Overnight Visitors: Unknown

Claim to Fame: Everywhere you turn in Banff and Jasper, a string of magnificent monoliths looms overhead—huge, endless, stupefying, and occasionally frightening. And those are just the tour buses. Wait'll you see the Rockies. Millions of people—particularly Japanese and European tourists—do so every summer. In July and August, you'll swear they're all there at once, turning North America's most heavily bejeweled alpine crown into Saturday-before-Christmas at the Edmonton mondo-mall.

Fear not: Visitors arriving even slightly off-season—or stubborn midsummer tourists willing to hoof it or paddle a few extra miles—can still find moments of mountain bliss in Canada's first and still-best national park.

Where Everyone Goes: In and out of the Cave and Basin National Historic Site, Ralph Lauren, the Body Shop, and Joe Btfsplk's Diner in the town—okay, city—of Banff; up to Lake Louise for an afternoon; then up and down the 143-mile-long Icefields Parkway to Jasper, scurrying to get back for a tee-time or teatime at the Banff Springs Hotel. That's actually not such a bad road map for the less-rushed, more-adventurous traveler: Crowded or not, the **Icefields Parkway** (93 North) truly is one of the most magnificent drives on the planet, with a dizzying series of 10,000-foot-plus, glacier-draped peaks on either side.

And with only a small amount of map-squinting and pit-sweating, the same Parkway pavement leads to lands where the Greyhounds don't roam.

Out There: Bring your boots. In general, the woods get lonely even several miles off the pavement here. In the town of Banff, smart summer campers avoid the main campground (Banff's Tunnel Mountain) and head for the outskirts.

Johnston Canyon Campground, a half-hour northwest on the winding, scenic Bow Valley Parkway, is more private and laid-back, particularly for tent-campers. It's a great family spot: Day-trip possibilities include a mostly boardwalked hike up Johnston Canyon (easy for all ages) and pick-a-length cycle trips in either direction up the scenic Bow Valley Parkway. Watch out: Traffic is usually heavy here in summer, but the speed limit is low (about 25 to 40 miles per hour throughout), shoulders are ample in most places, and the pullout lunch spots offer magnificent views of the Bow River and a dozen surrounding peaks. Keep an eye out for elk, bears, and wolves along the riverbank.

Two hours north along the Icefields Parkway, tour buses stack up by the hundreds at the Icefield Centre, and most RVs herd into nearby Wilcox Creek Campground. Slip right between them into the **Icefield Campground** (22 spots, pit toilets, tents only). This is a stunning spot, with a view across the valley to Athabasca and Andromeda, two 12,000-foot-plus glacier-capped peaks at the edge of the Columbia Icefield. But this campsite's true beauty is hidden behind it, where a series of short-but-steep way-trails lead up the ridge and connect with the Wilcox Pass Trail (best for older kids, age 12 and up).

Although this trail is within sight of the main highway, it's one of the most rewarding day hikes in Jasper, with herds of bighorn sheep on the ridgeline just above the campground and views across the valley. Families with younger children can start at the official Wilcox Pass Trailhead a half-mile south on Icefields Parkway, which bypasses the steep way-trails above Icefield Campground.

Farther north around Jasper town-site, avoid the well-worn tourist path between Whistlers Campground and Maligne Lake by taking a daylong bike-and-paddle trip to **Patricia and Pyramid lakes.** Park in Jasper and set off by mountain bike on Pyramid Lake Road (rentals are available at Free-wheel Cycle on Patricia Street in the center of town). It's 4.2 miles (mostly uphill, but not steep) on a paved, lightly traveled road to Patricia Lake, where several easy hiking trails skirt the aspen-dotted shoreline.

Continue on to Pyramid Lake and the **Pyramid Lake Resort** (403-852-4900), where there are rental canoes and rowboats. Strong paddlers can circumnavigate the lake in an hour or two, but even newbies can paddle the mile or so to the small island connected by a footbridge to the east shore. Watch for elk (numerous) and moose (rare) on the downhill bike ride back.

Resources: For general information, call 403-762-1550. The main number of **Jasper National Park** is 403-852-6161.

—RON C. JUDD

Glacier National Park

Gateways: Whitefish/Columbia Falls, Montana, on U.S. 2 to Apgar Visitor Center, and St. Mary Visitor Center on U.S. 89 from the east.

Annual Visitors: 2 million

Annual Overnight Visitors: 358,637

Claim to Fame: Glacier, 1,584 square miles of sheer cliffs and slack jaws on the U.S.-Canadian border, is a true twenty-first-century type of wilderness: It likely leads North America both in grizzly encounters and bumper-to-cycle-rack highway-gaper jams. A puny percentage of park visitors get the granola scared out of them by a personal grizzly greeting every year; most of them prefer the experience to Glacier's daily campsite-acquisition wars. Somehow, though, Glacier's rarefied Rocky Mountain air sends most people home giddy—particularly those who dare to venture even a short way off the beaten path.

Where Everyone Goes: They should issue elephant tails at the Apgar Visitor Center, so circuslike is the chain of rigs journeying along the park's primary roadway, the **Going-to-the-Sun Road** between Lake McDonald and St. Mary. The average visitor never ventures more than 15 feet off this spectacular, 51.2-mile north-south glorified trail over Logan Pass. It's easy to see why: The roadway provides a year's worth of extraordinary mountain scenery in one 3-hour trip, and really is the best (and only) way to sample all of Glacier's magnificence in a single day. Needless to say, most camp-grounds and trailheads along the route are jammed from June through August. Like it or not, the drive is a must: Follow the hordes to the summit of 6,680-foot Logan Pass, where a board-walk-covered trail leads 1.5 miles over alpine meadows, crossing the Continental Divide, to a grand vista of Hidden Lake. Few places in North America offer as much alpine splendor less than 1 hour from the car.

Out There: Your strategy is simple: Bring the Subaru, not a Winnebago, and treat the Going-to-the-Sun Road as a means, not an end. There are relatively untrammeled areas on the far west, north, and east borders of the park, two of which can be reached without ever even setting foot on the Going-to-the-Sun Road.

A good example: The **Polebridge area** on the park's northwest side. From Apgar near the main park entrance, Camas and North Fork roads (rough gravel for a good portion of the distance; annoying, but a grand RV eliminator) lead to Polebridge and two of the loneliest campgrounds in Glacier, Kintla Lake and Bowman Lake (no reservations). Both are tent-camping domains set on fjordlike lakes in the North Fork Flathead River drainage, with excellent nearby day hiking, canoeing, fishing, and backpacking. Kintla Lake, in particular, is a hidden gem. The lower campground is small (13 sites) and unimpressive, but you can hike up to a separate backcountry camp at the head of the lake (6.3 mostly flat miles), an ideal family destination (snare a free backcountry permit at the Apgar Visitor Center). Great next-day hikes from there include the family-friendly jaunt to Upper Kintla

THE FUN FILE: WHAT TO DO ON A RAINY DAY

Uno. It takes up almost no room in a pack (it is, after all, nothing more than a deck of cards) and can entertain for a good hour or two.

Friendship Bracelets. Take up to six strands of foot-long embroidery thread and knot them to a safety pin. Fasten the pin to your jeans, then braid the strands or try more elaborate knot designs.

Take Turns Reading Aloud. *The Hobbit* or books from *The Narnia Chronicles* are richly fantastical; Edgar Allan Poe is always deliciously scary; Roald Dahl is a delight for all ages.

Whittling. This, of course, is an activity with age considerations. But older kids can create bows and arrows, trucks, boats, whistles, and dolls.

Postcards. Don't forget pens, pencils, and markers to decorate the borders or draw pictures of what the kids have seen. —*Lisa Twyman Bessone*

Lake (2.7 miles), fairly level and good for kids age 7 and up, and the long, steep haul (stronger, older kids only) to spectacular Boulder Pass (8.7 miles). Kintla Lake is Glacier's best canoeing/kayaking venue. Paddlers can easily make the journey from the campground to the upper-lake backcountry camp in a day. Warning: Mosquitoes are relentless here in midsummer.

A less primitive, more crowded alternative on the east side is **Two Medicine Lake,** the only major area without overnight lodging. The large Two Medicine campground can be a zoo in midsummer, but it's worth investing half a day to fight for a spot. Once in, many days of nearby exploring await. A quaint old tour boat—always a hit with the kids—journeys up Two Medicine Lake several times a day, allowing memorable hikes to Upper Two Medicine Lake (an easy, 4.5-mile round-trip to a stunning primitive campground

with a 1-night limit). There's good trout fishing here; rent rowboats, small outboards, and canoes through **Glacier Park Boat Company** (406-257-2426).

For a 2- or 3-day backpack easy enough for the whole family, end your obligatory Going-to-the-Sun adventure at St. Mary, near Glacier's northeast border. Stop for a night at Rising Sun or St. Mary Campground, then get up early for a trek up the nearby Red Eagle Lake Trail. Unlike most Glacier hikes, this one goes around—not up—the park's spectacular peaks. Total elevation gain on the 7.7-mile walk to nice campsites at the lake is 300 feet, so even kids as young as 7 or 8 will be able to handle it. Get an overnight permit at the St. Mary Visitor Center.

Resources: For campground and backcountry permit information, call 406-888-7800. Rent camping gear from **Rising Sun Outdoor Adven-**

tures; 406-892-2602 summers, 406-862-5934 off-season. Helpful guides include *Glacier National Park and Waterton Lakes National Park* (The Mountaineers). For information and reservations at the park's lodges and inns, call 602-207-6000.

—RON C. JUDD

Yellowstone National Park

Gateways: In Montana, U.S. 20 leads to the West Entrance, U.S. 89 goes to the North Entrance, and U.S. 212 heads to the Northeast Entrance. In Wyoming, U.S. 14/16/20 goes to the East Entrance and U.S. 89/191/287 leads to the South Entrance.

Annual Visitors: 3.1 million

Annual Overnight Visitors: About 2 million

Claim to Fame: This 2.2-million-acre park, which occupies the northwestern corner of Wyoming and spills over into Idaho and Montana, is big enough to impress even the most jaded families. There's plenty of scenery (mountains, canyons, rivers, and lakes), more than 10,000 weird geothermal features (spewing geysers, burping mud pots, steaming hot springs), and the greatest concentration of wildlife in the Lower 48 (bison, moose, elk, deer, pronghorn antelope, and bighorn sheep), all seemingly trained to assume Kodak Moment poses until traffic snarls.

Where Everyone Goes: The park's five entrances funnel motorists onto the Grand Loop Road, which twists and turns for 142 miles through the heart of Yellowstone, passing attractions like the Lower Falls of the Yellowstone River; Mammoth Hot Springs; and, yes, Old Faithful. (Echinus Geyser in the Norris Basin, about 30 miles north of Old Faithful, is less crowded and almost as reliable, spewing to 80-foot heights about once an hour.) Hit the road before 10 A.M. and after 4 P.M. to avoid the heaviest traffic. For a more informed view of the must-see wonders along the Grand Loop, hire naturalist Ken Sinay of Northern Rockies Natural History, a kid-savvy guide who can deliver the goods on your megafauna wish list from a touring van equipped with spotting scopes and binoculars ($120 per person for a family of four for a full day).

Out There: Take a couple of days to navigate the Grand Loop, then light out for the wilderness. The **Yellowstone Institute** organizes 3-day outings for families with children 6 and older. Naturalists lead wolf prowls ($142 a day for adults; $79 for kids 16 and under) from June 21 to 23 from the Pebble Creek or Slough Creek campgrounds in the northeast corner. From July 7 to 9, a horsepack trip in the Hellroaring Creek region near the north-central boundary takes in the Grand Canyon of the Yellowstone ($600 per person).

Children 8 and older can take on the undemanding but scenic **Cascade Lake Trail**, a fairly level 16-plus-mile route that arcs west from Canyon Village through forests and across meadows to four backcountry lakes. Limit the first day to a 3-mile hike into

113

Cascade Lake. On day 2, hike up 9,397-foot Observation Peak (6 miles round-trip) for panoramas of central Yellowstone before settling in at Grebe Lake (another 3.7 miles), well-stocked with rainbows and whitefish. You could also go 1 mile farther west to Wolf Lake and 3.7 miles to Ice Lake before returning.

Backcountry-bound families with anglers age 6 and older can arrange a "drop camp" at **Slough Creek** or **Pebble Creek.** An outfitter escorts you on horseback along an easy 2-hour trail ride up Slough Creek, sets up a fully equipped tent camp, then rides out with the horses. After a few days of superb catch-and-release fly-fishing, the wrangler returns to lead you out.

If your children are old enough to walk 3 to 6 fairly level miles a day (8 or older), consider a llama trek through the backcountry. Children will enjoy a customized 5-night trek with **Llamas of the Yellowstone** (406-587-2661) from Old Faithful southwest to roadless Bechler country, aka Cascade Corner, where numerous waterfalls spill off the Pitchstone and Madison plateaus.

Relax hike-hardened muscles by "hot-potting"—soaking in the stretches of the Bechler River, its Ferris and Gregg forks, and other streams warmed by the region's 400-plus hot springs. A naturalist accompanies each trek, and one evening a buckskin-clad "mountain man" (actually a biologist), carrying an unloaded long rifle and a bundle of furs, drops by the camp to jaw about the park's colorful natural and human history. Bechler country works best in late summer, when it's drier and less buggy.

Canoeing or kayaking in the **Southeast Arm of Yellowstone Lake** is a "dream trip." Hire a motorboat to take you and your canoe from Bridge Bay Marina across the lake for a drop-off at The Promontory (about $80). From there, paddle 8 leisurely miles down the sheltered Southeast Arm, stopping at shoreline campsites. From the safety of your canoe you can watch grizzlies fishing for cutthroat trout at the mouths of spawning streams. Return to The Promontory for your prearranged pick-up (another $80).

Resources: **Northern Rockies Natural History** (406-586-1155) prepares personalized Yellowstone itineraries. Call the **Yellowstone Institute** at 307-344-2294. Request a backcountry travel planner from the **Backcountry Office** (307-344-7381). To set up a canoeing trip, contact **AmFac Parks and Resorts, Inc.** (307-344-7311).

—DAVID DUNBAR

THE SOUTH

Great Smoky Mountains National Park

Gateways: Oconaluftee Visitor Center near Cherokee, North Carolina, and Sugarlands Visitor Center near Gatlinburg, Tennessee.

Annual Visitors: 9,080,422

Annual Overnight Visitors: 517,918

Claim to Fame: Split almost equally between North Carolina and Tennessee, Great Smoky's 520,000 acres are not mighty or imposing but calm, filled with subtleties—soft-sculpted hills, slow-moving streams, and paths of cloistered quiet.

The cape of white that inspires the name isn't smoke but fog and clouds, forever swirling and shifting among the tightly woven forests and valleys and peaks that turn purple at sunset. Families love the Smokies because of the countless places to picnic and fish, summits to scale, old homesteads to explore, and stunning views around every turn.

Where Everyone Goes: The two-lane, 32-mile **Newfound Gap Road** (U.S. 441) cuts north to south through the heart of the park and crosses the mountains, connecting the two gateways. On summer weekends, driving is frightfully slow, and the vapors you experience won't be fog but exhaust. Still, every family must drive the road to reach 6,643-foot Clingmans Dome (from Newfound Gap Road, a quarter-mile south of the Tennessee line, turn onto Clingmans Dome Road), the highest point in the Smokies. Just as popular is **Cades Cove,** a near-flat hamlet of early-1800s hewn log and simple wood homes on the western side of the Smokies, 25 miles off Newfound Gap Road from the Sugarlands Visitor Center. Come to Cades Cove on Wednesday or Saturday mornings and rent bicycles; until 10 A.M., the 11-mile, scenic Cades Cove Loop Road is closed to motor vehicles.

Other popular stops include **Sugarlands Visitor Center** on the northern edge of the park, which has pioneer exhibits, and the **Pioneer Farmstead,** with the remains of primitive farm buildings set among wildflower meadows on the southern border of the park.

Out There: Start your day early to enjoy the overlooks and walkways in solitude. Later in the day, veer off the main roads, searching out remote trails that curl through the park. Trails to try: Roaring Fork Motor Nature Trail (off U.S. 441, about 4 miles south of Gatlinburg), a paved, 5-mile loop through forested hills, with numbered roadside stops including an 1865 log cabin and a waterfall called "The Place of a Thousand Drips."

At night, stay in one of the park's many remote campgrounds (ten of them are developed). On the eastern rim of the park, **Cataloochee Campground** was once the Smokies' biggest settlement but is now just wilderness, pale green flatlands, and ridges, with last century's farmsteads, churches, and schoolhouses tucked into the valleys.

Ten-mile Cove Creek Road is the easiest way to Cataloochee Campground (no reservations, so arrive midweek; campsites are full on weekends), though more than half the drive is over gravel. Kids like the Boogerman Trail, a 6.5-mile trek that forms a loop with the Caldwell Fork Trail through poplar and hemlock forest into an enclosed cove. Along the way you'll see vestiges of pioneer farms. There are shorter, easier trails, suitable for children age 3 to 7, including a self-guided nature trail. And there's Cataloochee Creek, with some of the best trout fishing in the park.

Southwest of Cataloochee, off Balsam Mountain Road, **Balsam Mountain Campground** (no reservations) has the Smokies' highest camping, 5,310 feet up, and is wonderfully cool on midsummer nights. It also offers one of the park's premier hikes: The 2.6-mile (one-way) Flat Creek Trail, with its grassy carpets of ridge forest, a double waterfall, and myriad stream crossings, begins just south of the campground.

Also off the main road, **Cosby Campground** (no reservations; in the northeast corner of the park, 2 miles south of the town of Cosby) has a self-guided nature trail great for kids 3 and older. Teens can try the 5.3-mile (one-way) Snake Den Ridge Trail and its views of waterfalls.

The park has one lodge, **LeConte Lodge**, in the north-central section of the park atop Mount Le Conte, accessible only via a fairly rugged 5.5-mile hike (one-way) suitable for kids 12 and over. From the trail you'll see boulders improbably hinged on bluff walls, streams dotted with stepping stones, and black bears nosing around for handouts. Take the shortest route, the Alum Cave Trail (along Newfound Gap Road, 8.6 miles east of the Sugarlands Visitor Center) and climb 6,593 feet to find the lodge's hand-hewn cabins and outhouses (think rustic) set on the Smokies' third-highest mountain.

The bad news: LeConte Lodge books up a year in advance; reservations are taken every October 1 for the following season. However, cancellations are common, so keep calling and be flexible with your dates. Nightly rates are $66.50 per adult and $58.50 per child age 4 to 10 (11 and older pay the adult rate), including breakfast and dinner; accommodations are rooms or private cabins.

If LeConte is full, try **Fontana Village** (off North Carolina 28 just outside the park's western edge), a family tradition since 1947. Parents and kids can play to-gether or apart; there's horseback riding, mountain biking, canoeing, crafts workshops, nightly dances, and bonfires. You can book a motel room, rustic cabin, or contemporary two- or three-bedroom condo ($79–$189).

Resources: The park's main number is 423-436-1200, but it's a maddening, automated line. You're better off stopping at one of the visitor centers—Oconaluftee, Sugarlands, or Cades Cove—which have excellent maps and volumes on park pursuits. Reach **LeConte Lodge** at 423-429-5704 and **Fontana Village** at 800-849-2258. Especially helpful: *Mountain Roads & Quiet Places* and *Hiking Trails of the Smokies*, both published by the Great Smoky Mountains Natural History Association. Three of the park's ten campgrounds take reservations for mid-May through October stays; call 423-436-1226 or **Destinet** at 800-365-2267.

—STACY RITZ

THE NORTHEAST

Acadia National Park

Gateways: Mount Desert Island: Maine 3, 20 miles south from Ellsworth. Isle au Haut: 4 miles by ferry from Stonington. Schoodic Peninsula: Maine 186, about 10 miles south from West Gouldsboro.

Annual Visitors: 2.8 million

Annual Overnight Visitors: 169,443

Claim to Fame: The first national park east of the Mississippi, Acadia is prototypically eastern in character: compact, civilized, tightly regulated, fetching in its details rather than grandly overpowering. By no means could you call it a wilderness. The core of the park, on Mount Desert Island, was donated in the 1910s by wealthy summer residents hoping to save their beloved coastal Maine retreats from further development. Its modest 35,000 acres are today a far-flung patchwork of spruce forest, lakes, pink granite peaks, rocky coastline, and small islands, liberally sprinkled with still-private landholdings and a half-dozen or so charming seaside villages. For most Acadia visitors, Bar Harbor and the other bordering villages are as big a draw as the bears, blueberries, lobsters, and loons of the park itself.

Where Everybody Goes: Acadia draws almost as many visitors as Yosemite, more than twenty times its size. The vast majority congregate in a daily summer gridlock along the 20-mile **Park Loop Road,** peering from their car windows at attractions such as Thunder Hole, a seaside rock formation that booms and hisses under certain wave and tide conditions; Sand Beach, where the bold and/or foolhardy swim in 54-degree water; and Jordan Pond, where you can take tea on the lawn of the historic inn, the Jordan Pond House. Cadillac Mountain, a 1,530-foot knob of granite overlooking the Porcupine Islands, is a traditional spot for sunset-viewing.

Out There: "Backcountry" is not a term that applies to Acadia. No place in the park is more than 3 miles from a road, and the two main campgrounds are set up for cars and RVs, not hikers. Overnight backpacking is prohibited. But since most Acadia visitors are tethered to their cars, it's surprisingly easy to escape them during the day. One way is a **bike excursion** along the 45-mile network of car-free carriage roads, most of which wind through the forest south and west of Eagle Lake. The broken-stone roads are wide, smooth, and graded gently enough for an 8-year-old on a one-speed BMX. To avoid the Eagle Lake crush, head for the 4.5-mile Hadlock Brook Loop, which crosses three ornate stone bridges and skims the shore of Upper Hadlock Pond. Rent mountain bikes for $10 to $16 a day at Acadia Bike and Canoe in Bar Harbor. In the Western Mountain section of the park, the 1.5-mile **hiking trail** from Seal Cove Pond to the top of 1,071-foot Bernard Mountain, suitable for kids as young as 6, cuts across broad granite ledges and has sweeping views of Blue Hill Bay. Older kids may prefer the 2-mile round-trip Perpendicular Trail up nearby Mansell Mountain.

Isle au Haut is a remote section of the park on a small island 16 miles by boat southwest of Mount Desert. Take the 55-minute ferry ride from Stonington (round-trip, $20 for adults; $10 for kids under 12). If you don't have time to cover all 17 miles of hiking trails, be sure to take the Goat Trail, which winds for 1 mile along the southern coastline atop cliffs and past tide pools. Isle au Haut's five lean-to camping shelters ($25 permit fee; reservations request forms accepted after March 31) are just steps away from a summer ferry stop at Duck Harbor.

10

Beach Vacations

What's summer without a little sand between the toes, the sounds of lapping waves and squawking gulls, and that ever-present smell of cocoa butter wafting on the breeze? A beach vacation may be the obvious summer game-plan, but that doesn't mean any beach will do. We steered clear of wall-to-wall terry cloth and honky-tonk boardwalks in search of old-fashioned summer havens where the beaches are safe (toddler-tested and re-laxing to loll by), but not so sedate that

Esprit de Shore

the kids are restless after the first hour. All these beaches offer plenty of action, from water-skiing to boardsailing, bicycling to in-line skating, and are sure to keep your kids busy—and away from your own plot of sand.

THE WEST COAST

Seaside
Oregon

The Big Picture: You might think a traditional beach vacation this far north in Oregon would be out of the question, but a lifeguard stand and boardwalk offer compelling evidence to the contrary. Seaside is on a particularly scenic stretch of Oregon's rugged coast, just above Tillamook Head. Its broad, flat beach—studded with playground equipment and volleyball standards—would be the envy of many a sand-starved southern California coastal community. Dating back to 1908, the Prom—short for Promenade, Seaside's concrete boardwalk—follows the beach for 1½ miles.

Things to Do: Few actually risk total immersion in Seaside's frigid 55-degree water without wetsuits. Kids happily splash around in the surf, however, and people play on the beach in other ways—sandcastle-building, kite-flying, skimboarding on the hard, wet sand, and pedaling around on low-to-the-ground beach tricycles. The waves are good for surfing and bodyboarding, and surfboards and wetsuits can be rented at **Cleanline Surf Shop** (503-738-7888). **Outdoor Fun for All** (503-738-8447) rents bikes, mopeds, in-line skates, and kayaks. Kayaking is safe and easy in Nehalem Bay, an estuary of the Necanicum River that flows through town. Boardsailors point their sails to Fort Stevens and Youngs Bay, 20 miles north on the Columbia River. Hikers head to Ecola State Park, 7 miles south, for matchless views from trails out to Ecola Point and Tillamook Head.

Where to Stay: The Shilo Inn (doubles, $168–$220; 503-738-9571) is a five-story hotel with a heated pool and fitness center. Two Prom-side contenders are the **Hi-Tide Motel** (doubles, $120; 503-738-8414) and the **Best Western Ocean View Resort** (doubles, $80–$172; 800-234-8439).

For More Info: Seaside Chamber of Commerce and Visitors Bureau; 800-444-6740.

Carlsbad
California

The Big Picture: Within 1 hour's drive of Disneyland, Sea World of California, and The San Diego Zoo, Carlsbad projects the less-harried character of a self-styled village by the sea, with Old World architecture, inland lagoons, and

STAYING SAFE: CHOOSING A SUNSCREEN

If SPF 15 is good, then SPF 30 must be twice as good, right? So why bother with the weak stuff at all, when you could just slather on the high-powered sunscreen and be done with it for the day? Or are the high-SPF screens overkill?

On average, it takes 30 minutes for the skin to redden from the sun (even less time at high altitudes or middle latitudes). An SPF of 2 will double that time to an hour. An SPF of 35 protects 35 times as long, or 17-plus hours (only in the Arctic Circle is the sun even out that long). But high SPFs aren't a rip-off because they protect you against increased UV rays. For every 1,000 feet of elevation gain, 4 percent more UV radiation is bombarding your skin. (For the mathematically impaired, that means that at 10,000 feet you're absorbing 40 percent more harmful rays than you would at sea level.) Reflection from sand increases UV radiation by 17 percent, while water can reflect an additional 100 percent.

The best rule of thumb is to minimize sun exposure between 10 A.M. and 3 P.M., when the radiation is strongest, and keep infants under 6 months out of the sun entirely—their skin is especially vulnerable to sunburn. Invest in a sunscreen with an SPF factor of at least 15 (the consensus minimum protection) that will block both UVA and UVB rays. And remember that most sunscreens take up to 30 minutes to start working. Reapply liberally and frequently; while sunscreens may indeed be waterproof, they're typically toweled off after a swim. Don't forget a lip balm with sunscreen; lips are skin, too. Finally, pack a wide-brimmed hat to prevent scalp-burns.

long, skinny beaches. The town and surrounding flower-growing region are a riot of eye-catching fields and gardens. Four miles downcoast is South Carlsbad State Park, where a blufftop campground overlooks the beach.

Things to Do: A wide concrete walkway runs along Carlsbad State Beach, where people jog, cycle, and skate at all hours. The summer surf is tame on this lifeguarded ribbon of sand and pebbles, making it safe for families. **Witt's Carlsbad Pipeline** (619-729-4423) sells surfboards, skateboards, and bodyboards (they'll rent you the latter as well). Agua Hedionda Lagoon—south of Carlsbad State Beach on either side of Carlsbad Boulevard—is a good spot for swimming, fishing, and water-skiing. **California Water Sports** (619-434-3089), on the lagoon at Snug Harbor Marina, rents kayaks, Wave Runners, and water skis, and offers water-skiing lessons. Batiquitos Lagoon, east of South Carlsbad State Beach, is an ecological reserve with miles of shoreline trails.

Where to Stay: Top-of-the-line in Carlsbad is the **La Costa Resort & Spa** (doubles, $225; 619-438-9111), a world-famous golf-and-tennis getaway where there's Camp La Costa for kids 5 to 12. **Carlsbad Inn Beach Resort** (doubles and suites, $140–$198; 800-235-3939) is less expensive and closer to the beach. Camping at **South Carlsbad State Beach** will place you even closer to the waves, but reservations (call Destinet at 800-444-7275) are essential.

For More Info: Carlsbad Convention & Visitors Bureau; 800-227-5722.

THE SOUTH

Gulf Shores
Alabama

The Big Picture: Alabama nearly gets elbowed out of the coastal picture by Florida's Panhandle, but its small stretch of gulf coast, with the low-key resort community of Gulf Shores as its hub, comprises 32 miles of soft, white beaches and water that's comfortably swimmable 8 months a year. And it's not totally resortified; extensive tracts of beach and woodlands have been preserved at Bon Secour National Wildlife Refuge and Gulf State Park.

Things to Do: Sportfishing is king in the Gulf Shores area, which calls itself the Red Snapper Capital of the World. From Little Lagoon to Lake Shelby, Cotton Bayou to Perdido Bay, and out into the blue waters of the open gulf, world-record snappers, cobias, and triggerfish are hauled in.

Charter a fishing boat at **Perdido Pass Marina** ($500 for a 6-hour trip for six people; 800-844-6481), 8 miles east of Gulf Shores at Alabama Point. Rent watercraft in the marina at **Perdido Pass Parasail & Waverunner** (334-981-5505). **Bon Secour National Wildlife Refuge** (334-540-7720) occupies the peninsula west of town, where migratory birds make landfall after a 600-mile trans-gulf flight. Beautiful beaches, 3 miles of trails, a small lake, and scads of tired flycatchers and hummingbirds can be found here. Part of **Gulf State Park** (334-948-7275) is a state-run resort with three freshwater lakes, a 2-mile beach, an 825-foot fishing pier, and five short hiking trails.

Where to Stay: A building boom on Alabama's Gulf Coast keeps bringing new properties to Gulf Shores, such as an all-suites addition at the **Holiday Inn Hotel & Suites** (doubles, $130; suites, $225; 800-662-4853). **The Lighthouse Resort Motel** (doubles and apartments, $71–$145; 334-948-6188) claims 620 feet of private beach. **Gulf State Park** has its own 144-room beachfront hotel (doubles, $99; 800-544-4853), plus seventeen rental cabins on Lake Shelby and a whopping 468 campsites ($11–$25 per night).

For More Info: Alabama Gulf Coast Convention & Visitors Bureau; 800-745-7263 or 334-968-7511.

Siesta Key
Florida

The Big Picture: Less commercial than most of Florida's developed barrier is-

lands, 8-mile-long Siesta Key is one bridge removed from Sarasota—close enough to hop into town for food and fun, far enough to confer a sense of island quietude. Siesta Key's claim to fame is its bright-white quartzite sand that's been pulverized to the consistency of powdered sugar, especially on 2.8-mile Crescent Beach in the island's midsection. From May to September endangered loggerhead and green turtles nest on the island.

Things to Do: The Gulf of Mexico, needless to say, is an inviting swimming hole (average summer water temp is 85 degrees). Crescent Beach is great for walking and running; Turtle Beach, farther south, is best for shelling. Snorkelers can poke along the reef off Point of Rocks looking for snook and grouper. **Sweetwater Kayaks** (941-346-1179) leads tours of the gulf and bay; on some you'll paddle alongside dolphins ($35 per person for

2 hours). For mechanized fun, **All Watersports** (941-921-2754) rents boats and watercraft (Jet Skis, $45–$65 per hour; motor boats, $25 per hour), and offers charter fishing, water-skiing, and diving trips. **Siesta Key Parasail** (941-349-1900) specializes in its namesake activity ($45 per person). A wide walking/biking path makes Ocean Boulevard and Beach Road safe for cyclists and in-line skaters. Everything from bikes to boats can be rented at **Mr. CB's Saltwater Outfitters** (941-349-4400).

Where to Stay: Captiva Beach Resort (doubles, $325; 800-349-4131) and **Sara Sea Inn at the Beach** (doubles with kitchenettes, $85; 941-349-3244) both have pools and are within 500 yards of the beach. Many families rent condos for a week or longer ($600 and up); for a list of available properties, contact the Siesta Key Chamber of Commerce (see below).

For More Info: Siesta Key Chamber of Commerce; 941-349-3800.

Hilton Head Island
South Carolina

The Big Picture: Twelve miles of sandy ocean beaches are the big draw to this tennis-shoe-shaped island deep in the South Carolina low country. In some places, the flat, hard-packed beach is 600 feet wide. The west side of Hilton Head is rimmed with salt marshes and lagoons; in between are dense stands of subtropical trees—oaks, pines, bays, and palmettos. Alligators, bobcats, and 250 species of birds share Hilton Head with duffers and condo-dwellers, and some 800 acres of wildlife preserves manage to keep the place relatively unspoiled.

Things to Do: There are 29 golf courses and 300 tennis courts, but the beach beats 'em all. The sand is hard enough for bicycling; for rentals try **Hilton Head Bicycle** ($10 per day; 803-686-6888) and **Peddling Pelican Bike Rentals** ($10 per day, $25 for 1 week; 803-785-5470). **Shore Beach Service** (803-785-3494) rents catamarans, aquacycles, fun cycles, Boogie boards, and more. April through October is offshore fishing season for grouper, king mackerel, and shark. Arrange half-day fishing trips for up to six people at **Harbor Town Yacht Basin** ($195–$365; 803-671-2704) and **South Beach Marina** ($250–$300; 803-671-3060); both also rent out watercraft. You can hike along several miles of trails in 650-acre Sea Pines Forest Preserve, home to herons, egrets, and ibis.

Where to Stay: Hilton Head's high-end hotels—such as the towering beachfront **Westin Resort** (doubles, $120–$290; 800-228-3000)—make life easy on families by providing a camplike children's program with arts and crafts, swimming, and games. The island has thousands of hotel and motel rooms as well as villas and homes for rent. For listings, contact the Visitors Information Center (see below).

For More Info: Hilton Head Island Chamber of Commerce and Convention & Visitors Bureau; 803-785-3673.

THE MID-ATLANTIC

Cape May
New Jersey

The Big Picture: A hard-packed, white-sand beach runs for 3 miles in this well-mannered Victorian-style community, which protrudes like a pointing finger into Delaware Bay. Perched on the Atlantic Flyway, Cape May is considered one of the best birding sites in the world. You might see a half-million robins fill the sky or spot rarer species like peregrine falcons and northern harriers. There's an asphalt boardwalk and bikeable back roads that pass through rural farmland and nature refuges; the beach itself is pounded by 2- to 3-foot waves. Compared with its noisy upcoast neighbors on the Jersey shore, Cape May unfolds like a flickering reel from the nineteenth century.

Things to Do: Bird-watching is a year-round obsession in Cape May. For the low-down on shorebird, raptor, and songbird migrations—plus info on guided walks—call the **Cape May Bird Observatory Hotline** (609-884-2626) or drop by the headquarters on East Lake Drive. The **Village Bicycle Shop** (2 Victorian Village Plaza; 609-884-8500) rents everything from two-wheelers to surreys. You can pedal the quiet side streets checking out the Victorians (there are 600 houses on the National Register of Historic Places) or head out to Cape May Point State Park, 3 miles south of town. Park visitors climb the 199-step Cape

May Lighthouse and hike the three short trails that meander over freshwater marshes and soft-sand beaches. Kayak tours of Cape May's sounds, tidal creeks, and harbor are led by **Aqua Trails** (2- to 4-hour trips, $30–$50; 609-884-5600).

Where to Stay: The venerable **Marquis de Lafayette** (doubles, $148–$228; 800-257-0432) has occupied its ocean-view spot for decades. A three-story motel adjoins the six-story, all-suites hotel with heated pool. To arrange a stay, call the **Cape May Reservation Service** (609-884-3191), which represents 70 percent of the town's B&Bs, hotels, motels, and guest houses.

For More Info: Chamber of Commerce of Greater Cape May; 609-884-5508.   —PARKE PUTERBAUGH

11

Ranch Vacations

Howdy Dude

My horse was a brown-and-white pinto named Shorty, and I had a terrible crush on a wrangler named Jack Neal," my old friend Bonnie said the other day. The summer we were 12, she spent 3 weeks at a Wyoming dude ranch, while my family took me to the New Jersey shore. Four decades later, I recall almost nothing about that summer, but Bonnie remembers every detail about her ranch vacation. "My mom let me wear the same shirt every day, a blue-plaid, western-cut thing with pearl snap buttons that made me feel like a cowgirl. I went riding with my dad for hours on end, and I still know the names of all the wildflowers that Jack pointed out to us."

The appeal of this classic American vacation hasn't changed much over the past 40 years. Most kids—even the most street-savvy and cool—still become besotted with "their" horses and taken in by the whole Wild West thing, especially the chance to rub chaps with real cowboys. (Caution: Older teens may find some dude-ranch staples, like hayrides and square dances, hopelessly hokey.) It's best to wait until your children are at least 6, however, before hauling the family out to a ranch; younger kids usually aren't long-legged or strong enough to enjoy the half-day rides. Parents, meanwhile, have the option of playing cowboy novitiate or not; in the latter case, they can kick back on the lodge porch, hike, or cast for trout in a nearby stream, confident that their kids are supervised and out giddy-upping on the range.

Like horses, there are many different breeds of dude ranches. At one end are the no-frill, working cattle operations that take in paying guests: You stay in rustic quarters (usually separate cabins), share simple meals with the ranch hands, and spend your time helping out with day-to-day chores—driving cattle to summer pastures, branding calves, and checking fences. Some kids are enthralled by the gritty reality of ranch life, but playing cowpoke for a week isn't everyone's idea of a vacation. At the other end are the Relais & Chateaux of dude ranches, with luxurious rooms westernified with lodgepole furnishings and Navajo rugs and options

like spas, exercise rooms, pools, and tennis courts.

Most of the hundreds of dude ranches scattered throughout the mountain West, however, are somewhere in the middle. These are casual, kid-loving places where you stay in a private cabin and share meals with other guests in the main lodge. Some are small with no set schedule, while others are bustling family operations that treat guests to a barrage of organized cowboy and noncowboy adventures (e.g., breakfast rides in the mountains or rafting trips in nearby parks). Many have a children's program, and some even have swimming pools and hot tubs.

Our ten family ranches, spread around Montana, Wyoming, Colorado, and Idaho, cover the range from gritty to gourmet. All have excellent riding programs, with gentle, sure-footed horses, plus spectacular Rockies settings that will jangle your spurs.

—NANCY DEBEVOISE

63 Ranch
Livingston, Montana

One of the oldest working dude ranches in the West, the 63 has been owned by the same family since 1929 and is listed on the National Register of Historic Places. The rambling log lodge is the genuine article, left over from the early glory days of dude ranches. These days it's stuffed with studded leather and Molesworth furniture, big-game mounts of elk, deer, moose, and bear, old Indian blankets and cowboy regalia, and a plentiful supply of well-worn western novels.

Since the 63 is set in a stunning landscape of snow-saddled peaks, glacier-formed canyons, forested mountain flanks, and rolling grasslands, you probably won't spend too much time lounging around the lodge. This is a place where you could spend 2 weeks in the saddle and never see the same view twice. Riders can amble up into the rugged Absaroka-Beartooth Wilderness for 100-mile vistas or head out into open rangeland for off-trail gallops. Or you can tag along with wranglers to the high pastures above the ranch where the 63's cattle spend their summers.

While most ranches won't allow children under 6 on trail rides, the 63 lets kids as young as 4 ride with their parents. When youngsters aren't glued to their horses or shadowing cowboys, they're yanking fish out of the stocked trout pond, messing around in the rec room or hanging out in the kids' te-pee. After dinner it's nostalgia time: old-fashioned parlor games, square dancing to records, wagon rides, snipe hunts, and nature walks.

If fish are almost as high on your list as horses, this is the place. A trout stream cascades down from the mountains through the ranch, and most of Montana's fabled blue-ribbon trout streams are within an hour's drive: the Yellowstone, Madison, Firehole, West Boulder, and Main Boulder rivers.

Guests stay in appealingly rustic, simply furnished cabins tucked into the pines. Built in the 30s, 40s, and 50s, the

Inside Skinny

City Slickers

At a dude ranch, it's not unusual to see folks doing what has come to be called the saddle-sore swagger: A gait that's a cross between a 103-year-old man and John Travolta in *Staying Alive*, resulting from knee, hamstring, and buttock muscles turned to plywood after hours in a saddle. The best remedies are a hot bath, aspirin, and some Ben-Gay. But the key is to stick with it. "It takes some getting used to," says Iris Behr of Hidden Creek Ranch. "As long as it's not so painful you can't walk, it's best to warm up the next morning and get back on the horse."

The Boots, Mars

Cowboy boots are best for riding because the heel prevents the foot from slipping through the stirrup, while the tapered toe lets the boot slide out of the stirrup, which prevents you from being dragged by the leg if you're jettisoned from the saddle. To break them in, try this trick: Fill boots with warm water and a dash of vinegar, let them soak about 30 minutes, then dump the water and wear the boots until they're dry on your feet.

The Cowboy Way

Insiders can spot a "dude" a mile away. While cowboys wear jeans over their boots, dudes wear theirs tucked in. Iris Behr's suggestion: Put the jeans over your boots before you put them on, then step into the whole outfit at once. You'll look as genuine as the rest of the wranglers—until you get on the horse, that is.

129

Wilderness Horsepack Trips

On the first morning of my first wilderness horsepack trip, I awoke to the murmur of voices and the crackle of the campfire outside my tent. As I unzipped the flap to peer at the world, a gloved paw reached around the side of the tent and tucked a mug of hot coffee into my hand. With that one gesture, all my trepidation about saddle sores, snow squalls, and short rations vanished. Clearly, one can find comfort—even luxury—on a wilderness pack trip, not to mention the thrill of exploring pristine Rockies backcountry in a time-honored fashion—a cowboy fantasy come to life.

Guided horsepack trips are ideal for families who love the idea of exploring wild country but cringe at the thought of shouldering a heavy pack, eating freeze-dried glop, and relying on topo maps to get them in and out of unfamiliar territory. It's easier to ride up and down steep trails than it is to hike them, especially for children, and packing gear on horses provides luxuries that backpackers can only dream about: fresh food, roomy tents, camp chairs, and wood stoves. Best of all, you're in the company of cowboys who know the turf intimately and can share hours of campfire stories about the terrain, the critters, and the local legends.

Most outfitters will book families with children as young as 6, but kids who are a little older and stronger will probably have a better time—as will their parents. Teenagers discover they can survive quite easily sans telephones and TVs, while adults find that the camaraderie of the trail can smooth over a surprising variety of parent-child rifts.

Backcountry horsepack trips aren't for everyone. The vast mountain preserves of the Rockies are wild and remote; it takes some long days in the saddle to earn access to their farther reaches. But if you're in reasonable shape and willing to learn some new moves, horsepacking can be a memorable family adventure. The following outfitters all provide kid-friendly guides, mountain-wise horses, and comfortable camps.

Allen's Diamond Four Ranch Wilderness Outfitting
Lander, Wyoming

The Diamond Four's pack trips roam 100,000 acres of high country in Wyoming's storied Wind River Range, home to the largest active glaciers in the Lower 48.

Outfitter Jim Allen schedules a variety of specialty trips each summer, ranging from custom family outings to "Long Rider" adventures that teach adults and teenagers basic horsepacking and low-impact camping skills. Trips vary from 4 to 14 days in length, take as few as four guests, and are tailored to the group's riding abilities and interests.

Most trips head into the Popo Agie Wilderness along the Continental Divide, site of some of the Rockies' most remote high country. One popular destination is the Cirque of the Towers, a semicircle of 12,000-foot granite spires that soar into the sky around Lonesome Lake.

Campsites are near streams for fishing and bathing, and offer a number of choices for hikes, picnics, and day rides. In addition to two-person domed tents with large rain flies, camps are equipped with a canvas wall tent and small wood stove.

The Diamond Four's season runs from June through September. Standard group pack-trip rates are $175 per day for adults and $150 per day for kids under 18. The outfitter recommends that children be at least 7 years old. Call 307-332-2995 for information and reservations.

—NANCY DEBEVOISE

Lass and Ron Mills Outfitting
Augusta, Montana

These guides teach conservation ethics on their 5- to 8-day wilderness pack trips—ideal for families who like to learn as well as play on their vacations. Most trips include a variety of hands-on nature activities, and some are accompanied by a geologist, botanist, historian, or fly-fishing expert.

The classroom is Montana's Bob Marshall Wilderness, which sprawls over more than a million acres of roadless high country that includes the Rocky Mountain Front and the Continental Divide. The trips visit dramatic sites like the Chinese Wall, an immense limestone reef that rises above the landscape like a giant tidal wave. "The Bob" is home to bighorn sheep, mountain goats, bald and golden eagles, black bears, elk, and moose—and more-elusive creatures like wolves, wolverines, cougars, and grizzly bears. Longer trips include as many as 5 days in camp; most families spend these layover days fishing in nearby streams, hiking to fossil sites and old homesteads, or heading off on sunset rides to scenic lookouts.

Nine trips are scheduled between June 10 and September 2; children as young as 6 are welcome. Rates are $185 per day for adults and $150 per day for each child under 18 accompanied by an adult. Call 406-562-3335 for information and reservations. —Nancy Debevoise

A. J. Brink Outfitters
Gypsum, Colorado

This 30-year veteran guides 8-day pack trips into pristine alpine terrain that ranges from 10,000 to 13,000 feet in altitude. One of the favorites is the Maroon Bells area of Colorado's Snowmass Wilderness, with seven peaks over 14,000 feet, impressive big-game herds, and spectacular Schofield Basin, "the flower garden of the Rockies."

On moving days, riders spend an average of 5 hours in the saddle. Still, it's not an endurance contest; plenty of stops are scheduled for short hikes and picnics to break up the ride. And most trips include 3 layover days, giving parents and kids a chance to ride or hike to nearby peaks and lakes, stalk wild trout in area streams, and explore abandoned mining towns. Camps are cushy by wilderness packers' standards, with roomy canvas sleeping tents and a large wall tent that keeps cooks, wranglers, and guests warm, dry, and out of the weather.

Three trips depart for Maroon Bells between July 22 and August 16; rates are $880

per person for 8 days. While it is recommended that kids be at least 10 years old, children as young as 7 are welcome if they have at least some riding experience. Call 970-435-5707 for additional information and reservations. —Nancy Debevoise

H. T. Outfitters
Vail to Aspen, Colorado

By car through sinuous Glenwood Canyon, it's 2 hours from Vail to Aspen. By horse, down the length of the Sawatch Mountains, it takes 4 to 5 days. Along the way you picnic in the wildflower meadows of Sawmill Park, skirt three sides of New York Mountain, splash across a dozen ice-cold streams, and climb to the summit of 11,765-foot Mount Yeckel. Once over the top, grab your binoculars and you can make out the ski slopes of Aspen Mountain to the southwest.

You're bound to be saddle sore, so plan on a well-earned soak in the wood-fired sauna at the Polar Star Inn, one of three backcountry huts that are used for overnights (all are part of the Tenth Mountain Division hut system linking Vail and Aspen). Your group takes over the cabins, while guide Pam Green tends to the grub and wranglers tend to the horses. All you have to do is spread your sleeping bag on your bunk's foam mattress and wait for the stir-fried rice and shrimp skewers to appear. The third night you chuck your bedroll for the clean-sheet luxury of the Fryingpan River Ranch.

Twelve to twenty miles a day on horseback can add up to 5 or 6 long hours in the saddle, which isn't every kid's idea of a good time. For your first trip, you might consider a 2- or 3-day outing that covers part of the route or heads north from Vail into the Flattops. Even with that precaution, kids under age 10 should have a strong horse background; the minimum age is 7.

The 3-day ride costs $970 per person (you stay at the two huts nearest Vail); 4- and 5-day trips cost $1,150–$1,175 (with overnights at two huts and the ranch). Call 970-926-2029 for information. —Susan Kaye

THE FUN FILE: TRAIL LORE

Watch Birds. Pack binoculars and keep a bird log. The classic field guides are the Peterson series (Houghton Mifflin), and *The Nature Company's Guide to Birding* (Time-Life Books) is a terrific resource book.

Forecast the Weather. Learn about forecasting in Cliff Jacobson's *Camping Secrets* (ICS Books). Frogs croak and the smoke from your campfire hangs low when rain is on the way, but a heavy dew in early morning suggests 12 hours of good weather. Keep a journal of your own predictions, then record what actually happens.

Do Scat. Young kids get jazzed about excrement, which happens to be all over the trails. Paul Rezendes's *Tracking and the Art of Seeing* (Camden House Publishing) provides all the information required to get out there and find your own evidence of animal life.

Keep a Flower Journal. Wildflowers die a nanosecond after being picked, so pack markers and a journal and sketch the flowers you find. Bring along a flower book to identify what you're drawing.

Sweep for Bugs. Bring a small net on a pole and a bug book. Gently brush through the grasses and wildflowers. Catalog in a journal all the bugs you find, then let them go. (See chapter 21 for nifty bug gear.) —*Lisa Twyman Bessone*

---

cabins (some log and some frame) have from one to four bedrooms and a bathroom. The cost of a 7-day stay, including all meals, is $895 per adult, with a $50 weekly discount for children under 11. Call 406-222-0570. —NANCY DEBEVOISE

Pine Butte Guest Ranch
Choteau, Montana

If you're the type of person who likes knowing the name of every flower, bird, animal, and rock you trot past, you're in luck at Pine Butte: A full-time naturalist is on hand to lend a slightly academic tone to the dude-ranch experience.

Set in dramatic wild country on the eastern front of the Rockies, the ranch looks west into the vast mountain strong-

hold of the Bob Marshall Wilderness and east into the roaming countryside of the high plains. The Nature Conservancy owns the ranch and the nearby Pine Butte Swamp Preserve, 18,000 acres of protected wetlands and pristine prairies. Together, the two properties safeguard an astonishing array of wildlife: deer, beaver, bighorn sheep, bear, coyote, and numerous bird species—such as sandhill cranes, long-billed curlews, and eagles.

Guests stay in cabins built of native stone and wood and decorated with hand-crafted lodgepole furniture. Most have two bedrooms, two baths, and a fireplace; some have living rooms as well.

On morning and afternoon rides into the mountains, kids can fish in alpine lakes, check out beaver ponds, and search for ancient sea fossils. Each day the staff naturalist guides hikes focusing on native plants, birds, mammals, geology, and paleontology. For dinosaur freaks, the ranch schedules an all-day outing to Egg Mountain, a world-class dig where novices can help experts uncover dinosaur bones, eggs, and nests.

Guests who'd rather hang out at the ranch can swim in the heated pool or poke around in the Natural History Center, a large cabin filled with nature books, maps, fossils, photographs, and information on the natural history of the area.

Weekly rates are $1,050 for adults and $800 for children 12 and under. There's no minimum age (baby-sitting can be arranged for younger kids). For information and reservations, call 406-466-2158.　　　—NANCY DEBEVOISE

Sweet Grass Ranch
Big Timber, Montana

When you get directions for this ranch in the heart of southern Montana, you'll know this is the place you've always wanted to find: "From the general store, follow the road to the left. It turns to gravel, then to dirt, crosses a creek bottom, climbs a ridge, and passes to the left of an old white house. You'll have to open and close several gates, depending on where livestock is."

Don't expect any coddling at this bonafide ranch that's been in the same family for five generations. Each day you can join a trail ride into the Crazy Mountains of south-central Montana, or opt for chores instead—you can haul blocks of salt to the Angus in the high pas-

tures, grain the horses, slop the pigs, milk Mooca, the resident cow, or help check the fence line. Activities at Sweet Grass are unstructured so as to best suit the interests of the twenty weekly guests. (Of course, chores are optional for guests. You could just kick back.)

Youngsters fit right in at this home on the range, though there are no special programs except perhaps playing hide-and-seek astride horses. Ages 6 and up ride alone or with their parents; the theory is that if they're up for it, they can ride as far as adults. No one ever said the West was for sissies.

Cabins, some with private baths, form a horseshoe around the main lodge, a welcoming two-story log building that's on the National Register of Historic Places and has four additional guest rooms. For accommodations with a private bath, weekly rates start at $800 for adults; $350 for ages 4 to 6; under 4 are free; gratuities are extra. For more information, call 406-537-4477.

　　　　　　　　—SUSAN KAYE

Hidden Creek Ranch
Harrison, Idaho

Hidden Creek is an upscale ranch with a not-so-hidden emphasis on conservation ethics and American Indian traditions. The ranch encourages its guests to think green by stocking the log cabins with eco-friendly linens and soaps, serving ranch-grown organic produce, and sprinkling many activities with subtle lessons about the importance of living lightly on the land.

Unlike many ranches, Hidden Creek offers in-depth riding instruction to those who want to improve their skills. A guest rodeo at week's end gives kids and grown-ups a chance to show their stuff in events like barrel racing, pole bending, and team relays.

But if you're only pretending to like horses, you won't be chained to the saddle at Hidden Creek: There are guided nature hikes, fly-fishing lessons in the ranch's pond, mountain biking on groomed trails or nearby logging roads, boating on nearby lakes, archery, and trapshooting.

It's impossible to imagine a bored kid at Hidden Creek. Several age-appropriate children's programs keep youngsters and teenagers entertained with riding, hiking (including a trip to an old gold mine), biking, swimming in the pond, fishing, crafts, nature studies, campfire storytelling, and tepee overnights. Television is banned, for obvious reasons, at most dude ranches, but Hidden Creek opens its otherwise off-limits video library to kids on occasional rainy days.

Hidden Creek's "week" is 6 nights long. From June to August, rates are $1,420 for adults (double occupancy) and $955 for children 3 through 11. There's no charge for infants and toddlers, and discounts are available for groups of eight or more. Call 208-689-3209.

—NANCY DEBEVOISE

Moose Creek Ranch
Victor, Idaho

With wild mustangs in the stable and the Tetons right out the back door, this 15-acre ranch serves up the genuine West. What really sets Moose Creek apart is that it rejects the concept of the pampered dude. Instead, the aim is to teach guests basic horse sense along with basic horse care. From day one, you'll be working alongside wranglers to groom and saddle your own steed (the chores are optional, of course). Even kids eventually master the intricacies of latigos, cinches, and bridles.

The Van Orden family that owns the ranch works through the "Adopt a Wild Mustang Program" to rescue mustangs; once trained, they become exceptionally sure-footed trail horses. Four to six of the mustangs pull an 1800s town coach on the jouncy, 40-minute ride to the town of Victor.

All five Van Orden offspring pitch in with the operation, so vacationing children can see how it's done. From about age 7 on (the ranch has accepted kids as young as 4), kids ride with their parents, thundering up Plumer Loop for views of the Grand Teton or on the sunset ride. Ages 6 and under have one-to-one supervision for pony rides, games, crafts, and hikes into the canyon, although they're welcome to ride with adults if they're up to it. Also on the roster is a whitewater raft trip on the Snake River (minimum age for rafting is 6).

Moose Creek accepts thirty to thirty-six guests a week; they stay in knotty-pine cabins at the edge of Targhee National Forest. One popular option for lodging is a secluded log ranch home with five bedrooms, three baths, and two living rooms (four-person minimum required).

The weekly cost for cabins is $1,045 for adults; $860 for ages 8 to 12; $675 for ages 3 to 7 (kids under 3 are free), plus an additional 20 percent for tax and ser-

COWBOY
VS.
DUDE

To the untrained eye—or the eye trained by Hollywood—it can be hard to tell a real cowboy from a dude. But no matter how authentic the outfit or the attitude, there are unmistakable differences:

COWBOY

The cowboy rolls his own cigarettes.

The cowboy's belt buckle is big enough to display his initials.

The cowboy two-steps.

To the cowboy, "ranch" is a noun.

The cowboy would never, ever eat or wear eggplant.

The cowboy has boot spurs.

The cowboy wears plaid.

The cowboy eats everything with ketchup.

DUDE

The dude rolls his abs.

The dude's is big enough to receive DirecTV.

The dude twelve-steps.

To the dude, "ranch" is a flavor.

The dude would, and drive it, too.

The dude has bone spurs.

The dude wears Burberry.

The dude eats everything with aïoli.

—Ryan Underwood

THE HYSTERICAL PARENT

What If My Kid's Horse Decides It's Rodeo Time? Wranglers look for horses to put in their lines that are "bomb-proof" (their description, not ours) because they don't underestimate their clients' inexperience or the severity of the term "liability." Be honest about your family's riding experience and you'll be assigned horses commensurate with your abilities.

What If the Horse Takes a Spill? Horses are sure-footed creatures, and rarely fall unless human riders interfere. Trust the horse to know what to do. These aren't cars with rack-and-pinion steering; horses can pick a line down the trail much better than you can.

Those Horses Are Too Big; Can't You Give My Kids a Pony? Wrong. Ponies are imps that delight in mischief. But horses the size of buildings can maneuver their bodies to keep kids from falling off, even when they pound the horses' sides in an attempt to get them to gallop. When it comes to horses, bigger is better.

If Someone Gets Hurt Aren't We Days Away from Help? A horse can cover some serious ground in a hurry. For most of the trip the horses have been walking; a galloping horse can cover the same distance in a fraction of the time.

—*Lisa Twyman Bessone*

vice charge. The ranch home runs $100 more per person. Call 800-676-0075.

—SUSAN KAYE

Absaroka Ranch
Dubois, Wyoming

The Absaroka is a secluded hideaway at 8,000 feet in the mountains of northwest Wyoming. The ranch takes just 18 guests, making it ideal for families who like the homey feel of small places.

Miles of superb riding country stretch away from the corrals, much of it gentle enough to permit lots of cantering and an occasional gallop. The Absaroka's rolling hills lead to the foothills of Ramshorn Mountain, about 5 miles away. For a ranch of its size, the Absaroka's horse operation is lavishly staffed with horses and wranglers. Three rides take off from the ranch each morning and afternoon: a sedate amble for beginners and those who prefer a leisurely pace; a walk-trot ride for those with fair riding skills; and a fast ride for skilled thrill-seekers. Guests with time and enthusiasm to spare can spend a few days before or after their ranch stay on a guided wilderness horsepack trip.

Except for daily rides, the ranch has no set schedule. Instead, the staff organizes guided hikes, fishing expeditions, river trips, and other doings in response to the guests' daily whims. Owners Emi and Budd Betts delight in organizing deliciously corny after-dinner activities like three-legged races, campfire sing-alongs, cowboy poetry, and outings to local rodeos and square dances.

A 7-night stay (from Sunday to Sunday) costs $1020 for adults and $920 for kids 12 and under, based on a four person occupancy. Discounts are available for families of five or more who share one of the exceptionally comfortable two- and three-bedroom log cabins. Call 307-455-2275. —NANCY DEBEVOISE

Double Diamond X Ranch
Cody, Wyoming

In late spring, it's a zoo in the South Fork Valley, 34 miles south of Cody. Entire herds of pronghorn antelope, deer, and elk stop to drink in the Shoshone River, which runs within a couple hundred yards of the Double Diamond X, and bighorn sheep roam in the forested Absaroka Range to the west.

Kids as young as 3 have made the rounds in the riding ring, but it takes three adults to make it happen—one on each side and another holding the reins. Counselors lead a full program for the kids, with at least one ride a day, along with games on horseback and feeding and grooming chores with the wranglers. One day kids might learn a cowboy song on the guitar, and the next jump on a hay wagon pulled by Samson and Delilah, two magnificent Percherons. They'll hear stories about Wyoming's Cowboys and Indians, make picture frames out of bark, and still have time for swimming, softball, hiking, and even parents. They can also use the heated pool, and fish in the pond or at a fishing camp on the river.

There are Thursday overnights ($150 extra) for kids whose riding skills pass muster; on Fridays everyone takes part in the family trail ride.

Most weeks, all thirty-two guests steal away for a day in Cody, poking through the Buffalo Bill Historical Center and Old Trail Town and taking in the rodeo. Rates for 1 week in a cottonwood-shaded cabin with two bedrooms, bath, a porch, and a log interior are $1,460 per adult; $1,020 per child age 6 to 14; $550 per child under 6. Rates for rooms in the Trailhouse Lodge are $1,210 for adults, $800 for kids 6 to 14, and $550 for under 6. Taxes and a service charge add nearly 15 percent. Call 800-833-7262.

—SUSAN KAYE

Vista Verde Ranch
Steamboat Springs, Colorado

In a valley surrounded by aspen- and pine-forested mountains, Vista Verde offers guests the best of both worlds, combining working-ranch traditions with dude-style fun. The ranch runs 80 head of cattle, corrals 60 horses, and raises lots of farm animals—pigs, lambs, chickens, and ducks—and at the same time provides comfortable accommodations. Guests stay in posh, rustic log cabins, most of which have a master suite for parents and a sleeping loft or second bedroom with its own bath for kids (some of the cabins also have Jacuzzis). In a bow to its sophisticated clientele, the ranch is staffed with a professional chef and equipped with a spa, exercise machines, and a sauna.

Unlike many dude ranches that crowd a dozen or more riders of varying abilities onto each trail ride, the

Vista Verde takes groups of no more than five guests on their choice of slow, medium, and fast rides that range from 1 to 6 hours in length. The ranch caters to adventurous spirits with rock-climbing instruction at a fairly tame rockface down the road, mountain biking, and even hot-air balloon flights. There are also supervised kids-only rides, hikes, swimming excursions, archery, treasure hunts, panning for gold at nearby Elk River, and tepee overnights.

In June and September the rates for a 7-night stay are $1,450–$1,550 per adult and $950–$1,050 for children under 12. In July and August, the rates are $1,650–$1,750 per adult and $1,150–$1,250 per child. Prices are slightly higher during the cattle drive. Call 800-526-7433 or 970-879-3858.

—NANCY DEBEVOISE

C Lazy U Ranch
Granby, Colorado

Call it the Mild West: In a well-tamed spot on Willow Creek, 2 hours north of Denver, is C Lazy U—part ranch, part resort. You'll find no rough edges here: Navajo rugs hang on lacquered log walls; neat rows of saddles and bridles fill the oversized barn; and guests are soothed with massages, saunas, whirlpools, and dips in the heated swimming pool.

With 170 horses in the stable for 115 guests, you're assured of a mount at all times. Various levels of 2- to 3-hour rides leave daily at 9 A.M. and 2 P.M. Separate programs for ages 3 to 5, 6 to 12, and teens include early mealtime for both lunch and dinner and after-dinner cookouts, hayrides, and games. Ranch weeks run Sunday to Sunday, beginning with tack and riding instruc-

tion and moving on to trail rides and riding games. By Thursday, teens overnight at McQueeries Ridge while younger kids spend all day on the trail. Families ride together on Friday, and everyone competes in the Saturday afternoon "Shodeo" to demonstrate their newly acquired skills.

But for the saddle-weary there are plenty of other options: You could scramble up Mount Baldy on the ranch's southern flank for views of the hard-edged summit of 14,256-foot Longs Peak. Or plan a day of guided fly-fishing, golfing on renowned Pole Creek, tennis, trap and skeet, or rafting the Colorado River.

Families stay in one-, two-, and four-unit log cabins with one to three bedrooms, most with fireplaces and some with private Jacuzzis, but none with a phone or TV. Following ranch tradition, meals are family-style but far from hot dogs and mounds of baked beans; more typical would be Black Angus prime rib or jalapeño-stuffed mountain trout.

Average rates are $1,725 per week; $1,525 for age 5 and under; you'll pay an additional 20 percent for tax and service charge. Call 970-887-3344.

—SUSAN KAYE

Lost Valley Ranch
Sedalia, Colorado

White-faced Herefords graze the upper meadows, some 120 quarter horses nicker in the pastures, and a team of beer-commercial Clydesdales pulls wagons up narrow mountain roads. It's a working ranch, all right, but for you, there's no work in sight. Your week at Lost Valley, a AAA four-diamond property, is a family-fest of tennis, swimming, and volleyball squeezed in between morning and afternoon trail rides. Although the ranch is an easy 90 minutes northwest of Colorado Springs, the country you'll explore seems as isolated as when a cowboy homesteaded the Goose Creek property in 1883.

Lost Valley accommodates ninety-eight guests, and three counselors and three wranglers handle the agenda for three age groups of kids (6 to 7, 8 to 10, and 11 to 12) that includes picnics, hikes, and an all-day trail ride through 28,000 acres of Pike National Forest. Kids ride with their own age group except during the thrice-weekly family rides; teens hang together or with the adults, then dash off for tubing in mountain streams or a haywagon ride to a breakfast cookout. Three- to five-year-olds have their own fun, with pint-size excursions, a picnic away from the ranch, and corral rides with parents leading the horse. Bring a rod to fish in Goose Creek, a 2½-mile trout stream.

Back at the ranch, you'll chow down on home-style cooking with plenty of fresh vegetables and even more desserts. Families stay in one- to three-bedroom cabins, each with a porch swing and a living room with a stone fireplace. Weekly rates are $1,495 for adults, $1,350 for teens, $1,095 for ages 6 to 12, and $850 for 3- to 5-year-olds, including gratuity; tax is 4.5 percent. Call 303-647-2311.   —SUSAN KAYE

Horse Sense

Because of the years I spent in 4-H raising and showing horses, I can say with authority and without reservation that pigs are smarter and a hell of a lot more trustworthy and, were pigs only taller and faster, I'd much prefer to have one of them beneath my saddle than some commonly addlebrained, backbiting horse.

So why do I recommend that parents set their treasured offspring upon a horse and, with them, embark upon a trail ride? Simple: As dumb as horses are, they are still one of the great ways to access the outdoors. Moreover, the trail ride is an American institution—a rare time-conduit that can transport your children and you back to the roots of a nation founded on horseback. And there is one more consideration: At some time in everyone's life, it will become necessary to ride a horse, and the sooner our children learn how to deal with the ornery things the better off they will be.

The first trail ride I took with my two sons was along the Pacific coast of Costa Rica, and I know that they remember it more fondly than I do—perhaps because it was my gristly little horse that chose to bolt, sprinting me out of control through a sleepy little fishing village ("¡Ándale, gringo! ¡Ándale!") until it finally slowed from sheer exhaustion. My sons loved that. They thought it was funny.

A better trail ride, though, was in Colorado, where we rode beneath snowy peaks and camped beside streams. Even I had to admit that horses were the common denominator that carried us to a place in which the three of us were closer than we had ever been.

—RANDY WAYNE WHITE

139

12

Learning Vacations

Summer 101

The very idea of a learning vacation is enough to make a kid gag. Once you're free from school for the summer, who wants anything to do with learning? Well, most of the vacations I've taken in my 14 years have been educational ones, and I've sure never found myself cooped up in a classroom.

My family bought into learning vacations in part because my dad, Thane, runs the education department at the Cincinnati Zoo. I joined the Junior Zoologist Club, and one trip we took was to Belize. Hiking through the Cockscomb Basin Jaguar Preserve, I stood a few feet away from two of the world's most venomous snakes, the fer-de-lance and the coral snake. We also snorkeled in Ranguana Cay, part of the second-largest coral reef in the world. At school, you pretty much just sit in class; on a learning trip, you're out in the field having this great adventure. And because you live it, you don't soon forget it.

But don't think the only way you can have a good time is to travel halfway around the world. There are so many exciting places right here at home. Like New Jersey: Every year, my parents, two sisters (Shailah is 11 and Lily is 7), and I pile into our minivan for the 14-hour drive to Cape May. This is on the main route for the southern migration of butterflies, songbirds, owls, and hawks. And, sure, my dad is the official animal expert, but it's my mom, Kath, who has gotten hooked on birds. Which proves, I guess, that even parents can be taught a thing or two on a learning vacation.—CAITLIN MAYNARD

THE WEST COAST

Pacific Northwest Marine Adventure Camp

Any summer camp that starts with a ferry ride or seaplane flight across Washington State's sparkling Puget Sound to a pristine island in the outer San Juans is getting things off on the right foot. The Island Institute knows how to keep kids—and tagalong parents—happily occupied for a full week. During the institute's Marine Adventure Camp, families whale-watch, hike, fish, wade, swim, cruise, dive, snorkel, and sea kayak, all in the name and company (your campmates will be naturalists and marine biologists) of good science. From day one, your family is plopped into the water to investigate shore-based animal and plant life; wade and snorkel the tide pools and kelp beds; and observe whales, otters, and seal rookeries aboard sea kayaks or a 43-foot expedition boat. You'll then recover your land legs on island hikes in search of nesting bald eagles and deer who aren't the least bit bashful around humans. During free time, families can take off as a group and explore the islands, scout out one of the *Free Willy* movie locations (right off Spieden Island), or record their marine discoveries with underwater photos and fish prints, an ancient Japanese art using textile ink that, by the way, makes for great T-shirt designs.

Facilities are rustic but comfy: Campers sleep on beds in roomy, safari-style tents (BYO sleeping bag), eating group meals and taking hot showers in a spiffy new lodge that also has a Jacuzzi and shelves full of bird and fish books. A few private cottages are available at an additional cost. Camp weeks run Saturday to Friday ($895 per person, with significant discounts for families; 6- to 8-year-olds come for half-price; kids 5 and under stay free), with a 3-night getaway option ($395) as well as single-day activities. The program runs weekly from June through the end of September, with a few weeks set aside for advanced camping programs (ages 18 and older) and a special Project Orca for teenagers. All meals, activities, and equipment are included, except scuba diving, which is available as an option. Boat charters and year-round programs for private groups are also available. The institute offers a 4-hour resort course for kids 12 and up ($75) and a full 2-week certification course for ages 15 and up ($1,640) in August. Call the Island Institute at 800-956-ORCA.

—KATHY MARTIN

THE SOUTHWEST

Crow Canyon Archaeological Center

Most kids love a treasure hunt, especially if their quarry is a real-life trea-sure. At Crow Canyon Archaeological Center, a campuslike work-study complex situated in the middle of the homeland of the ancient Anasazi Indians, your family can delve into prehistory in search of artifacts.

During two special Family Weeks, parents and kids age 12 and up attend classes and workshops on Anasazi life and lore; learn to properly wash, sort, and analyze artifacts in Crow Canyon's laboratory; then spend a couple of days out in the field actually digging.

You'll also learn the delicate art of excavation with trowel and whisk broom at Shields Pueblo, an Anasazi site that has seen little previous excavation. (All artifacts are turned over to Crow Canyon.) The week concludes with an all-day guided tour of the exquisite cliff dwellings in Mesa Verde National Park.

Dirt-diggers of all ages stay in four-bunk, Navajo-style wooden hogans. Cost is $795 for adults, $475 for kids 12 to 18, including meals. Families usually stay together in one hogan, but Crow Canyon can't guarantee it. Family weeks begin August 3 and 10. Call 800-422-8975.   —DAVID NOLAND

Desert Southwest Archaeology Expedition

Sure, it's educational. But the real reason you're here is more primordial: to make like a kid and dig in the dirt. The Anasazi excavation expeditions offered by eastern Arizona's White Mountain Archaeological Center will give you and your kids a hands-on orientation to the mysteries of the ancients who lived here 1,000 years ago. Among the Raven Site Ruin's two kivas and 800 rooms, high on a knoll above the Little Colorado River, families can devote a day, several days, or a week to excavating prehistoric trash—pottery shards, bone tools, shell pendants, stone fetishes—from the ruins of Anasazi middens. They can hike in the volcano-studded White Mountains to see petroglyph and shrine sites; work in the field lab cleaning, sorting, and cataloging the daily finds; tour the ethnobotanical garden to see what the Anasazi farmers grew (corn, squash, beans, sunflowers, wild grapes, prickly pears); or perfect their coil-and-scrape technique, a prehistoric method for making pottery. Evening lectures by staff archaeologists enliven the history of the area, a significant Indian trading community inhabited as early as A.D. 1000 and as late as A.D. 1450 by the Anasazi and Mogollon Indians.

The White Mountain Archaeological Center is 4½ hours east of Phoenix, near the New Mexico border. Six-day programs run Monday through Saturday from May 1 to October 15 and cost $59 per day for adults, including lunch; $37 for kids 9 to 17. Tent-camping is available at the center within walking distance of the site ($12 per night), so are a few self-contained RV camping areas. You can camp at Lyman Lake State Park (520-337-4441), 6 miles north of the center, or let a field staffer recommend one of the motels in nearby St. Johns or Springerville. Call 800-814-6451 or 520-333-5857 for information and program reservations.

It's worth noting that Arizona's White Mountains are a spectacular—

National Wildlife Federation Conservation Summits

To paraphrase Bill Cosby's old Noah's Ark routine, "Right…what's a conservation summit?" Answer: an annual weeklong workshop in environmental education specifically designed for families with kids as young as 3. (Childcare is available for kids under 3.) The **Adirondacks Summit,** held July 5–11, offers classes, field trips, and workshops on topics such as black bears, wildlife ecology, and nature photography. Adults' and kids' programs are conducted separately in the mornings, with family activities—canoe trips, nature hikes, a bat-box construction project—scheduled for the afternoons.

Summiteers stay in a YMCA lakeside retreat with digs ranging from dorm-style bunkhouses to a historic inn. Lodging rates for the week (meals included) range from $419 to $594 for adults, $230 to $258 for kids. Registration fee is $400 for adults, $200 to $325 for kids depending on their ages. Non-NWF members pay an additional $50 for kids, $100 for adults.

For the more adventurous, there's an NWF Summit in **Seward, Alaska,** June 21–27. Activities include boat excursions in Resurrection Bay to watch whales, sea lions, seals, and sea otters; a field trip to Exit Glacier; and a lecture on the *Exxon Valdez* oil spill. Attendees stay in B&Bs, motels, or at a local campground. Room rates range from $60 to $120 per night for double rooms, including breakfast. Costs for the meal plans are $100 to $210. For more information on both summits and assistance in booking rooms in Seward, call 703-790-4265.

—DAVID NOLAND

and largely undiscovered—range; there's great trout fishing in the Little Colorado, elk and pronghorn antelope graze in forest clearings and the high-desert grasslands, and hiking opportunities abound in nearby Apache-Sitgraves National Forest. If you've got a few extra days of vacation time, I suggest a stay in the tiny alpine village of Greer, and a road trip at least partway down the old Coronado Trail, to Alpine or perhaps Morenci.   —KATHY MARTIN

Southwest Language Immersion

Language study high in the Rockies of northern New Mexico? Sounds like torture—if you think it means conjugating irregular verbs in a fluorescent-lit classroom while sunny mountain trails and bracing outdoor air beckon. But at the Santa Fe Language Institute's Family Spanish Immersion Program in Taos, New Mexico, you and your offspring will learn to *hablar español* while you hike and picnic in the spectacular Sangre de Cristo Mountains, with nary a vocabulary quiz to distract you. The institute's modus operandi is to immerse adults in the language via conversational dialogue and role-playing, not grammar, while the kids learn at their own pace through Spanish games and stories.

During the 5-day vacation, you'll work on fluency in the spoken language and Southwestern and Latin American culture: Historians, folklorists, and the Mexican consul are guest speakers, and your field trips include tours of a nineteenth-century Spanish colonial hacienda, Taos Pueblo (where you might catch a traditional dance), and other cultural and historical sites of the Southwest. Your base, the Hotel Edelweiss, in the heart of the Taos Ski Valley, is only a minute or two from trailheads and chairlift rides up the mountain. And there's horseback riding and Rio Grande rafting nearby.

Included in the Family Spanish Immersion Program are accommodations, instruction, materials, excursions, and meals, including gourmet Spanish-style dinners for parents (Anne Marie Wooldridge, an owner of the Hotel Edelweiss, trained with the White House pastry chef) and a special menu for the kids. Day care for kids under 3 runs about $5 per hour per child. Call 800-983-6469 for this year's program dates and prices.   —KATHY MARTIN

Texas Wildlife Safari

Across the savanna they come: a small herd of wildebeests, followed by a pair of gemsbok and a lone greater kudu. Zebras nibble the prairie grass. A cheetah pops out of the woods as a white rhino basks in the sun. This scene unfolds right in front of your open safari vehicle—deep in the heart of Texas.

At the Fossil Rim Wildlife Center in the Texas hill country, your African-style family safari takes place on a range that's home to 1,100 free-roaming exotic and endangered animals. This 2,700-acre ranch, 1½ hours southwest of Dallas, participates in the Species Survival Plan, a worldwide managed-conservation program, and serves as a breeding ground for ten endangered species: cheetah, Grevy's zebra, two kinds of rhino, two types of oryx, addax antelope, and three wolf species.

But you'll also get up close and personal with giraffes, llamas, gazelles, sandhill cranes, emus, ostriches, prairie chickens, white-tailed deer, jackrabbits, and armadillos of the native Texas variety. Most visitors settle for the 2-hour, self-guided driving tour, but during a family overnight Conservation Camp you'll travel with a naturalist guide in an open Land Rover to areas that aren't on the Scenic Wildlife Drive; take nature hikes and night walks; hunt for fossils; visit the vet clinic; touch a rhinoceros; and feed giraffes by hand. Itineraries are tailored to group interests: If the kids are fans of *Canis lupus*, you'll spend more time with the wolves; if they're fascinated with the Arabian oryx, you'll bone up on oryx life. Even toddlers can get chummy with a pot-bellied pig, goats, sheep, or tortoises at the petting pasture.

You'll spend nights in screened bunkhouses on a hill overlooking the animals' valley ($58 per person per night; BYO sleeping bag); you can also bring your own tent and sleep outside ($48 per person). Sorry, no kid discounts—dinner and breakfast are included, though. A Wilderness Camp overnight option features a 5-mile guided hike to a remote campsite ($58 per person per night; BYO backpack and sleeping bag; tents are provided).

Both camps operate year-round for groups of ten or more (bring your neighbor's family or ask the center to set you up with a smaller group), and you can stay from 1 to 6 nights. Ask about the center's annual Wolf Howl evening in June, which includes seminars, a campfire dinner, wolf-lore tales, and a wolf-calling contest; other special summertime events include a Star Watch and a "Rhino Rap." Call 817-897-2960.   —KATHY MARTIN

THE ROCKIES

Rocky Mountains Natural History Adventure

Old Wild West meets new Wild West during the Nature Place's weeklong Colorado Natural History Adventure. From base camp on a 6,000-acre property at 8,600 feet in the Rockies, prehistory groupies can dig for fossils and investigate 35-million-year-old tree stumps at Florissant Fossil Bed National Monument, while the social studies set reenacts the human history of the area by touring an 1800s homestead, where they dip candles, bake bread, and press apples for cider. Then everyone can try newfangled activities like a high-ropes course, darkroom photography, or an astronomy program with a 17.5-inch telescope.

In between old and new come the classic adventures: canoeing and kayaking, wildflower hikes, bird walks, and the optional bagging of a Fourteener. And by the closing campfire sing-along, most families will have joined at least one field research team in mapping bird and mammal nests, surveying pond and stream life, or collecting bugs.

The Nature Place, 40 miles west of Colorado Springs on the back side of Pikes Peak near Florissant, is part of the Colorado Outdoor Education Center, designated a National Environmental Study Area by the National Park Service. Families sleep in studio apartments with fireplaces, kitchenettes, lofts, decks, and picture windows with views of the

Rockies; apartments sleep four (larger groups should request two apartments).

The main lodge serves home-cooked meals in a large dining room with a view of Pikes Peak and has an indoor pool, Jacuzzi, and exercise/weight room, plus outdoor tennis and volleyball courts and a putting green. But you'll likely find the younger set loitering in the Interbarn, a kid-friendly ecology center with rocks and fossils, a walk-in plant cell, and a seismograph. Family programs run from June 28 to July 4, July 12 to July 18, July 28 to August 3, and August 11 to August 18; cost is $745 for adults, $530 for ages 5 to 15 (kids under 5 are free), including all meals, facilities, and field trips. Call 719-748-3475 for more information.

—KATHY MARTIN

Outward Bound's Colorado School

Take the philosophy of personal empowerment, mix in the group-bonding factor of teamwork and leadership, and fry it all up in stressful situations and you've got the idea behind Outward Bound, the granddaddy of all wilderness schools.

OB's Colorado School offers a 7-day Family Alpine Adventure in the heart of the Rockies. From a base camp near Leadville, "patrols" of two or three families spend the first few days in confidence- and trust-building activities like rock climbing and rappelling.

Accommodations at the base camp may be tents, tepees, or a bunkhouse. On day three, you and the kids will shoulder packs for a 4-day backcountry expedition that includes a climb of a nearby 14,000-foot peak. The trek concludes with an overnight "duo," a par-ent-child variation on OB's traditional "solo" time of solitude and reflection. Courses start June 15, July 13, and August 10. Cost is $895 per person; the minimum age is 14.

OB also runs 5- to 7-day family rafting courses (minimum age 14) down the Green and Colorado rivers in Utah. Rafters paddle and set up camp, and each person has a chance to captain a raft through a major rapid. Some courses include rock-climbing instruction. Cost is $595–$945. Call 800-477-2627.   —DAVID NOLAND

THE SOUTH

Southeast Sea Turtle Watch

It's the ultimate science project: witnessing a prehistoric ritual of an ancient reptile. On Pritchards Island, a wild barrier island off the South Carolina coast just north of Hilton Head, this solemnity is an every-night occurrence from late May through mid-August. Huge loggerhead sea turtles drag their 300-pound bodies across the hard-packed sand to dig nests with their flippers and lay clutches of precious eggs before making their exhausted way back to the water.

On Wilderness Southeast's 4-day Turtle Watch program, you patrol 2½ miles of beach, observing and meeting with scientists who are recording the nesting patterns of this threatened species, protecting the loosely buried eggs from other animals, and sometimes helping the mama reptiles back to the water.

During the day you can sleep late, explore Atlantic salt marshes, hike maritime oak and palm forests, and comb the beach for some pristine additions to your seashell collection. Rather than the sunning throngs and golf addicts you'd rub shoulders with at Hilton Head, most of your daytime company will be wading birds: Pritchards Island remains pretty much in its natural state.

Families sleep in dormitory-style rooms in the University of South Carolina's Pritchards Island Research House; bring your own sleeping bags. The recommended minimum age for the trip is 12, but younger children who are sturdy walkers and up for staying up late will do fine—you'll just need to make arrangements with Wilderness Southeast.

Remember that this is the Southeast: Daytime summer temperatures can reach the 90s, and the sun is intense—so pack plenty of sunscreen and protective clothing. But at night, when you'll spend most of your time on the beach, temperatures are generally in the 60s. One trip is scheduled for 1997: July 28–31. The cost is $525 for adults, and $475 for kids, including meals and transportation between the island and Savannah. Call 912-897-5108.

—KATHY MARTIN

13

It may be the best of all worlds: a camplike array of things to do, plus the presence of Mom and Dad…in measured doses. Even the chummiest of families find it difficult to hang together for an entire vacation, but at a multisport resort, you don't have to. If the notion of learning some new skill with your progeny, like rock climbing or boardsailing, seems a prescription for embarrassment, there's usually plenty of opportunity to slip off and drown a worm on your own or take a solo swim, saving the bonding for a nature hike or mealtime.

Multisport Resorts

Independence Days

However much togetherness you opt for, you can be grateful that the kids are enjoying great-outdoors alternatives to video games and MTV. And that both generations inevitably discover that common ground is actually quite a large place, particularly when it has lakes and hiking trails, rocks and rivers, and a place to come back to that feels, for a while at least, a lot like home. —BOB HOWELLS

THE WEST COAST

Strathcona Park Lodge
Campbell River, British Columbia

Equal parts resort and outdoor education center, Strathcona is something of an adventure camp for families. The setting is a private, 160-acre spread next to Strathcona Park—a 550,000-acre wilderness in the heart of Vancouver Island—with snowcapped peaks, steep, glaciated slopes, old-growth forests, and deep, cold lakes. The lodge is a complex of chalets and cabins fronting Upper Campbell Lake. Guests can select from a daily "Best of Adventure" menu that includes classes in canoeing, kayak touring, and sailing; rock climbing; a ropes course; and a wilderness skills clinic. Courses are $41 (U.S. dollars) a day for adults, $23 for a half-day; $32 a

day for kids 16 and under, $18 for a half-day (no age limit, but parents must accompany kids), and are taught by pros—most are grads of the Canadian Outdoor Leadership Training Programme, a 100-day course based at the lodge. If your clan numbers four or more, save money and hire a private family guide at $114 per day.

Another option is one of three Family Adventure weeks (one in early July, another late that month, and the third in mid-August; adults, $473; kids, $303; all-inclusive) in which kids and parents participate in climbing, kayaking, wilderness etiquette instruction, and an overnight canoe journey.

Of course, you can skip the tutorials and opt for hiking in the high country, where turquoise waterfalls tumble into glacial tarns. There's good mountain biking on logging roads outside the park and fishing for cutthroat and rainbow trout on the lake. Or you can rent kayaks or canoes ($6 per hour, $22 per day) and paddle the lake on your own. Accommodations are in lodge rooms ($53–$83) or cabins ($83–$114) that sleep from two to ten. They're equipped with full kitchens, but there's little reason to cook when mountains of wholesome food are served buffet-style in the Whale Room for about $22 a day for three meals (kids under 12 are half-price). Call 604-286-3122. —BOB HOWELLS

Otter Bar Lodge
Forks of Salmon, California

Imagine a family whitewater resort so small and intimate that the Partridges and the Bradys together would fill it, with no room left for Alice. Otter Bar Lodge, set along northern California's Salmon River in the middle of the 1.7-million-acre Klamath National Forest, has four double rooms in the main lodge and three one-room cedar cabins that can accommodate six people. All cabins have hardwood floors; lodge rooms have French doors, large windows, and private decks.

In weeklong sessions from April through September, adults and kids as young as 10 can gorge on nonstop semi-private kayak lessons (three students per instructor) on the Salmon (Class II–V) or the nearby Klamath (Class II–IV). Experts prefer the high water of spring; beginners typically choose July, August, and September. In the sessions at the end of July or the beginning of August, kids camp out all week at their own riverside refuge atop a totally awesome jumping cliff. Prices are $750 for kids on their own, $650 with their parents.

In August and September, Otter Bar adds mountain biking to the menu. Nearby are hundreds of miles of dirt roads and single-track trails suitable for all skill levels; the lodge provides instruction and Specialized Rockhopper Comps with front suspension. Or you can just hike, snorkel, fish for steelhead, or watch the river roll by. Cost is $1,450 per person for the kayak sessions, $1,290 for mountain-bike weeks, including meals, equipment, and instruction. Call 916-462-4772 for more information. —DAVID NOLAND

THE SOUTHWEST

Enchantment Resort
Sedona, Arizona

For those who think of Sedona as a repository for T-shirt shops, garish paintings of desert sunsets, and New Age crystal-gazers who've changed their names to Moonstar or Runs-With-The-Wolves, there's a pleasant surprise in store: surreal Boynton Canyon, the red-rock fantasyland that conceals luxurious but unpretentious Enchantment Resort. Five miles from town, the complex of fifty-six tasteful suites and casitas makes a good family base for exploring the region's rock formations, ancient Indian ruins and petroglyphs, and starkly lovely high-desert vistas. Enchantment carefully blends into the landscape; in partnership with the U.S. Forest Service, it works to promote conservation and education, and provides regular guest programs on topics ranging from forest-fire prevention (complete with a visit from Smokey) to leave-no-trace camping.

Outdoor activities are best undertaken before 10 A.M. or after 3 P.M. (At 4,500 feet, Sedona's average summer temperatures, while in the 90s, are surprisingly comfortable, but the high-desert sun is strong.) Leaving from the resort, an easy 2-mile hiking trail through the canyon reveals stunning rock formations and plenty of critters—mule deer, javelina, jackrabbits, and eagles. The concierge can point you to other nearby trails through the rock formations and canyons that range from easy to strenuous.

Mountain bikes are available at the resort ($10 per hour, including helmet and map); there are no dedicated trails, but bikers are welcome along hiking trails as well as the area's many lightly traveled paved and unpaved roads leading to Sinagua Indian ruins.

The ruins, of course, are what imbue the region with its sense of timelessness and mystery: Montezuma's Castle, a well-preserved cliff dwelling;

The Best Off-Season Deals

How to Save Money 101: Go to winter high-season destinations during summertime low season for discounts of up to 60 percent. Here are four kid-oriented resorts that are just as much fun in the down season.

✦ **Smugglers' Notch, Vermont.** A bored kid is hard to find at this Vermont ski resort, where in summer kids can paddle a canoe, learn to rock climb, or spend an afternoon hiking to a Green Mountain summit. Kids' programs are organized into five age groups (from 6 weeks to 17) and water slides, a kids' lagoon, and two toddlers' pools keep everyone busy. Be aware: The resort tends to sell out, so book by mid-April. Summer rates: $1,335–$1,585 for a family of four, including most kids activities, in July and August for a 5-night midweek stay in a one-bedroom condo. Family deal: Save 20 percent or more by going before July 1 or during the last week in August. Phone: 800-451-8752.

✦ **Club Med Eleuthera, Bahamas.** In the best Club Med Family Village tradition, there are four age-ranked kids' groups (age 1 to 11), circus instruction, scuba experience for kids as young as 4, and both a gorgeous beach and a protected bay to explore. For adults, it's the usual buffet of Club Med activities. Summer rates: $931 per person for adults, $651 for kids for a 7-night stay including all meals and most activities. Family deal:

Kids 5 and under stay free (one child per adult) in May, June, September, and October. Phone: 800-258-2633.

✦ **Marriott's Marco Island Resort and Golf Club, Florida.** Down on Florida's southwest coast, this is a designated bird sanctuary and barrier island and the stomping grounds for the Beach Bandits kids' program (ages 5 to 12). Besides supervised pool activities, kids bird-watch for bald eagles and spot manatees, and cruise on air boats in search of alligators. Summer rates: $104–$174 per night per room (for up to five people). Beach Bandits costs $29 per day. Family deal: Book at least 21 days in advance and prepay for the lowest rate. Phone: 800-438-4373.

✦ **The Pointe Hilton Resort at Squaw Peak, Arizona.** Just 10 miles from the Phoenix airport, this resort is adjacent to the 16,000-acre Phoenix Mountains Preserve, the perfect place for kids to learn about desert ecology and geology. The kids' program, for ages 4 to 12, also takes advantage of the Hilton's Hole-in-the-Wall River Ranch, with its water slides and tubing. Summer rates: $89–$159 per room per night. Family deal: Hilton's Bounce Back Rate ($125), good for a family of four in a two-room suite, with complimentary continental breakfast for everyone, is good from May 26 to September 20. Phone: 800-876-4683.

—Everett Potter

Tuzigoot, a collection of hilltop houses; and Walnut Canyon Ruins, where ancient dwellings cover the walls and floor of the canyon. Jeep tours to these and other historical sites, all within a 2-hour drive or less, can be arranged through the concierge or by calling **Pink Jeep Ancient Expeditions** (800-999-2137 or 520-282-2137). The resort also arranges horseback trips for all skill levels ($25 per hour; $98 for a full day with lunch), including themed rides to

Indian ceremonial grounds ($42 per person) and a cowboy barbecue under the stars ($50 per person).

Enchantment's Camp Coyote has programs for kids 4 to 12 that include nature walks, treasure hunts, Indian sandpainting, and on-site sports: swimming, tennis, and golf. Rates are $44 for a full day, $29 for morning only, $36 for the afternoon, $34 for evenings 5 P.M. to 9 P.M.

Families stay in spacious, well-appointed one-bedroom suites ($365–$425) or two-bedroom casitas ($535–$625) that include a kitchen, a deck with barbecue grill, and a living room; kids under 12 stay free with their parents. The resort also has two restaurants and a health and fitness center. For reservations and information call 800-826-4180 or 520-282-2900. —NANCY ZIMMERMAN

Sundance
Sundance, Utah

Robert Redford's version of the Wild West is a cottage decorated with Navajo rugs and Native American crafts; a view of Mount Timpanogos and the Wasatch Range through your windows; and access to the mountains by way of foot, mountain bike, or horseback. The dried wildflowers in your room are Sundance-grown, and the seventeen-ingredient granola in your minibar is Sundance-made. It all carries a filmmaker's stylized touch, but the manipulation is welcome.

Amid the orchestration, the beauty of the place is undeniable. And, yes, a river runs through it (a stream, actually; fly-fishing for fat browns is done nearby on the Provo River). Ride horseback through the 6,000 acres, glimpsing deer and elk en route to 350-foot Stewart Falls, then feast on lunch packed by the Sundance chef (2-hour ride with food, $65). Or ride the new quad lift (full-day, $12) up a flank of Mount Timp to mountain bike on 25 miles of private single-track, hooking up with more rides in Uinta National Forest (mountain bike rentals, $25–$35 per day; guided tours available). A new tepee is headquarters for the complimentary Sundance Kids program for ages 6 through 12. It's actually three programs in sequence: Native American/Environmental Day, with native games, crafts, and storytelling; Recreation/Adventure Day, with horseback riding, hiking, and camping in the woods; and Theater Workshop Day, when kids create and perform an original story based on their previous days' experiences.

As for evenings, you can lie back and watch free Redford videos (among others) in your room, attend screenings of films from the Sundance Festival on Fridays and Saturdays, or partake of live outdoor summer theater (past years' shows have included *West Side Story* and, for the kids, *Mirrette*).

In the same spirit as Sundance granola, the Tree Room uses local organic herbs, veggies, and critters in special dishes that change weekly, such as campfire-style stuffed trout with four different mushrooms and saffron rice. Entrées there run $20–$25; $7–$15 will get you pizza and pasta in the Grill Room. Accommodations are in cottages (double-occupancy rooms, $175 per night; junior suites, $265; suites, $325) or two- to four-bedroom mountain cabins ($475–$950 per night). Ask about special family rates. Call 801-225-4107 for additional information.

—BOB HOWELLS

THE ROCKIES

The Peaks at Telluride
Telluride, Colorado

With its four-level spa complex, The Peaks exudes mountain chic—though you won't feel out of place here wheeling a dusty mountain bike or ushering a brood of pool-wet urchins through the lobby. You are, after all, in Telluride, ringed by the 14,000-foot peaks of the San Juan Mountains, and diving into the spate of mountainy things to do is all but mandated. Hike out the door on 2-hour trails to the Tomboy Mine Ruins or to Bridal Veil Falls, the longest free-fall cascade in Colorado. Rent a mountain bike from the in-house shop ($20 per day, $45 for a guided day trip) and head off on single-track rides, like the 16-mile Deep Creek Loop, or on Jeep roads in the Uncompahgre National Forest. Fly-fishing for brown or rainbow trout is best on the nearby San Miguel River; call **Telluride Outside** (800-831-6230), which also runs raft trips on the Class III–IV Gunnison River and the Class III Dolores, plus daylong Jeep tours of San Juan mines and ghost towns. Tours depart the lobby daily at 8 A.M.; $85–$95 per person; reservations required.

Back at The Peaks, you've got a 1-acre spa to explore, with a 25-foot indoor climbing wall, Cybex weight room, and indoor lap pool. Kids spend time in the KidSpa, which offers two programs: the Explorers Package (half-day, $25; full-day, $40; lunch included), where 2½- to 5-year-olds get to cook, swim, hike, and make T-shirts; and the Mountaineers Package, with gold-panning, horseback riding, aerobics, swimming, and hiking for 6- to 11-year-olds (half-day, $40; full-day, $60; lunch included). Doubles run $150–$350; kids under 12 free; $20 for each additional person (call 800-789-2220 for more information).

—Bob Howells

Keystone Resort
Keystone, Colorado

If it's crucial that your Western vacation spot have a frontier sensibility, skip Keystone. But if you like the idea of being surrounded by the high wilderness peaks of the Continental Divide and the cold, clear waters of the Snake River while you vacation under a virtual bubble of comfort, it would be hard to do better than this Summit County Colorado ski resort just 1½ hours from Denver. Families can take advantage of all the services that a top ski destination offers—child care, intra-resort transportation systems, well-run activities desks, and a broad choice of accommodations and dining spots—while they go biking, hiking, fishing, and sailing.

Keystone Village surrounds a 5-acre man-made lake full of paddleboats, kayaks, canoes, windsurfers, and novice fly-fishermen practicing their casts. In-line skates and bikes can be rented at the lakeside Sports Shaq. Big-boat sailors, anglers, and more advanced windsurfers head for Lake Dillon, a large reservoir a few miles from Keystone. Bike trips on paved bike paths to

154

Glorified Baby-Sitting? Hardly.

Big hotel chains love to tout their kids' programs, but many consist of little more than a box of Crayolas and a roomful of tiny chairs. Others simply exalt Barney and other television gods, leaving your kids oblivious to the fact that they're surrounded by the desert, the Caribbean, or the mountains. But there are notable exceptions. One quick indicator of quality is the ratio of counselors to children: One counselor to ten kids is fine, though on field trips and during water activities a one-to-six ratio is safer. Here's what a few far-sighted hotels have come up with.

When it comes to beach resorts, the **Fontainebleau Hilton Resort and Towers** in Miami Beach runs a program for ages 5 to 12 with nearly nonstop action: beach games, pool Olympics, sand-castle contests, relay races, and scavenger hunts. Plus, each week there are field trips to Miami's planetarium and seaquarium. There's no charge for the program but lunch is extra. Phone: 800-445-8667.

At **Radisson's Arrowwood Resort** on Minnesota's Lake Darling, kids can join Camp Arrowwood and saddle up a horse, paddle a canoe, or hike through the great North Woods. The program for ages 5 to 12 also takes advantage of Arrowwoods' children's library and indoor and outdoor pools. The cost is $15 per child per day (20 percent discount for two or more kids), including a picnic lunch. Phone: 800-333-3333.

What's new at the **Hyatt Regency Scottsdale at Gainey Ranch** is Family Camp (available on July 4 and Memorial Day and Labor Day weekends), which gets Mom and Dad involved as well as Hopi storytellers, Mexican vaqueros, and Native American dancers. Start training

now for water volleyball and waterslide splash competitions. On other days 3- to 12-year-olds can join Camp Hyatt Kachina for nature walks, movie-making, and Navajo sand painting ($54 per day, including lunch). Phone: 800-233-1234.

At the oceanfront **Westin Resort** on South Carolina's Hilton Head Island, 4- to 12-year-olds in Camp Wackatoo aren't lolling around on the beach. Instead, they're flying kites, playing volleyball, taking Jazzercise classes, cooking, and walking the sand with a naturalist ($40 per child, including lunch; $25 for second child). Phone: 800-999-4975.

Desert Discovery Day, French lessons on a Macintosh, and a 165-foot waterslide are what 5- to 12-year-olds will be up to in the Funicians Kids Club at **The Phoenician,** Sheraton's Scottsdale property. There's a different theme daily and a private kids' clubhouse. A full day costs $50 and includes lunch. Phone: 800-325-3535.

Kids learn trampoline tricks, try out scuba gear, and go water-skiing at Florida's **Club Med Sandpiper**, north of West Palm Beach. This Family Village caters to babies as young as 4 months, and has three age-separate programs for kids 2 to 11. There are activities from 9 A.M. to 9 P.M. and no extra charges. Phone: 800-258-2633.

—EVERETT POTTER

155

Dillon (about a half-hour ride) and Frisco (about 45 minutes away) are perfect for families. More ambitious riders can make the challenging and hilly hour-long trip to the restored mining town of Breckenridge, Keystone's neighboring ski resort. There are guided llama pack trips along Keystone's summit, white-water rafting trips, trail rides on horseback, swimming in one of eleven resort pools—even skiing at nearby Arapahoe Basin, where the season can last into early July.

Keystone's Children's Center provides day care for children 2 months and older, and Kamp Keystone entertains kids 3 years and up with nature hikes, gold panning, cookouts, fishing, swimming, gondola rides, and more. A Keystone daily activities pass, which allows guests to sample a variety of resort activities, including a gondola ride, an hour of tennis, and rentals of in-line skates, mountain bikes, canoes, and kayaks, starts at about $27.

Lodging choices include the Keystone Lodge, the resort's handsome centerpiece (doubles, $200), and 900 equally architecturally correct hotels, condominium units, and private houses clustered around the lake and in the surrounding forest. Units designed especially for families with young children, just steps away from the lake and the pedestrian village, can be found in the Lakeside Condominiums. For a more secluded setting, The Pines, about 1 mile from the lake, is a good choice. All outlying lodging is served by a free shuttle bus system.

Children 18 and under stay free with their parents in either the Keystone Lodge or a condo. In June, July, and August, 6 nights in a two-bedroom, two-bath condo located 1 mile or less from Keystone Village start at $682 for a family of four. A deluxe two-bedroom unit by the lake starts at $1,053. Call 800-468-5004.

—MEG LUKENS NOONAN

Lone Mountain Ranch
Big Sky, Montana

Ain't no dogies at this ranch, so don't call it "dude," but a stable of ninety steeds can keep a family busy riding the range in fringe-of-Yellowstone country—that is, when they're not hiking with a naturalist, fly-fishing with a guide, or banding birds with an ornithologist. Nestled in a valley of the Spanish Peaks range about 20 miles from the northwestern corner of the national park, Lone Mountain sprawls across 160 acres of glorious alpine country that its owners unassumingly encourage guests to learn about and appreciate.

Besides daily rides, a family week at Lone Mountain is filled with high-country hikes, llama walks, excursions to Yellowstone, and fly-fishing clinics, while other activities are reserved for the small-fry: animal-tracking, making plaster casts, map-and-compass courses, campouts, and low-to-the-ground rope-and-balance maneuvers. Between epiphanies, kids can hang in their own yurt or do crafts in the HideOut.

A 1-week package ($1,900 for the first adult; $1150 for additional guests over age 5; kids 2 to 3 are $400; 4 to 5, $800) includes all meals and most activities; one of twenty-three hand-hewn-log cabins that sleep two to nine; or space in the new, six-bedroom Ridge Top Lodge—which can also be reserved for big family gatherings. Call 406-995-4644. —BOB HOWELLS

THE MIDWEST

Gunflint Lodge
Grand Marais, Minnesota

Set amid the sprawling North Woods of northeastern Minnesota and water-linked to the million-acre Boundary Waters Canoe Area Wilderness, Gunflint is both country inn-style home base and outfitter for paddling, fishing, hiking, and wildlife-watching excursions. Moose, wolves, and deer thrive in the balsam-fir forests, and Gunflint Lake and its neighbors harbor plentiful walleye, lake trout, and smallmouth bass. What began as a fishing lodge in the early 30s has grown to a comfortable, woodsy resort for eighty guests, with a main lodge and twenty-five knotty-pine cabins (most with a kitchen and private sauna or hot tub). The pine-paneled walls of the main building are festooned with carved birds and voyageur artifacts, and there's a big stone fireplace and huge picture windows overlooking the lake. The place has been run by the Kerfoot family since its beginning, retaining a "welcome to our place" feel with a strong family orientation that appeals to parents.

Every cabin comes with a canoe, and the Kerfoots can steer you to easy paddles, such as an 8-miler that traces an early *voyageur* route. Fishing guides are always available, and Trek moun-tain bikes can be rented ($15 a day) for rides on forest roads and cross-country ski trails. A daily schedule of free family activities includes naturalist-led walks in the woods for viewing and calling wildlife (yes, the moose do answer—sometimes), evening paddles in search of beavers, kids-only hobo hikes (with lunch wrapped in a bandanna and hung from a stick), and half-day fishing outings for kids. Or you can relax and splash on Gunflint's private sandy beach.

You can book a cabin with full, modified, or no meal plans, but be forewarned that pancake breakfasts, picnic lunches, and such hearty dinners as barbecued walleye and pan-roasted duck breast are hard to resist. Daily rates, including meals, are $256–$331 for two, plus $65–$90 for each additional person. A 1-week family package for four is $2,350–$3,310 ($300 for each additional family member), all-inclusive. Gunflint is 48 miles up the Gunflint Trail from Grand Marais, the eastern road-access corridor to the Boundary Waters. Call 800-362-5251.

—BOB HOWELLS

Ludlow's Island Resort
Lake Vermilion, Minnesota

Numbered are the days when simple fun like fishing off the dock, picking blueberries, and roasting marshmallows will be cool enough for increasingly sophisticated 10-year-olds. But at Ludlow's Island, image goes by the wayside the minute the kids are out of the car—they're too busy hiking, water-skiing, kayaking, boating, and exploring the rocky shorelines of northern Minnesota's Lake Vermilion.

157

Do-It-All Sampler Trips

If life for your family works best when it flits from activity to activity like an MTV video, booking a "sampler" trip may make you a hero. This way, if one kid is screaming to go rafting and the other is set on mountain biking, you can be the great compromiser and make everyone happy. Herewith, a summer's worth of multisport trips.

On Escape the City Streets's 5-day hike/bike trip, you'll pedal through Utah's remote Red Canyon crossing a meandering stream exactly forty-four times. While that particular day should appeal to any kid who likes serious mud, other days are just as good—biking through the red sandstone rocks around Bryce Canyon, hiking up the famously claustrophobic walls of the Zion Narrows, and cliff-jumping into the Virgin River. Outfitter: **Escape the City Streets**, 800-596-2953. Cost: $655–$855 per person. Family deals: Kids under 16 (one child per adult), half-price; students, 15 percent off. Departures: July 7, August 18, September 8.

Backroads' new 6-day family trip through Puget Sound employs so many modes of transport your kids will be too winded to whine "Are we there yet?": They'll bike through the tulip beds of Skagit Valley, ferry between the San Juan Islands, hike through forests of Douglas fir, and kayak along coastal inlets where orcas hang out. Stay at a variety of secluded inns, or opt for a camping trip. Outfitter: **Backroads**, 800-462-2848. Cost: $1,698 inn-to-inn, $798 for campers. Family deals: Kids 6 and under, 40 percent off; 7–12, 20 percent off; 13–17, 10 percent. Departures: inn-to-inn, July 13; camping, July 27.

The ideal 10-day turf and surf combo begins at Idaho's Hayden Creek Ranch with 4 days of horseback riding, fly fishing, mountain biking, and hiking through the Lemhi Mountains of Salmon Na-tional Forest. Then you head downstream to the Salmon River for 5 days of shooting Class III rapids. There's also a river-bluff rappelling lesson. Outfitter: **Wilderness River Outfitters and Trail Expeditions**, 800-252-6581. Cost: $1,700 per person. Family deals: 30 percent discount for children 12 and under. Departures: July 4 and 12.

For kids who prefer paddling their own boats, thank you, Coastal Adventures runs a 6-day backpacking/sea kayaking tour of Nova Scotia's coastal archipelago. Sea kayaks are the stealthiest way to slide up behind seals, and spot the eider ducks, osprey, and cormorants that nest here. On shore you can explore the abandoned settlements and graveyards left behind in the last centuries by European fishermen. Outfitter: **Coastal Adventures**, 902-772-2774. Cost: $660 per person. Family deals: Ten percent discount for families of four or more. Departures: June 29, August 7.

Once you set up camp at Madeline Island's Big Bay State Park, the hub of Trek and Trail's 5-day family exploration of Wisconsin's Apostle Islands, your kids can pedal along Madeline's paved roads, or paddle kayaks to hikes on Lake Superior's most secluded islands. Outfitter: **Trek and Trail**, 800-354-8735. Cost: $469 per person. Family deals: Half-price for kids under 12. Departures: Every Sunday from Memorial Day through Labor Day.

If you have any doubts that a multisport trip could please every member of your clan, **The Road Less Traveled** can customize a trip for groups of eight or more that can include everything from kayaking Utah's Green River to hiking past Anasazi ruins to climbing the Grand Teton—variety that ensures even the most quarrelsome siblings will find something to agree on. Prices vary; call 312-348-4100.

—Laura Billings

Situated on three separate land parcels on skinny Wa-Kem-Up Narrows, Ludlow's Island is the premier resort for families who want the crisp, cool weather and birch and pine wilderness adjacent to the Boundary Waters Canoe Area Wilderness, but also want more luxuries than will fit in a canoe. The lodge's eighteen pine- and cedar-lined cabins are equipped with full kitchens, one to five bedrooms, two to five full baths, a fireplace, and a barbecue grill.

You can explore the 40-mile-long lake with a Lund fishing boat (one included with each cabin rental) and troll for walleye, bass, northern, and muskie (independent fishing guides can be hired for $85–$200 per day). Or, hike the 1½-mile shoreline trail, take a sauna, then cool off with a swim. You also can rent a water-ski boat ($40 per hour; $120 per day), a pontoon boat ($50 per hour; $140 per day), or use the paddleboats, sailboats, kayaks, and canoes free of charge. There are also outdoor tennis and indoor racquetball courts.

On the occasional blustery day, relax in the cabin while the kids learn how to make Native-American dreamcatchers and other crafts with Ludlow's Island staff. Most kids will want to spend at least 1 night on the camping island, a small satellite island within yelling distance. Ludlow's provides the gear—you provide the ghost stories.

Although there are no restaurants at the lodge, you can order take-out before 5 P.M. from a restaurant 5 miles away that will boat-deliver to the lodge. And the on-site Gourmet Pantry supplies groceries and sundries and also provides free woks, ice cream-makers, and board games.

Weekly prices range from $1,350 to $1,850 per couple; daily prices from $260 to $370 per couple. Charges for children staying in the same cabin are $150 per week for age 16 and over; $75 for ages 3 to 15; and $30 for age 2 and under. The lodge is open from May 9 to October 5. Call 800-537-5308 or 218-666-5407.   —STEPHANIE GREGORY

THE SOUTH

Nantahala Outdoor Center
Bryson City, North Carolina

Think of it as the anti-Disneyland: a self-contained family vacation paradise where the thrill rides are managed by God, not Michael Eisner. The Nantahala Outdoor Center complex includes the world's largest kayaking school, a rafting operation, more than 40 miles of single-track mountain-bike trails, and a 134-bed complex of lodges and cabins.

Twenty-plus kayak courses and clinics target everyone from "apprehensive beginners" to wave-riding rodeo experts. While parents roll and surf, kids 10 to 18 can participate in 3- and 4-day kayak clinics ($540–$685, all-inclusive), in which kids can bunk with their folks or stay in kid-only digs.

Accommodations include a dormitory-style base camp with bunk rooms that sleep two to eight people; five plain wooden cabins with two, three, six, or ten bedrooms; and a standard-issue motel.

NOC also offers a NORBA-sanctioned mountain-bike camp for kids ages 10 to 15; the 3-day (for ages 10 to 12) and 4-day (for ages 13 to 15) sessions cost $495 to $620, all-inclusive. Parents, meanwhile, can ride the vast network of dirt roads in nearby Nantahala National Forest and the single-track network of the Tsali Recreation Area. And right outside NOC's front porch, of course, is Great Smoky Mountains National Park.

For family togetherness, try NOC's 1-day "sampler" programs ($75 per person) of whitewater kayaking, canoeing, sea kayaking, mountain biking, rock climbing, or a ropes challenge course. Minimum age for the samplers is 13, except for the ropes course (age 12) and mountain biking (no minimum). Call 888-662-1662 or 800-232-7238 for rafting and lodging information.   —DAVID NOLAND

THE NORTHEAST

Topnotch at Stowe Resort and Spa
Stowe, Vermont

Like an oversize New England country inn laced with a dash of Baden-Baden, Topnotch is the hostelry equivalent of a binge-purge cycle: Go out and get sore (run, bike, ride, hike, skate); come back and slither into a whirlpool while a heated waterfall tumbles onto your shoulders. Set in 120 acres of woods in the Green Mountains, Topnotch anchors one end of the paved, 5½-mile Recreation Path that links the resort to Stowe village. The conduit is gentle enough for all ages of bikers and skaters; rent either conveyance at the Topnotch Mountain Bike Club (mountain bikes, $21 per day; in-line skates, $15) and ask about guided rides.

Out-the-door hiking can lead 4 miles to the top of Mount Mansfield (4,393 feet) and a view of most of New England. Or let hooves do the walking—horses are stabled in a 200-year-old barn for guided trail rides three times a day ($22). Fly-fishing is good in the West Branch River; Topnotch can steer you to an experienced local guide. Children are provided for through the Kids Program, which runs from July 4 through Labor Day. Kids ages 5 to 12 can play outdoor games, go on nature hikes, paint, and play in the pool for $30 a day, including lunch. Other nearby kid-lures include an alpine slide on Mount Mansfield and—everyone's favorite—the Ben & Jerry's ice cream factory 10 miles away in Waterbury.

Besides the waterfall whirlpool, Topnotch's 23,000-square-foot spa has an indoor lap pool, heated outdoor pool, Cybex weight room with all the trimmings, and a menu of massages and wraps. Minimum age for the spa is 16. The two-tier main dining room, Maxwell's at Topnotch, serves "new Vermont cuisine"—local organic vegetables, venison, and trout ($18–$30), while Papa Jake's has a lighter menu for $7–$10. Double rooms are $190–$270 (kids 12 and under are free); add $50 per person for breakfast and dinner. Call 800-451-8686 for information.
—BOB HOWELLS

The Balsams
Dixville Notch, New Hampshire

The longevity of the Balsams stems from its ability to change with the times.

Instead of relying on its majestic location at the base of Dixville Notch or its 131-year history to attract families, the property has transformed itself into a civilized summer resort, utilizing all 15,000 acres to present a panorama of sporting activities. In 1995, the resort inaugurated its mountain bike center, which rents bikes (adults, $10 per hour; kids 6 to 16, $5) and leads groups on 48 kilometers of single-track, double-track, and dirt-road rides. A good family trip is the double-track Roller Coaster Trail, which sweeps down the side of the golf course through a shady forest of fir and spruce.

Another 20 miles of trail are designated for hiking. Children 5 to 13 can make friends on guided walks around neighboring Lake Gloriette (a 1.4-mile loop), while teenagers and adults should opt for the 1½-mile Sanguinary Ridge Climb. The trail clings to the north wall of Dixville Notch, a mountainous pass of castellated granite, carved by glaciers and ice beds into fantastic formations.

Other sporting options include trout fishing in Lake Gloriette, a full 18-hole golf course, clay and all-weather tennis courts, beach volleyball, badminton, and basketball. At dusk, drink cocktails on the manicured back lawn, then indulge in a six-course gourmet dinner. For children, there are counselor-led all-day programs; activities change weekly depending on kids' ages and interests. Resort rates range from $298–$400 per night, per couple, including lodging, all meals, and sports amenities. To calculate the daily rate for children, multiply their ages by $7. Call 800-255-0600. —STEPHEN JERMANOK

Northern Outdoors
The Forks, Maine

How wild and remote is Northern Outdoors' setting? Well, a road sign a few miles south of the 100-plus-acre resort proclaims, "Moose Crossing Next 50 Miles." Whether or not you witness Bullwinkle's browsings, you can count on seeing forests that spread for a few million acres, with some of the best whitewater in the Northeast roiling nearby.

The Kennebec is Northern's primary lure: Twelve miles of Class II–IV water with enough froth to get your heart rate up, but without the overwrought challenges of *The River Wild*—your PG-age progeny will love it. Most families take the 1-day trip through Kennebec Gorge ($79–$114; kids 8 to 15 half-price). The day's foamy climax is Magic Hole Wave, a recirculating hydraulic that'll stand a 16-foot boat (but not yours) on end. Even cooler is the Family Overnight Adventure ($224 for adults, $124 for kids under 16), with a tame-water paddle, camping, lobster cookout, and raft trip through the gorge. Bouncier outings on the Penobscot and Dead rivers have minimum age requirements of 12 or 15, depending on the stretch of river to be run. But you have tamer options, too. Hire a guide for smallmouth bass fishing ($84–$198 per person), take a 1-day rock-climbing course or a ropes course ($75; minimum age 12), or rent your own two-person inflatable kayak ($20–$25; minimum age 8).

The lodge includes four motellike lodge rooms that sleep up to six ($20–$80 per person, depending on the size of your group) and ten kitchen-outfitted "logdominiums" that sleep up to eight ($25–$40 per person). Tent sites are $8 a night. There are also some new cabins, a condominium, and a cottage; call for more information. Everyone hangs out in the main lodge, where reruns of the day's rafting video are shown, and nonpaddling deadbeats are resoundingly booed. Call 800-765-7238.

—BOB HOWELLS

FLORIDA & THE CARIBBEAN

Hawk's Cay Resort
Duck Key, Florida

It would be tempting for a family to camp out at Hawk's Cay beach, a white-hot skirt of sand with a fringe of coconut palms and a perfect circle of lagoon where kids can splash in Florida's tropical calm. But Hawk's Cay Resort, the only lodging on private, 60-acre Duck Key, has much to lure both parents and kids from the beach.

You can cruise around the Keys' backcountry in a rubber pontoon boat while a naturalist points out great white herons, cormorants, and mangroves whose roots are nurseries for baby shrimp and snapper (adults, $25; kids under 12, $15). You can also snorkel or scuba dive offshore coral reefs (snorkeling, $30 per person; scuba diving, $35 for one person, $10 each additional person, minimum age 12); join a catamaran sail ($25 per person); fish the flats, reef, or blue water (half-day charters, $275–$550); or play at the eight-court tennis "garden" ($3–$5 per person, per

hour). Or you might haul your clubs to the nearby 70-par golf course.

Take the kids to see Atlantic bottlenose dolphins at the Dolphin Interaction Program (minimum age 10; $70 per person), offered three times daily for groups of up to four. You'll touch, feed, and give hand signals to the dolphins with the help of the resort's trainers; it's best to book the program 30 days in advance.

Most relaxing for the whole family: a bicycle outing (rentals, $3 per hour) across Duck Key (about 7 miles of paved roads). Kids 5 to 13 can join the Island Pirate's Club ($20 per child, per day, with lunch) for tiki boat races, fishing trips, backcountry outings, and "No Parents Allowed" parties. Wednesday, Friday, and Saturday evenings, the club meets for pizza and games ($15 per child). Meanwhile, Mom and Dad can choose from inventive Italian at Hawk's Cay's Porto Cayo eatery or fresh sea fare at WatersEdge.

The resort is low-key elegant, with 160 spacious rooms and 16 suites (doubles, $150–$400 early May through mid-December; kids under 18 stay free in parents' room). Call Hawk's Cay Resort at 800-432-2242 for reservations.

—STACY RITZ

Club Med
Eleuthera, Bahamas

It's hard to say which is more appealing: a valentine-pink sandy beach stretching along the transparent turquoise of the Atlantic, or the indescribably cute sight of a formation of floppy-finned, scuba-tanked tykes about to plunge through that same water into an effusion of elkhorn coral and parrot fish. On Eleuthera, Club Med sheds its swinging-singles image, but not its activity-crammed formula—here, though, it comes wrapped in a family bundle. Three Kids Clubs keep the little ones occupied while the adults go fishing, diving, or pink-sand lounging. In the Baby Club, infants play on the beach, nap, and feed fish in the aquarium-clear water of the club's marina. Petit Clubbers (2 to 4) might build pink castles between boat rides. Mini Club kids (4 to 12) get to snorkel, take scuba lessons, and go water-skiing.

Adults can sail, snorkel, water-ski, and take scuba lessons (extra charge). Certified divers will want to take an excursion to Harbour Island and down to a coral plateau rife with sea whips, sea rods, curious groupers, and angelfish.

Accommodations are clean and simple, brightly Bahamian-hued in greens, blues, and, of course, pink. Weekly rates, including meals and all activities, are $931 per adult and $518 per kid under 12; one kid (5 and under) per parent goes free between April 13 and June 22. Call 800-258-2633.

—BOB HOWELLS

14

I drive for a living. I'm a car writer—what some call an "automotive journalist." Touring and testing, hammer down and crankin'... driving as an end in itself. Then I started traveling with passengers. Neither my wife nor my small daughter was a car guy.

At first, the kid was content if I occasionally "squeaked" the wheels—a 6-year-old's description of using a V-8 to turn rubber into noise at a stoplight. But

Family Road Trips On the Road Again

soon she demanded more in the way of amusement. And I learned that there's more to driving than rolling up the mileage and sampling the understeer.

The easiest thing that a roadmeister can do to make family touring fun flies in the face of the all-American "Me father, you slime" principle, which restricts kids to the backseat. To keep everybody happy, you have to play musical chairs every hour, even if this means Dad gets to warm the jump seat, Mom takes the conn, and the kids navigate. You also have to stop often. Remember that a diner with a jukebox selector in every booth can be a major diversion for a child, a snake farm a source of delightful nightmares for years to come, a Big Johnson T-shirt display the high point of an entire vacation.

And ultimately, remember that one reason you're in the car is the freedom it provides. Be flexible. Change plans. Remember that road-tripping is America's own unique form of unscheduled mass transit. If you're going to stick to a timetable, why not fly?—STEPHAN WILKINSON

THE WEST COAST

Washington's Olympic Peninsula

Before you even shut the hatchback, face the truth about family road-trip-

ping. Highway robbery is bad. Highway bribery? Essential. Think about it: If you were a junior camper cooped up in the car for days with parents, pets, and a Porta Potti, what would it take to buy your contentment? Something pretty awesome when the seat belts come off, that's what. Like a loop around the Olympic Peninsula, the island of mountain and ocean splendor separating Puget Sound from the Pacific.

Day One

Edmonds to Port Angeles. **Mileage:** About 77. **Drive Time:** 1½ hours. **Route:** Take the Washington State Ferry from Edmonds (20 miles north of Seattle) to Kingston. Follow signs to Hood Canal, then travel west via Washington 104 and U.S. 101 to Port Angeles, which marks the northernmost entrance to Olympic National Park.

Stopovers & Side Trips: From Port Angeles, follow signs to Hurricane Ridge, 17 miles away. At the top, about 5,200 feet, hike the **Hurricane Hill Trail,** a moderate, 3-mile round-trip to a summit with unforgettable views, plus the occasional encounter with Olympic marmots and black-tailed deer. For gear and advice, consult **Olympic Mountaineering** in Port Angeles (360-452-0240).

Bedtime: Heart O' the Hills Campground ($10), 5 miles south of Port Angeles on Hurricane Hill Road, is a good choice.

Day Two

Port Angeles to Lake Crescent. **Mileage:** About 25. **Drive Time:** 45 minutes. **Route:** Continue southwest on U.S. 101 to Lake Crescent, an eerily deep glacier-carved lake nestled in the Olympic Mountains.

Stopovers & Side Trips: Scout a site at Fairholm Campground, on the lake's western shore. A new stern-wheeler-type boat plies the icy waters of **Lake Crescent** all summer, with an Olympic National Park naturalist aboard (the boat departs throughout the day from funky old **Lake Crescent Lodge**; call 360-928-3211). From Fairholm Campground, follow North Shore Road around the lake to the trailhead at its end and set out on foot or mountain bike on the **Spruce Railroad Trail.** The 10-mile round-trip is mostly flat and passes old railroad tunnels and bridges.

Bedtime: Fairholm Campground ($10) is nice, but often full in midsummer. The **Lake Crescent Lodge** (doubles, $88–$99; cabins, $130–$140; $10 each additional person; 360-928-3211) is delightful, with floors that have gotten creakier every year since FDR slept there.

Day Three

Lake Crescent to Rialto Beach and back. **Mileage:** 120 (round-trip). **Drive Time:** 3 hours. **Route:** Continue south on U.S. 101 to the logging town of Forks, then follow signs west to Rialto Beach, across the Quillayute River from La Push, a coastal fishing village.

Stopovers & Side Trips: A road meanders for about 1 mile through a cool, quiet forest along the Quillayute River to **Rialto Beach,** one of the most scenic in the Northwest. You can drive here,

but it's more fun to cycle (bike rentals, $8 per hour, $22 per day at **Pedal-n-Paddle** in Port Angeles; 360-457-1240).

Bedtime: Same as day two. For dinner try the Smokehouse Restaurant, north of town near the La Push turnoff.

Day Four

Crescent Lake to Hoh River. **Mileage:** 70. **Drive Time:** 2½ hours. **Route:** Continue 13 miles south of Forks on U.S. 101 to the park's Hoh River Visitor Center, about 20 miles east on Hoh River Road.

Stopovers & Side Trips: Even the biggest trail grumps like the **Hoh River Trail.** It's nearly completely flat, and overhead loom thousands of old-growth Douglas fir, hemlock, and Sitka spruce. Go as far as you want, stop for lunch along the river, watch for stealthy Roosevelt elk, then return.

Bedtime: Grab a campsite at one of three campgrounds between the Hoh Visitor Center and U.S. 101.

Day Five

Hoh River to Kalaloch. **Mileage:** 20. **Drive Time:** One-half hour. **Route:** Head south on 101.

Stopovers & Side Trips: The draw in Kalaloch is the beaches; at **Beach 6,** several miles north of the campground, smelt run along the beach in summer. Kids especially enjoy snagging the sardinelike fish in buckets.

Bedtime: Site-sleuthing is crucial here; if the main camping area is full, the South Beach overflow area, about 3 miles south on 101, has primitive sites even closer to the beach. Another option is the beachfront **Kalaloch Lodge** (rooms, $111; suites, $121; cabins, $121–$186; 360-962-2271; book early), which has lodge-style rooms and duplex-style cabins with kitchenettes.

Day Six

Kalaloch to Westport. **Mileage:** 120. **Drive Time:** 2 hours. **Route:** Head about 90 minutes south on U.S. 101 to Aberdeen/Hoquiam, and then drive 30 miles west around Grays Harbor on Washington 105 to the fishing town of Westport.

Stopovers & Side Trips: Two formerly lonely beachcombing spots here— **Westhaven State Park** and the unnamed beach just beyond **Westport's** downtown jetty—have grown into surfing spots, with dozens of neoprene-clad boardriders bobbing around like seals. One stop at **The Surf Shop** (360-268-0992), on the main drag just east of the waterfront strip, will get you going. Kids who are strong swimmers can get a 1-hour personal lesson for $20. And Westport's boat harbor is filled with fishing boats that offer charters for salmon, halibut, rockfish, and tuna, as well as whale- and wildlife-watching tours inside and outside Grays Harbor. Try **Neptune Charters** (800-422-0425; full-day bottom-fishing trips, $53, plus $7 for tackle and gear; full-day salmon fishing, $55.50, plus $7 for tackle and gear) They also offer "guaranteed" whale-watching ($19.50 adults; 12 and under, $12.50)—if you don't see whales, they'll take you out again.

Bedtime: Scout for a campsite at **Grayland Beach** ($16–$20 per night)

or **Twin Harbors State Park** ($11–$16, plus $6 reservation fee); call 800-452-5687 to reserve.

Day Seven

Westport back to Seattle. **Mileage:** 120, or 170 via ferry. **Drive Time:** 2 or 5 hours. **Route:** Follow U.S. 12 east to I-5, then drive north to Seattle—or follow the more leisurely route as follows.

Stopovers & Side Trips: Leave U.S. 12 at McCleary and take Washington 108 north through Shelton, following U.S. 101 north along the west shore of **Hood Canal.** The route offers scenic views, roadside campgrounds, and other sights on the slower trek north back to where the loop began: on Washington 104, just west of the Hood Canal Bridge.

Bedtime: If you have an extra day, consider an overnight stop at one of this highway's fine campgrounds, such as **Dosewallips State Park** (campsites, $5–$10). —Ron C. Judd

California's North Coast

It's just 65 miles north of San Francisco, but Bodega Bay still looks like it did when Hitchcock filmed *The Birds* there. This is your starting point for a 5-day coastal ramble, mostly on two-lane blacktop hugging steep mountains that plummet to the sea. Many people blast through in one or two white-knuckle, carsick days, but this is a coast for dawdling. The route takes you slowly up the Pacific Coast Highway past the most remote parts of the California shoreline, inland to the heart of the Eel River canyon and redwood country, and back to the beach again at Arcata, a quirky timber town in Humboldt County 300 miles from San Francisco.

Day One

Bodega Bay to Salt Point State Park. **Mileage:** 32. **Drive Time:** 1½ hours. **Route:** North from Bodega Bay on the Pacific Coast Highway (California 1).

Stopovers & Side Trips: If you start your trip on a Friday, get off on the right foot with a tour of the University of California's **Bodega Marine Laboratory** (open Fridays from 2 P.M. to 4 P.M.), a major aquaculture research center where kids will love the gurgling tanks and fascinating experiments.

Twelve miles north of Bodega Bay in Jenner, the mouth of the **Russian River** is a large harbor-seal rookery filled with quickly growing pups in the summertime; orange-vested volunteers will lend you binoculars and keep you a safe distance from the seals. Everyone knows about the Spanish history of California, but how many know that this part of the state was settled by Russians? **Fort Ross State Historic Park** ($6 per vehicle; 707-847-3286), 12 miles north of Jenner, is a reconstruction of a Russian fort and Orthodox Church built here in 1812.

Once you reach **Salt Point State Park** (707-847-3221), about 8 miles farther, check out the tide pools in Gerstle Cove, then hit the 1.6-mile trail up the blufftop to Stump Beach.

Bedtime: Camp at **Salt Point State Park** ($12–$16 per night, reservations recommended; call **Destinet,** 800-444-7275).

Inside Skinny

Camp Etiquette

Since car-camping is done in close quarters, be sensitive to others around you. Don't blare music, keep it down late at night, and ditto in the early morning hours. Of course, if the Winnebago next to you is still in full party roar when you're trying to turn in, revenge is only a few hours away. When your kids wake up at the crack of dawn, send them over to play, extremely noisily, under one of the 'bag's windows.

Books on the Fly

Cracker Barrel Restaurants Old Country Store Inc., a chain of 246 nationwide restaurants clustered predominantly in the Southeast, has what in our humble opinion ranks as one of the all-time great motorist services. Each restaurant keeps up a lending library of books on tape. Diners can check one out, spend miles spellbound by the prose of authors like Stephen King or E. Annie Proulx, then return the tapes to a different Cracker Barrel hours down the road.

Smooth Sailing

The seas aren't the only place stomachs get woozy. Carsickness is the bane of parents, but we've found relief in a can. Smooth Sailing, currently being targeted at the boating set, is said to be effective in curing any type of motion discomfort. Blended from natural papaya, pineapple, and passion fruit concentrates, it contains no drugs or caffeine and is sweetened with fructose. Carsickness aside, it's a healthy alternative to the sodas that kids tend to swig in the back seat on extended trips.

Day Two

Salt Point to Manchester State Beach. **Mileage:** 40. **Drive Time:** 2 hours. **Route:** North on California 1.

Stopovers & Side Trips: At the border of Sonoma and Mendocino counties in the town of Gualala, the **Gualala River** runs parallel to the Pacific for just under 2 miles. The dirt road on the left on the north side of the California 1 bridge leads down to sandy beaches and freshwater swimming holes, a perfect midway stop.

After a swim, continue 14 miles to **Point Arena;** beyond the tiny town, turn left onto Lighthouse Road to visit the tall concrete lighthouse that was built to replace a brick lighthouse that tumbled during the famous 1906 San Francisco earthquake. Keep your eyes peeled for migrating whales, which often round Point Arena close to shore.

Bedtime: Manchester State Beach, 4 miles north of town, is a first-come, first-served primitive campground stretched along a long sandy beach with dunes.

If being without a reservation makes you nervous, book a campsite ($27–$34 per night) or a cabin ($39–$49 per night) at the **KOA campground** (707-882-2375 or 800-562-4188) near Manchester Beach on Kinney Road.

Day Three
_____

Point Arena to MacKerricher State Park. **Mileage:** 40. **Drive Time:** 2 hours. **Route:** North on California 1.

Stopovers & Side Trips: About 20 miles north of Point Arena stop at **Van Damme State Park** to show the little tykes something they'll surely appreciate—a unique pygmy forest where the average old-growth cypress tree is 4 feet tall and the tallest tree in the for-

est only 7 feet tall. If the quarter-mile loop trail leaves you wanting something more strenuous, the 4.7-mile (round-trip) Fern Canyon Trail follows Little River through a Jurassic Park–style grotto.

Six miles up the coast, whale-watching kids will love a stop at **Mendocino Headlands State Park.** Late in the summer, blackberry bushes along the blufftop trails provide a finger-staining feast.

Bedtime: MacKerricher State Park has 8 miles of beach, sand dunes, tide pools, and fine campgrounds spilling back into the woods ($16 a night, with hot showers; reservations recommended; call 800-444-7275).

Young bikers can practice their not-quite-ready-for-the-highway moves along the 8-mile Haul Road (no motor vehicles allowed), and Lake Cleone in the park is periodically stocked with trout for fishing.

Day Four
_____

MacKerricher to Richardson Grove State Park. **Mileage:** 64. **Drive Time:** 2 hours. **Route:** California 1 about 44 miles north to Leggett. From there take U.S. 101 about 20 miles north to Richardson Grove State Park.

Stopovers & Side Trips: You'll be leaving the coast soon after passing **Westport–Union Landing State Beach,** so take the time to walk down to any of the beautiful pocket beaches along this stretch.

After the junction with U.S. 101, stop for a swim in the Eel River at

Standish-Hickey State Recreation Area. For an excellent neck-craning hike to old-growth redwoods, take the 2.1-mile Big Tree Loop to the 1,200-year-old Standish tree—easy enough for anyone over 5 years old.

Bedtime: If you were able to reserve a site in **Richardson Grove State Park's Huckleberry Campground,** sleep peacefully under a grove of enormous coastal redwoods in one of the thirty-six sites there. Otherwise, the park has 133 less-secluded campsites near the Eel River ($16 per night; call 800-444-7275 to make reservations).

Day Five

Richardson Grove to Patrick's Point State Park. **Mileage:** 106. **Drive Time:** 2½ hours. **Route:** U.S. 101 north.

Stopovers & Side Trips: Only 11 miles north of Richardson Grove, **Benbow Lake** is a 123-acre reservoir created every spring on the south fork of the Eel River; you can rent a canoe or sailboat at **Benbow Valley Resort** (707-923-2777).

Farther up U.S. 101, Eureka is the biggest town on the north coast and an important port, but for a more interesting dose of local color stop off in **Arcata,** the home of Humboldt State University. Just east of town on 11th Street is the 25.8-acre Redwood Park, which backs up to the 600-acre Arcata Community Forest. Trail 8 is a good 1.7-mile loop through the woods near Jolly Giant Creek, but in this heavily used mini-wilderness, feel free to improvise on intersecting trails—it's hard to get lost for long. For hiking maps and information, call 707-822-8184.

Bedtime: In **Patrick's Point State Park** (707-445-6547), 123 campsites with toilets and showers are split between several campgrounds ($16 per night; call 800-444-7275 for reservations). In the morning hike the 2-mile Rim Trail to Agate Beach, littered with millions of the water-smoothed semiprecious stones.   —ANDREW RICE

THE SOUTHWEST

Arizona's Desert Loop

Arizona's southeastern corner, a mountain-rimmed retreat on the edge of the Sonoran and Chihuahuan deserts, is where Cochise held off the cavalry, and where Wyatt Earp gunned down the bad guys at the OK Corral. You can hike through the surreal rock formations of the Chiricahua Mountains, scope out the hummingbird colony in leafy Ramsey Canyon, or head out on a trail ride from one of the area's many guest ranches. One caveat: It gets hot here. Plan your outdoor activities for early in the morning or late in the afternoon.

Day One

Tucson to Sierra Vista. **Mileage:** 80. **Drive Time:** 1½ hours. **Route:** I-10 east to U.S. 80, south on U.S. 80 to Arizona 92, then east.

Stopovers & Side Trips: Rent a mountain bike at **Full Cycle** on East Speedway Boulevard ($20 per day; 520-327-3232) and head west on Speedway

The Zen of Car-Camping

Since you can haul as much stuff as your car can hold (and even if you drive a Hyundai, that translates into considerably more cargo space than even the roomiest expedition pack), car-camping is pretty much the Ritz-Carlton wilderness experience. You can sit on chairs around a campfire, dine on fresh fish and designer veggies while the kids down mac and cheese and applesauce, and sleep in condo-size tents with cushy air mattresses and pillows. And it's because of all these niceties that people run into trouble. Inevitably, you remember the cocktails but forget the frying pan.

The key to successful car-camping is organization. Families who do it often have what they call their car-camping box—all the essentials stored and ready to be tossed in the back of the station wagon. This not only expedites the packing process, but leaves little fear of for-

getting items. (One Martha Stewartesque tip is to use the dishwashing basin as the storage box.) Here's what your box should contain:

The Kitchen: skillet, pots, pans, or dutch oven, stove (go two-burner; portability is no object), spatula, pot holders, cutting board, sharp knife, paper towels, can opener, tongs (good for fishing aluminum-wrapped foods out of the campfire), grill grate (also for campfire cooking), matches, hammock (good for lounging and for drying dishes after meals), ziplock bags, large plastic garbage bags, water, water filter, aluminum foil, tablecloth (forest service picnic tables can get quite nasty), sponge and soap for cleaning dishes, dishtowel, cooler, cooking set with small bottles of oils and spices, and mess set (kids seem to prefer these to plastic plates and silverware).

The Campsite: multisystem tool, lantern, flashlight or headlamps, extra batteries, chairs, first-aid kit, duct tape, nylon cord and bungees (for jury-rigging things or hanging food), tarps, sleeping bags, pillows, pads, tent.

Entertainment: Frisbee, ball, travel versions of Guess Who and Sorry! en route, and Jenga (once you've arrived at your site).

over Gate's Pass to the Tucson Mountains for a close-up look at the saguaro, the tall, Gumby-like cacti native to the area. A paved road loops through **Saguaro National Monument**, and more than 20 miles of trails lace through **Tucson Mountain District**.

About 70 miles southeast of Tucson, **Tombstone** feels like a western movie set: Two-story wooden buildings line

the boardwalks of Allen Street, and locals wander about in full cowboy regalia. Check out the OK Corral, then try the *barbacoa* (Mexican barbecue) at **Don Teodoro's** (520-457-3647).

Next, head 16 miles west to **Sierra Vista**, home to Fort Huachuca, an active military post housing a history museum. **Ramsey Canyon Preserve**, owned by the Nature Conservancy, lies about 7 miles south on Arizona 92 ($5 donation; open 8 A.M. to 5 P.M.; call ahead for parking reservations). The 300-acre wilderness area is home to fourteen species of hummingbirds, Coues' white-tailed deer, and coatimundi.

Bedtime: The Nature Conservancy rents out six housekeeping cabins ($80 for one bedroom, $90 for two, based on double occupancy, each additional person $10; 520-378-2785). The nearby **Ramsey Canyon Inn** ($90–$105; 520-378-3010) offers bed, breakfast and, in the afternoon, prize-winning fruit pies.

Day Two

Sierra Vista to Bisbee. **Mileage:** 30. **Drive Time:** One-half hour. **Route:** East on Arizona 92.

Stopovers & Side Trips: Rise early and wear a red shirt to watch the hummingbirds (they love red); their population swells in summer. Then go hiking: The **Hamburg Trail** follows Ramsey Creek to Ramsey Vista (6,250 feet), which overlooks the gray cliffs of the narrow, winding canyon. A leisurely round-trip takes about 2½ hours. Backpackers can hike into the Miller Peak Wilderness Area to the **Crest Trail** on the Huachuca Ridge, a rugged hike suitable for older kids only. Mountain bikers can ride up the many canyons of the Huachucas— but be forewarned: The trails are steep. **Sun 'n' Spokes** in Sierra Vista rents bikes ($10 per day; $25 per week; 520-458-0685).

Next, head south on Arizona 92 to **Bisbee**, once a typical mining boomtown,

later a ghost town, and now a boomlet town attracting artists, escapists, and assorted iconoclasts. The steep streets, carved precariously into the side of a mountain, are lined with art galleries, antique shops, and bookstores.

Bedtime: Book a room at one of the local B&Bs. **The Bisbee Inn** on OK Street (doubles, $55; 520-432-5131) is a favorite.

Day Three

Bisbee to Douglas. **Mileage:** 24. **Drive Time:** One-half hour. **Route:** Southeast on U.S. 80.

Stopovers & Side Trips: The local museum portrays the town's colorful history; also tour the **Queen Mine**, a turn-of-the-century underground copper mine (adults, $8; children 7 to 11, $3.50, 3 to 6, $2; 520-432-2071). Road bikers can pedal the **Bisbee Loop**, a strenuous 60-mile circle through the Mule Mountains between Sierra Vista and Bisbee on Arizona 90 and 92.

If you make it to **Douglas** by lunchtime, try the huevos rancheros at the Saddle & Spur, where hundreds of ranchers have left their brands on the walls.

Bedtime: Its rooms aren't as grand as its marble lobby, but the historic **Gadsden Hotel** is the best in town (splurge on a suite, just $70; 520-364-4481). **Price Canyon Ranch** (520-558-2383), 42 miles northeast of Douglas on Arizona 80, is a working cattle ranch that takes paying guests where you can hike, fish, swim, and ride horses. The ranch has a 2-day minimum for cabins ($100 per person; discounts for children), but tent campsites ($6 per day for two people, plus $1 per extra person) and trailer sites ($10 per day for two people, plus $2 per extra person) are available for overnighters. There is also a "people barn" (single beds, shared bathrooms, and a kitchen; $200 per night per group) for large parties.

Day Four

Douglas to Willcox. **Mileage:** 77. **Drive Time:** 1½ hours. **Route:** U.S. 191 north to Arizona 181, east to Arizona 186.

Stopovers & Side Trips: About 35 miles north of Douglas, head east on Arizona 181 and then Arizona 186 into the heart of the **Chiricahua Mountains,** the ancestral homeland of the Chiricahua Apaches. Water has eroded the volcanic rock into weird formations—spires and needles that extend skyward like stone sentinels. More than 20 miles of trails wind though the park, so plan to spend at least a half-day hiking. The **Echo Canyon Loop Trail** is an easy hike suitable for all ages.

Bedtime: Campers can stay at the **Bonita Campground,** just north of the visitor center at **Chiricahua National Memorial** ($8 per night). The **Triangle T Guest Ranch** (cabins, $50–$65, per night, double occupancy; $15 each additional person; 520-586-7533), 23 miles west of Willcox, has 130 acres of land with hiking and horse trails (guided horseback tours, $16 per hour) and a swimming pool.

Day Five

Willcox to Tucson. **Mileage:** 80. **Drive Time:** 1½ hours. **Route:** West on I-10.

Stopovers & Side Trips: **Cochise Stronghold,** 12 miles southwest of Willcox off U.S. 191, where the Apache chief and his warriors eluded capture, attracts hikers and rock climbers. The granite domes in this rugged section of the Dragoon Mountains offer traditional climbing—no bolts. Be sure to stop at the **Amerind Foundation,** one of the region's best archaeology museums (adults, $3; ages 12–18, $2; under 12 free; 520-586-3666), in Texas Canyon just west of Dragoon.

Bedtime: Head back to Tucson. With its pink casitas and large swimming pool, the **Arizona Inn** is a restful place to end your trip (doubles, $110 in summer, $165–$195 in fall; suites, $210–$260; based on double occupancy, $15 per each additional person; 520-325-1541). Three miles northeast of Tucson, **Tanque Verde Guest Ranch** (520-296-6275) offers a program for kids age 4 to 11 that includes hiking, tennis, horseback riding, and arts and crafts. The price is $385–$430 per night for a family of four, plus $65 for each additional person.   —MICHELE MORRIS

THE ROCKIES

Boise to Farragut State Park, Idaho

Several summers ago, two 9-year-olds and I had a terrific time driving up the spine of Idaho from Boise to Coeur d'Alene. We slid down sand dunes, hiked through ponderosa pines, took a jet-boat into the country's deepest gorge. An almost entirely rural state, 40 percent of which is forest, Idaho encompasses more than 53 million acres that are bisected by eight world-class wild and scenic rivers and preserved in 1,575 parks and wildlife refuges.

Day One

Boise to Bruneau Dunes State Park. **Mileage:** 70. **Drive Time:** 1½ hours. **Route:** Southeast on I-84 to Mountain Home (exit 90), then south on Idaho 51 and east on Idaho 78.

Stopovers & Side Trips: Stop at the Peregrine Fund's **World Center for Birds of Prey,** about 6 miles south of I-84 on the south side of Boise. Ninety-minute tours run all day Tuesday through Sunday (208-362-8687). Continue south for a 56-mile loop through the **Snake River Birds of Prey National Conservation Area,** home to the largest population of nesting and breeding raptors in North America. Allow 3 to 4 hours to complete the loop, with time for picnicking at Celebration Park, short hikes, or even a half-day boat tour into the Snake River Canyon (contact **WSRT/ Birds of Prey Expeditions,** 208-922-5285; $50–$92 per person; second child under 12 free).

Bedtime: Camp at **Bruneau Dunes State Park** ($12–$15 per night; 208-366-7919) so you and your kids can climb the largest single structured sand dune in North America, rising 470 feet above a small lake.

Day Two

Bruneau Dunes to Ponderosa State Park. **Mileage:** 176. **Drive Time:** 3 hours. **Route:** Head back west along I-84 and then north on Idaho 55 along the Payette River's roiling North Fork.

Stopovers & Side Trips: Picnic about 60 miles north of the junction near **Banks,** where you can watch kayakers maneuver from water's edge. For a half- or full-day raft trip on Class II and III rapids, contact **Headwaters River Co.** (adults, $30–$71; under 12, $20–$45; 800-800-7238).

Bedtime: Head north along the Payette River Scenic Byway to **Ponderosa State Park** on a peninsula jutting into Payette Lake (reservations, $6; camping, $12–$15 per night; 208-634-2164).

Day Three

Spend an extra day rafting on the Payette River, or drive to Hells Gate State Park. **Mileage:** 166. **Drive Time:** 2½ hours. **Route:** Drive north on U.S. 95, cross the Salmon River near Riggins, and continue into Lewiston.

Stopovers & Side Trips: Take the short, self-guided auto tour of the **White Bird Battlefield,** part of the Nez Percé National Historical Park where, on June 17, 1877, the first battle of the Nez Percé War was fought. Park headquarters and a visitor center are located 10 miles east of Lewiston in Spalding on U.S. 95.

Bedtime: Hells Gate State Park lies along the bank of the Snake River (ask for a shaded campsite; reservations, $6; camping, $12–$15 per night; 208-799-5015). There's fishing, swimming, or in-line skating along paved paths.

Day Four

Arrange a daylong jet-boat trip into **Hells Canyon,** the deepest river gorge in North America; contact **Beamers Hells Canyon Tours** (adults, $90; ages 6 to 12, $45; under 6, free; 800-522-6966) or **Snake Dancer Excursions** (adults, $92; under 10, $55; 800-234-1941).

Day Five

Hells Gate State Park to Farragut State Park. **Mileage:** 144 miles. **Drive Time:** 2½ hours. **Route:** The drive along U.S. 95 north of Lewiston winds through the "Palouse," Idaho's rich agricultural region, where you'll truly see amber waves of grain.

Stopovers & Side Trips: Farragut State Park, about 110 miles from Moscow, lies on the shore of Lake Pend Oreille, so deep it was used as a Naval training site during World War II. There's fishing, hiking, biking, and swimming. Farragut also has 9 miles of flat-track, marked mountain-bike trails. Bike rentals are available in Coeur d'Alene or Sandpoint, 20 and 29 miles, respectively, from the park. **Schweitzer Mountain Resort,** 11 miles north of Sandpoint, has rentals (half-day, $20; full day, $28) and 8 miles of trails for summer rides. Get hiking and biking guides from the **Sandpoint Ranger District** (208-263-5111).

Bedtime: Stay at one of the two campgrounds at **Farragut State Park.** They have showers and a lake a quarter-mile away (campsites, $12–$15; reservation fee, $6; 208-683-2425).

—DEBRA SHORE

Rocky Mountain National Park, Colorado

Bisected north to south by the Continental Divide, with a third of its 415 square miles above tree line, Rocky Mountain National Park provides a generous dose of unmolested Colorado ideally suited to an active family vacation. Only 65 miles from Denver, the park encompasses more than 350 miles of hiking trails and some of the most renowned rock climbing and mountaineering routes in the West. The spectacular scenery includes dozens of pristine glacial lakes; large populations of deer, elk, bighorn sheep, beaver, hawks, and coyotes; and thousands of species of summer wildflowers.

Two cautions: Plan hikes so that you're below tree line by early afternoon to avoid lightning storms, and be prepared for sudden and drastic changes in weather. Up high, August snow is not unheard of. For weather, camping, and other updates, contact the park's public information office at 970-586-1206. An excellent introduction to the area is *The Insiders' Guide to Boulder & Rocky Mountain National Park*, by Reed Glenn and Clair Walter (Boulder Publishing Company and the Insiders Guide); for a good general guide to traveling in Colorado, check out *Frommer's Colorado*, by Don Laine (Macmillan Travel).

Day One

Denver to Grand Lake. **Mileage:** 85. **Drive Time:** About 2½ hours. **Route:** I-70 west to Empire, then north on U.S. 40 to Granby, then north on U.S. 34 to Grand Lake.

Stopovers & Side Trips: This is the long way from Denver to Rocky Mountain National Park, but it introduces you to the park via its less crowded (but no less spectacular) west side. **Grand Lake** is a relatively laid-back six blocks of resort—an alpine beach town at 8,367 feet—with a pleasant stretch of sandy shoreline.

Just outside town, the national park is a hikers' paradise, and visitor centers stock plenty of maps and guidebooks. Two especially thorough guides are *Rocky Mountain National Park: A Family Guide,* by Lisa Gollin Evans (The Mountaineers), and *Rocky Mountain National Park: Classic Hikes and Climbs,* by Gerry Roach (Fulcrum).

A safe bet for day hikers: Start at the **North Inlet trailhead,** about 1 mile outside town, then catch the trail to **Cascade Falls** (a gentle 7-mile round-trip through evergreens, aspens, and mossy cliffs good for kids about 8 and older).

Though mountain bikes aren't allowed on national park trails, there are plenty of routes in the surrounding national forest; **Rocky Mountain Sports** (970-627-8124) rents bikes ($22 per day, $8 per hour; kids' bikes half-price). For a few hours (or a day) on the water, **Spirit Lake Marina** (970-627-8158) rents fishing boats and **Boater's Choice** (970-

627-9273) rents canoes and fishing boats you can take out on Grand Lake.

Afterwards, plan a dinnertime picnic at Lake Irene, 15.8 miles into the park from the west entrance, to spot deer and watch the sun set behind the Never Summer Range.

Bedtime: The Rapids Lodge in Grand Lake (doubles, $45–$80; 970-627-3707), built in the early 1900s and restored with Victorian decor, abuts the rushing Tonahutu River; ask for a room on the creek side. **Grand Lake central reservations** (800-462-5253) can also help with booking accommodations.

Timber Creek Campground, 8 miles into the park on U.S. 34, has 100 sites available on a first-come, first-served basis for $12 a night, with a 7-night maximum stay.

Day Two

Grand Lake to Estes Park. **Mileage:** 50. **Drive Time:** 3 hours, including stops at roadside overlooks. **Route:** Trail Ridge Road (U.S. 34) east through the national park.

Stopovers & Side Trips: Trail Ridge, with 11 miles of road above tree line (it's the nation's highest continuous paved road), snakes through windswept, fragile alpine tundra 20 miles or so to 12,183-foot Fall River Pass. The road is usually open from Memorial Day to mid-October, weather permitting, and features many overlooks with jaw-dropping views of snowfields, tundra, and glacier-sculpted peaks, with marmots and

Family Values, Hollywood-Style

Planning to curl up in front of the tube before you take off? First, consider these VCR do's and don'ts: the five best movies to plop the gang in front of, and five better left on the Blockbuster shelf.

—Adam Horowitz

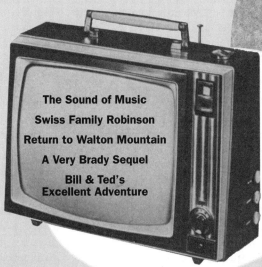

DO Watch

The Sound of Music

Swiss Family Robinson

Return to Walton Mountain

A Very Brady Sequel

Bill & Ted's Excellent Adventure

DON'T Watch

National Lampoon's Vacation

Throw Mama From the Train

Thelma and Louise

Bill & Ted's Bogus Journey

Alive

pikas in the foreground. There are numerous trailheads here, including one for the half-hour tundra walk that leaves from the **Alpine Visitors Center.**

From Fall River Pass on the eastern side of the Continental Divide, you begin the descent into **Estes Park,** the somewhat honky-tonk eastern gateway to the park, where you'll find lodging and restaurants. One of the best ways to take in the east side of the park is on horseback; **Hi-Country Stables** (970-586-3244 or 970-586-2327) has two locations within the park and offers 1-hour to full-day rides (1 hour, $18; 8 hours, $70; half-price for kids under 5).

Bedtime: The **Aspen Lodge** at Estes Park, 7 miles south of town on Colorado 7 adjoining a 3,000-acre ranch, offers hayrides, swimming, tennis, horseback riding, and a hot tub (3-night minimum; adults, $430 for a 3-night stay; kids 3 to 12, $260; under 3 free; meals included; call 800-332-6867).

Streamside Cabins, on a forested hillside overlooking the Fall River, offers nineteen units in five cabins, some with skylights, gas grills, steam rooms, and fireplaces—the sybarite's answer to camping out (call 970-586-6464 or 800-321-3303 for reservations and information).

Day Three

Estes Park to the Longs Peak Trailhead. **Mileage:** 22 (round-trip). **Drive Time:** 30 minutes. **Route:** South on Colorado 7 from U.S. 36 for 9 miles, then west for 1 mile on the road marked by a sign for the Longs Peak Ranger Station and Campground.

Stopovers & Side Trips: Longs Peak is the crown jewel of Rocky Mountain National Park—the park's highest peak (at 14,255 feet) and the northernmost "Fourteener" in the entire Rockies. For the well conditioned (suitable for ages 13 and up), the steep trail to **Chasm Lake** is an invigorating 9-mile round-trip hike to a glistening glacial tarn with excellent views of the hard-core alpinists scaling Longs' sheer east face— "the Diamond." Along the way you should make a stop at Columbine Falls, where the Roaring Fork River plunges more than 100 feet into a dark-blue pool.

Colorado Mountain School offers rock-climbing instruction and guided climbs in the park and the surrounding area for adults and kids 7 and older (970-586-5758).

For an alternate day's jaunt, **Colorado Bicycling Adventures** (970-586-4241) in Estes Park rents bikes ($20–$40 per day) and offers a no-exertion rush: a one-way ride downhill from the top of Trail Ridge Road ($65; minimum age 12).

Bedtime: The **Goblins Forest** backcountry campsite, marked by eerily gnarled pines 1.2 miles up from the Longs Peak trailhead, sits along the route to Chasm Lake and Longs Peak (permits required, $15; call the Backcountry Office, 970-586-1242).

Day Four

Estes Park to Denver. **Mileage:** 65. **Drive Time:** 1½ hours. **Route:** U.S. 36 south to I-25 south.

Stopovers & Side Trips: No out-doors-oriented vacation to the Front Range is complete without at least a good portion of a day spent in **Boulder** (32 miles from Denver), fondly known to locals as the "People's Republic." A stopover here should include a walk, run, bike, or skate along the 16-mile **Boulder Creek Path**, which winds through parks, under busy streets, and along a gurgling stream; Central Park, at Broadway and Canyon, is a good central access point.

The path also leads to the base of the **Elephant Buttresses** and **the Dome**, two especially popular climbing spots. Instruction is available through the **Colorado Mountain Club** (303-449-1135), the **City of Boulder Parks and Recreation Adventure Program** (303-441-4401), and the **Boulder Rock Club**, which also has two indoor climbing gyms (303-447-2804).   —MIKE GRUDOWSKI

THE MIDWEST

Lake Michigan Circle Tour, Michigan/Wisconsin

The Lake Michigan Circle Tour, a 1,100-mile circumnavigation of the only Great Lake entirely inside U.S. boundaries, claims some of the most kid-pleasing topography around: towering sand dunes, surf-washed beaches, hilly woodland trails, and maritime villages.

Day One

Chicago to Holland, Michigan. **Mileage:** 130. **Drive Time:** 2 hours. **Route:** I-80/94 east to I-90/94 east (Indiana toll road) to I-94 north to I-196 north.

Stopovers & Side Trips: Swim in the Lake Michigan surf, or hike up 180-foot-high sand dunes at **Indiana Dunes National Lakeshore** (219-926-7561), about 1 hour east of Chicago along U.S. 12. Next, pick raspberries, cherries, peaches, and plums at the **Lemon Creek Fruit Farm and Winery** (616-471-1321) in Berrien Springs, a 20-mile round-trip detour from St. Joseph, Michigan, via U.S. 31. At **Holland State Park** (616-399-9390 or 800-543-2937), along the lakeshore, you can spend the day beachcombing.

Bedtime: Camp in **Holland State Park** ($14 per night, plus a $5 reservation charge; 616-399-9390 or 800-543-2937). Or rent a housekeeping cabin in the woods near the state park from **Sunset Harbor Cottages** ($60–$79 per night; 616-399-9626).

Day Two

Holland to Traverse City. **Mileage:** 240. **Drive Time:** 4 hours. **Route:** U.S. 31 north to Michigan 22, which traces the Leelanau Peninsula shoreline to Traverse City.

Stopovers & Side Trips: Check out **Grand Haven's** boardwalk and beaches, a half-hour north of Holland. Stop in the twin cities of Montague and Whitehall, 15 miles north of Muskegon on White Lake, to pedal a portion of the 22-mile **Hart-Montague Bicycle Trail**; rent bikes and buy the permit sticker ($2 for individuals, $5 for families per day) right at the Montague trailhead at Bicycle Depot. Ten miles north is **Rainbow Ranch Riding Stables** (616-861-4445) in New Era, where you can book a trail ride along 250 wooded acres ($7.50 per hour). Then head for **Sleeping Bear Dunes National Lakeshore** (616-326-5134), 20 miles of the world's largest shifting sand dunes, where you can hike one of 13 trails, swim, or paddle the Lower Platte or Crystal rivers; rent a canoe inside the park from **Riverside Canoe Trips** ($23–$43 per day; kids under 5 free; 616-325-5622).

Bedtime: Sleeping Bear Dunes National Lakeshore offers two campgrounds ($10–$12 per night) and two backcountry campsites (no charge); call 616-326-5134. Or rent a cottage at **The Knollwood**, a motel with a private beach (doubles, $80; 616-938-2040).

Day Three

Traverse City to Mackinac Island. **Mileage: 105. Drive Time:** Under 2 hours. **Route:** U.S. 31 north to I-75 north to the Mackinac Bridge.

Stopovers & Side Trips: From Charlevoix, an hour north of Traverse City, take a ferry (616-547-2311) to **Beaver Island** for a morning of swimming, fishing, and touring lighthouses. Back on U.S. 31, head north. Ferries leave every half-hour for **Mackinac Island** (an 18-minute trip) from both ends of the bridge (Mackinaw City to the south and St. Ignace to the north); try **Shepler's** (800-828-6157) or **Star Line** (800-638-9892). On Mackinac, tour **Fort Mackinac** (adults, $7; kids under 12, $4; 906-847-3328), a British and American military outpost built in 1780. Then head for **Mackinac Island State Park**, where you can ride bikes

($3.50–$5 per hour from one of six bike shops on Main Street), in-line skate (rentals available on Main Street), or explore weird geological formations like Arch Rock and Sugarloaf.

Bedtime: You can splurge on a room in the **Grand Hotel** ($170 per adult based on double occupancy, including breakfast and dinner; children's rates, $35–$99, depending on age; 800-334-7263), which has a pool, tennis courts, golf course, and children's program (hike and picnic, $15 per child). But there are dozens of affordable B&Bs and hotels on the island, starting at $35 per night (there's no camping on the island).

Day Four

Mackinac Island to Manistique. **Mileage:** 90. **Drive Time:** 1½ hours. **Route:** Mackinac Bridge to U.S. 2 west.

Stopovers & Side Trips: Drive north into Michigan's wild, barely populated **Upper Peninsula**. At St. Ignace, detour 4 miles north on I-75 to **Castle Rock**, a lookout for a seventeenth-century Ojibway Indian village. Then head back to U.S. 2, which skirts Lake Michigan's scenic overlooks and deserted beaches as it passes through the Hiawatha National Forest. Just past Manistique, **Indian Lake State Park** (906-341-2355) offers swimming, fishing, and 5 miles of wooded hiking trails.

Bedtime: Camp along the shores of Indian Lake in the state park (campsites, $14, plus $5 reservation fee; 800-543-2937).

Day Five

Manistique to Door County. **Mileage:** 225. **Drive Time:** Under 4 hours. **Route:** U.S. 2 west to U.S. 41 south to Michigan 35 south to U.S. 41 south (again) to I-43 south to Door County's Wisconsin 57 and 42 north.

Stopovers & Side Trips: Door County has 250 miles of shoreline and five state parks, but the largest is 3,700-acre **Peninsula State Park,** just north of Fish Creek on Green Bay, where you can hike 200-foot-high limestone bluffs or cycle a 9-mile trail (rent bikes at **Edge of Park Inc.**; adults, $5 per hour; kids, $3; 414-868-3344). Or board a fishing boat and cast for walleye, northern pike, salmon, or lake trout; call the **Door County Fishing Hot Line** at 414-743-7046 for conditions and charter informa-

tion. During the late May and early June bloom, don't miss hiking through the 1,200-acre **Ridges Sanctuary** (414-839-2802) in Baileys Harbor across the peninsula from Fish Creek.

Bedtime: Pitch a tent in **Peninsula State Park** ($10–$20 per night; 414-868-3258 for reservations).

Day Six

Door County to Chicago. **Mileage:** 230. **Drive Time:** 4 hours. **Route:** Wisconsin 57 to Wisconsin 42 south to I-43 south to I-94 south.

Stopovers & Side Trips: At Manitowoc, 70 miles south of Sturgeon Bay, you can tour the World War II sub USS *Cobia* and view the model ship gallery at the **Wisconsin Maritime Museum** (adults, $6; ages 6 to 12, $4; a family rate of $18.95 includes two adults and any kids ages 6 to 17; 414-684-0218). Thirty miles south of Milwaukee in Racine, squeeze in one last hike at the **Riverbend Nature Center**, 80 acres of woodlands, grass fields, and ponds, or sign up for their naturalist-led 3-hour paddle on the Root River for groups of ten or more (414-639-0930).

—KATHY MARTIN

The Ozark Mountains, Missouri

South of St. Louis is a sparsely populated region where it's said that "the hills ain't too high, but the hollers sure are deep." Welcome to the Missouri Ozarks.

Part of a 60,000-square-mile plateau—the largest area of highlands between the Appalachians and the Rockies—the Ozarks are a rolling landscape of hills and forest, where pioneer cabins hide among the vast hardwood tree cover, and life takes on a slower pace. A 620-mile loop drive from St. Louis traverses the region, yielding plenty of opportunities en route for hiking, fishing, rafting, and exploring.

Day One

St. Louis to Ozark National Scenic Riverways. **Mileage:** 164 to Van Buren. **Drive Time:** 3 hours. **Route:** U.S. 67 south to Missouri 34 west to U.S. 60 west.

Stopovers & Side Trips: The **Ozark National Scenic Riverways** (573-323-4236) encompasses 100 miles of the Current River and 34 miles of its main tributary, the Jacks Fork, and is highlighted by cold springs, mysterious caves, richly hued forests, and limestone bluffs up to 200 feet high. The deep-green pools of the Current are perfect for casting for bass; daily or 3-day licenses can be purchased in any of the nearby towns. Fast-flowing but smooth, the river is also perfect for novice canoeists or floating in inner tubes. **Big Spring Canoe & Tube Rental** in Van Buren (800-567-8701) offers an 11-mile float, including canoe rental, equipment, and transportation, for $25 per person; "Cadillac" inner tubes (a deluxe version) rent for $10 per day per person.

A good spot for hiking is the **Between the Rivers section of the Ozark Trail**, which winds past cedar glades, springs, and sinkholes, with exceptional views of the Ozark landscape. The trailhead is located 4 miles west of Van Buren off U.S. 60.

A few miles south of the U.S. 60 bridge at Van Buren is **Big Spring**, the granddaddy of Ozark gushers. America's largest single-outlet spring, Big Spring discharges 277 million gallons of water per day into the river, enough to supply the needs of several midsized cities. A short walk from the parking lot leads you there.

Bedtime: The National Park Service manages seven campgrounds that offer car-camping facilities ($8 per night). Along the Current River, most families prefer **Big Spring** because of its proximity to Van Buren, which makes quick trips to town easier.

Day Two

Spend an extra day exploring the Ozark National Scenic Riverway; finish at Alley Spring Campground on the Jacks Fork River, or at Montauk State Park. **Mileage:** 34 from Big Spring Campground to Alley Spring; 50 to Montauk State Park. **Drive Time:** 1 hour direct; all day with stops for sight-seeing. **Route:** U.S. 60 west to Missouri 19 north to Missouri 106 west.

Stopovers & Side Trips: Before leaving **Big Spring**, check out the interpretive area that offers slide shows and information about the area's pioneer history.

Head next to **Coldwater Ranch** on Missouri 19, 3 miles north of the town of Eminence on Farm Road 208, for guided trail rides into the Ozark hills ($15 per person the first hour, $100 all day; 573-226-3723). At Round Spring, 13 miles north of Eminence on Missouri 19, you can accompany park rangers on a 2-mile guided tour of **Round Spring Cave**. The tour runs Memorial Day through Labor Day ($4 adults; $2 for age 12 and under).

At **Alley Spring,** 5 miles from Eminence on Missouri 160, visit a one-room schoolhouse and a historic roller mill that used to grind wheat and corn.

As an alternative, visit **Montauk State Park** (573-548-2201), about 30 miles north of Round Spring. Here, seven clear, cold springs form the headwaters of the Current River, which is regularly stocked with rainbow trout.

Bedtime: Alley Spring Campground offers good swimming in a pleasant, wooded setting ($8 per night). **Montauk State Park** has campsites (call 573-548-2201), motel rooms and sleeping cabins (both $44–$56 per night), housekeeping cabins ($65–$77 per night), and dining at Montauk Lodge (573-548-2434). All cabins have heating and air conditioning, and the housekeeping cabins are furnished with linens, cooking utensils, and dishes.

Day Three

Alley Spring Campground to the Eleven Point Ranger District of the Mark Twain National Forest to Gulf Island State Park. **Mileage: 124. Drive Time:** 3 hours. **Route:** Missouri 106 east to Missouri 19 south; then to U.S. 60 east (back through Van Buren) to Missouri 21 south for 23 miles to Missouri 142 west.

Stopovers & Side Trips: A wealth of outdoor-recreation opportunities await within the seven ranger districts of the 1½-million acre **Mark Twain National Forest** (573-364-4621). Although most roads through the forest are picturesque, the 4-mile

paved **Skyline Drive** in the **Eleven Point Ranger District** (573-325-4233) offers especially inspiring vistas of the surrounding hills and forested valleys. The Skyline Drive follows a ridgetop off Missouri 103 south of Van Buren.

There are hundreds of miles of trails along the way. The **Skyline Trail** follows ridges across the upper end of Sweezie Hollow and returns to Skyline Drive in 1.3 miles; the trailhead is located 1½ miles from Missouri 103 on Skyline Drive. **Songbird Trail,** a 1.2-mile loop, passes Watercress Spring, backwater sloughs of the Current River, small coves, bluffs, and the remains of Civil War gun emplacements. The trailhead is in Watercress Spring Recreation Area.

In the afternoon, drive southwest 48 miles from Doniphan in the southeastern corner of the Eleven Point Ranger District to **Grand Gulf State Park** (573-548-2201), 6 miles west of Thayer off County Road W. Often called the "Little Grand Canyon," the gulf was created when the ceiling of a giant cave collapsed. The intriguing canyon winds for 1 mile through vertical walls as high as 120 feet.

Bedtime: Greer Crossing Recreation Area (Missouri 19 north 8 miles). Campsites are $6 per night; call 573-325-4233.

Day Four

Greer Crossing Recreation Area to Sam A. Baker State Park. **Mileage: 80. Drive Time:** 1½ hours. **Route:** Missouri 19 north to U.S. 60 east; then 2 miles on Missouri 21 north to Missouri 34 east to Missouri 143 north.

Stopovers & Side Trips: Sam A. Baker State Park (573-856-4411), 4 miles north of Patterson on Missouri 143, is a family favorite. The 5,164-acre park comprises an expansive wilderness that surrounds Mudlick Mountain, a nature center, and a clear stream for summer splashing. Big Creek and the St. François River attract anglers and canoeists (rentals about $25).

There are numerous hiking trails in the area. Some paths take only a half-hour or so, but a more energetic family can tackle the 12-mile **Mudlick Trail,** a moderately strenuous loop route (good for ages 7 and up) that climbs from an elevation of 415 feet to 1,313 feet at the top of Mudlick Mountain. Here you can see the dramatic effects of harsh climatic conditions on a summit forest amid unobstructed vistas of the surrounding landscape.

Bedtime: Sam A. Baker State Park has 193 vehicular-access campsites ($6–$12 per night) with hot showers and a convenient coin-operated laundry.

You can also choose from seventeen modern housekeeping cabins ($44–$150 per night) and one sleeping cabin ($36 per night; reservations necessary; call 573-856-4223).

Day Five

Sam A. Baker State Park to Onondaga Cave State Park. **Mileage:** 112. **Drive Time:** All day, with stops. **Route:** Missouri 143 north to Missouri 49 north to Missouri 32; then Missouri 49 again to Missouri 19.

Stopovers & Side Trips: From south to north, there's a tight cluster of state parks, each worthy of a visit. First is Johnson's **Shut-Ins State Park** (800-334-6946), 8 miles north of Lesterville on County Road N, where you can prowl the Black River's unusual canyonlike gaps or shut-ins carved through Missouri's oldest exposed rock.

If you backtrack through Lesterville to Glover and head north on Missouri 21 for several miles, you'll find the new **Taum Sauk Mountain State Park** (573-546-2450), site of Taum Sauk Mountain—at 1,772 feet, Missouri's highest point. A few miles north, in Pilot Knob on Missouri 21, is **Fort Davidson State Historic Site** (573-546-3454). And 9 miles north on Missouri 21 west of Graniteville is **Elephant Rocks State Park** (573-546-3454), with giant red boulders dating back 1.2 billion years.

Bedtime: Onondaga Cave State Park (573-245-6576) has seventy-three campsites and a store. For more creature comforts, stay at the **Meramec Farm Bed & Breakfast** (doubles, $50–$65; ages 13 to 18, $15–$20; 6 to 12, $10–$15; dinner and/or breakfast included in some rates; under 6 free; 573-732-4765) 9 miles south of the town of Bourbon. The 460-acre cattle ranch, located along the Meramec River, has three rooms in a 114-year-old farmhouse and a cabin that sleeps three to eight. Farm-to-farm mountain biking is offered as well; rates vary.

Day Six

Onondaga Cave State Park to St. Louis. **Mileage:** 70. **Drive Time:** 1 hour. **Route:** I-44 east.

Stopovers & Side Trips: Before heading back to St. Louis, take a guided tour of Onondaga Cave to view the outstanding onyx formations (daily tours, $7; age 13 to 19, $5; age 6 to 12, $3; under 6 free).

At the **Eagle Hurst Resort & Dude Ranch** (800-257-2624), 1 hour south of the park on Missouri 8, there's horseback riding, family-style meals, free pony rides, tennis, swimming, tubing, and cottages for rent ($58–$65 per person per night).　　—LARRY RICE

THE MID-ATLANTIC

Virginia's Shenandoah Valley

Cited as one of the ten most beautiful drives in America by Charles Kuralt, the Blue Ridge Parkway/Skyline Drive route through Shenandoah National Park straddles the Blue Ridge Mountains past a panorama of dense mountain forest, rolling farmland, streamlaced hollows, and waterfalls.

Day One

Staunton to Shenandoah National Park. **Mileage:** 140. **Drive Time:** About 2½ hours. **Route:** From Staunton, at the intersection of I-81 and I-64, head north on I-81.

Stopovers & Side Trips: Stop at the **New Market Battlefield Military Museum** (adults, $6; ages 6 to 14, $3) and the Hall of Valor, a prime Civil War museum (adults, $5; ages 6 to 15, $2), both about 35 miles from Staunton.

Briefly take I-66 to the town of Front Royal and enter the northern gateway of **Shenandoah National Park.** The great park sprawls across 195,000 acres over the Blue Ridge and adjacent foothills in a southwesterly direction, with Skyline Drive its cloud-capped connector. There are 515 miles of trails and more than 75 scenic overlooks; a recommended starter hike leaving from the Skyland area at mile 41.7 is **Stony Man Nature Trail,** an easy 1½-mile round-trip to the second-highest point in the park (4,010 feet). Up at mile 31.6 is the 3.7-mile **Marys Rock Trail,** appropriate for kids of all ages

Bedtime: Noncampers can overnight at two rustic concessionaire lodges, **Skyland and Big Meadows,** with motellike rooms (doubles, $77–$91; suites with fireplaces $110–$150; 800-999-4714) or more rustic cabin rooms (doubles, $46–$84). There is a $5 charge for each additional person; children under 15 stay free in their parents' room. Campers can try **Big Meadows Campground** at mile 51 near the center of the park (campsites, $14 per day; call 800-365-2267 or 540-999-2243 for reservations).

Day Two

Shenandoah National Park.

Stopovers & Side Trips: Head up to **Hawksbill Mountain** at mile 45.6—at 4,051 feet the highest point in the park. It's a relatively steep, 2-mile round-trip trail, with views from the top extending across the valley to the west and the Alleghenies beyond. As an alternative, explore the park's 200 miles of designated horse trails at **Skyland Lodge** (guided tours, $18 per hour; call 800-999-4714).

Bedtime: Same as Day One.

Games People Play

Getting there is half the fun. Who ever coined that phrase obviously wasn't traveling with a carload of kids. Here are a few items from our bag of tricks that will help keep the "How much longer?" chorus at bay.

Magnavox Sideshow and Nintendo 64

High-speed TV. Once the stuff of "Night Rider" episodes, it's fast going mainstream. This television console ($769.95) fits between the front seats in minivans and super-utes like Suburbans and Tahoes, then plugs into the lighter with a three-accessory plug so you can still use the cell phone and radar detector. Anchored without drilling by brackets and straps, you can ditch the set when not in road-warrior mode. It can play videos or video games, like the still white-hot Nintendo 64 ($199.95; 800-422-2602) with its lap-the-field production quality and 3-D graphics. Best of all, the console comes complete with two headphones for some front-seat peace and quiet. It's available through Hammacher Schlemmer; call 800-543-3366.

Computer Software

If you sport a "Kill your Television" bumper sticker, the aforementioned item probably won't appeal. Consider buying a lighter-jack plug for your laptop, then checking out some of the newest software. LucasArts has nine titles of *Star Wars*–inspired games ($29–$45 each) that will be even hotter this summer with the re-release of the trilogy. *Oregon Trail* (The Learning Company, $49.99), which continues to top the charts despite its Stone Age technology, has gotten a 90s face-lift. The result is a jazzed-up version of the same great game—a

Conestoga wagon trip down the Oregon Trail. The younger set will enjoy still more adventures with Woody and Buzz Lightyear in Disney's *Toy Story* ($39.95), a CD-ROM that succeeds where so many have failed—it's actually as good as the movie.

Game Gear

Sega's answer to Nintendo's GameBoy, but with better graphics and a bigger price tag ($99 versus $49 for GameBoy). It's just as mobile (six AA batteries required for 4 to 6 hours of fun), and just as annoying to adults. All of which will make your kids love it.

A Backseat Survival Guide

This kid's travel kit is chock-full of the classics: License Plate, Connect-the-Dots, Hangman, Thumb Wars, and palm-reading games. It's "warranted for thousands of miles" according to the publisher, and endorsed by the Save The Parents Society. It contains some fifty games complete with markers, cool sticky game pieces for Parcheesi, and thread for hair-wraps and string games. Call Klutz Press (415-424-0739) for this and the complete Klutz catalog of titles.

Storytelling

Last spring, when our family took a 400-mile road trip, our friends let us borrow *Stories at the Tipi* (Trails West Publishing, $10.95; 800-566-9072) by Joe Hayes. This man should be canonized for his animated storytelling and wonderful material (natural phenomena explained with a new mythological twist). You get 80 minutes of interstate bliss.

—LISA TWYMAN BESSONE

187

Day Three

Shenandoah National Park to Wintergreen Resort. **Mileage:** About 60. **Drive Time:** 2 hours. **Route:** Head south on Skyline Drive to the end of Shenandoah National Park and the start of the Blue Ridge Parkway at Rockfish Gap.

Stopovers & Side Trips: Continue on the Parkway to mile 5.8 and stop briefly at **Humpback Rocks Visitor Center,** where you can view a reproduction of a mountain farm homestead. From there, make the quarter-mile climb up to Humpback Rocks, a popular landmark with great Shenandoah Valley views.

Seven miles down the Parkway, a left turn at Reed's Gap leads you to **Wintergreen Resort,** an 11,000-acre facility where you can play tennis, swim, go mountain biking on 8 miles of trails (half-day rentals, $21 for guests; $25 for nonguests) or go horseback riding (trail rides, $25–$30 per person).

Bedtime: Choose your accommodations at the **Mountain Inn** or condos within the resort (studios, $146; two-bedroom condos, $262).

Day Four

Wintergreen Resort.

Stopovers & Side Trips: Wintergreen's Nature Foundation runs field trips to collect wildflowers. Other activities include golf, trout fishing (5-day license, $6.50), and swimming and canoeing at Lake Monocan (canoe rental, $6 per hour). Later, hike up Crabtree Falls, a Blue Ridge landmark; the 2.8-mile loop is strenuous in places, but kids enjoy playing in a small cave en route.

Bedtime: Same as Day Three.

Day Five

Wintergreen Resort to Monterey. **Mileage:** About 125. **Drive Time:** 2½ hours. **Route:** Head south on the Blue Ridge Parkway through some of its most dramatic and primeval scenery, looking down from the steep ridge over the valley. Depart the high road at the intersection of U.S. 60.

Stopovers & Side Trips: Take U.S. 60 west about 40 miles to **Lexington,** a charming and historic college town. Continue on Virginia 39 through **Goshen Pass** on the Maury River, where you can picnic and swim from a boulder in a crystal-clear stream. At Warm Springs, take U.S. 220 north about 30 miles to **Monterey,** a remote village in rugged Highland County. Visit the Maple Museum, or catch your own rainbows at the Virginia Trout Company's pools.

Bedtime: Register at the **Highland Inn**, a classic Victorian house with an authentic country dining room (doubles, $49–$79; under 18 free in parents' room; 540-468-2143).

Day Six

Monterey back to Staunton. **Mileage:** About 45. **Drive Time:** 1 hour. **Route:** U.S. 250 east.

Stopovers & Side Trips: Stop for a hearty buffet lunch at the **Buckhorn**

Inn, a former stagecoach tavern built in 1811. Take in the **birthplace of Woodrow Wilson** a block away, and visit the **Museum of American Frontier Culture** (adults, $7; kids, $3; under 6 free), an outdoor museum comprising four actual working farms.

—JAMES S. WAMSLEY

THE NORTHEAST

New Hampshire's White Mountains

Considered one of the most beautiful highways in the Northeast, the Kancamagus is a perfect family road-trip. **Route:** With numerous overlooks, turnouts, trailheads, picnic areas, and campgrounds, it keeps the adults oohing at the scenery while providing enough activities to satisfy the kids' shorter attention spans.

Day One

Boston to Center Ossipee, New Hampshire. **Mileage:** 100. **Drive Time:** Under 2 hours. **Route:** I-95 north to New Hampshire 16.

Stopovers & Side Trips: One moment you're looking at scruffy gas stations on the highway, the next you're locked onto the most dramatic summit cone in the Whites, 3,475-foot Mount Chocorua. The ideal family base camp is **White Lake State Park**, about 5 minutes north of Center Ossipee at the junction of New Hampshire 16

and 25. The park has a 2-mile 'round-the-lake nature trail through pitch pine forest, good trout fishing (get licenses at the nearby Ossipee Lake Country Store), and canoe rentals ($5 per hour at the full-service camp store). It's a traffic-free 20-minute drive (at Conway, take 112 west from 16) to the scenic **Kancamagus Highway,** which has dozens of superb hiking trailheads along its 36-mile course (consult Robert Buchsbaum's family-oriented *Nature Hikes in the White Mountains*; AMC Books). One must in late summer is an afternoon at the **Swift River,** where you can do a cannonball or two into deep pools. Parking for Lower Falls is at the wide turnout on the westbound lane, 6.7 miles from the New Hampshire 16/112 junction.

Bedtime: White Lake State Park has 210 campsites with showers, including 13 right on the water (sites, $14–$20). For campsite reservations, call 603-271-3628.

Day Two

White Lake State Park to Loon Mountain Park to Sugar Hill. **Mileage:** 75. **Drive Time:** 1½ hours. **Route:** New Hampshire 16 to the Kancamagus Highway (112 west) to I-93 north to Franconia village and New Hampshire 117 west.

Stopovers & Side Trips: Loon Mountain Park in Lincoln, on the west end of the Kancamagus, is a perfect summer day camp.

Stop for maps at the **Mountain Bike Center** (603-745-6281, ext. 5566); rental gear includes mountain bikes (adults, $30 per day; ages 6 to 16, $25), in-line skates, skateboards, and horses (ext. 5450). Try the East Ridge Trail System and the 5-mile Black Mountain/Serendipity loop for a nice rolling beginner mountain-bike ride. More advanced, above-tree-line riding is accessible via the gondola (all-day bike-lift service, $18 for adults; $15, ages 6 to 16). The best option is the 10-minute Loon Shuttle bus (adults, $26 with bike rental; ages 6 to 16, $21) to the **Franconia Notch Bike Path,** an 8-mile paved spin that accesses a stunning array of waterfalls and lakes. The shuttle departs four times daily for Echo Lake, at the northern end of the bike path. Take I-93 north for 11 miles to the Franconia exit (38).

Bedtime: The Hilltop Inn (doubles, $70–$100; suites, $140; cottages, $200; 800-770-5695) in Sugar Hill, a few sky miles from Franconia center on New Hampshire 117, offers a homey suite on its second floor, plus a bottomless cookie jar on the first. Rates include breakfast.

Day Three

Sugar Hill to Pinkham Notch. **Mileage:** 70. **Drive Time:** 1½ hours. **Route:** New Hampshire 117 east to Franconia center, I-93 south to New Hampshire 3 and Twin Mountain. Take U.S. 302 southeast to New Hampshire 16 north.

Stopovers & Side Trips: Try one of the best bang-for-the-buck waterfall hikes in the Whites, Bridal Veil Falls. To reach the trailhead, take New Hampshire 116 south from Franconia

Village for 3.4 miles. Turn left on Coppermine Road and park at the turnout about half-mile down the road. The 2½-mile ascent follows an old, easy-grade carriage road to the base of the falls. Driving back into Franconia, stop at the tiny **Franconia airfield** (603-823-8881) for a glider flight over Mt. Lafayette ($55 for a 25-minute ride).

Bedtime: It's an hour-long drive to the 176-site **Dolly Copp Campground** (campsites, $14; for reservations call 800-280-2267), off New Hampshire 16, in the White Mountain National Forest.

Day Four

Pinkham Notch to North Conway. **Mileage:** 24. **Drive Time:** One-half hour. **Route:** New Hampshire 16 south.

Stopovers & Side Trips: Pinkham Notch, the headquarters for the Appalachian Mountain Club (AMC) and the starting point for most day hikes up Mount Washington, is invariably crowded; a good alternative is a hike on the other side of New Hampshire 16 into the Carter range, where there are fewer people and superb views of Washington and the entire Presidential range. For good topo maps and detailed trail descriptions, pick up the AMC *White Mountain Guide* at the AMC store.

Bedtime: Overnight at the **Nereledge Inn** (doubles, $59–$99; 603-356-2831) back in North Conway, just north of town off Main Street. It's a short hike from the cliffs at Whitehorse and Cathedral ledges, the best all-around rock-climbing area in the Whites. You can take lessons and rent gear from the

International Mountain Climbing School (603-356-7064). —TODD BALF

Cape Breton Island, Nova Scotia

Scottish-Canadian inhabitants here greet "from-aways" (visitors) with a Gaelic *Ciad Mile Failte,* or "a hundred thousand welcomes." Cape Breton's hospitality is outstripped only by the island's abundant opportunities for hiking, biking, fishing, sailing, kayaking, and whale-watching. Access is via a pair of linked routes. The 187-mile Cabot Trail loops around the finger projecting from Cape Breton's skeletal fist, a roller-coaster ride that passes beaches along the Atlantic shore, ventures into wilderness highlands, crests sea cliffs lining the Gulf of St. Lawrence, and then winds through the pastoral Margaree Valley. The 250-mile Bras d'Or Lake Scenic Drive encircles a lochlike inland sea that divides Cape Breton into highland north and lowland south.

Day One

Sydney to Ingonish Beach. **Mileage:** 76. **Drive Time:** 2 hours. **Route:** Highway 125 to 105 (Trans-Canada Highway) to the Cabot Trail.

Stopovers & Side Trips: At North River Bridge, about 45 miles from Sydney, drive 2 miles south of the Cabot Trail on Murray Road to **North River Kayak Tours.** Half-day and daylong paddles down the Murray River pass an abandoned 1899 paper mill that looks like an old monastery, and head up the sheltered coast toward St. Ann's

Bay, where there's a 90-percent chance of sighting bald eagles and, on a full-day tour, a 100-percent chance of a shoreline lunch of steamed mussels (902-567-2322; $63 per person for a full day; 10 percent off for three or more).

About 24 miles from North River Bridge, on a massive headland called **Cape Smokey,** a 3½-mile trail winds through a provincial park of birch, spruce, and fir to the edge of a 900-foot granite cliff, where eagles and hawks soar on updrafts. At **Ingonish Beach** you can alternate freshwater and saltwater swimming by crossing a narrow *barachois,* a natural breakwater of rock and sand.

Bedtime: Camp in the park at **Ingonish** (tent sites, about $11–$12 per night plus $6 entrance fee per family; 902-285-2691).

Day Two

Ingonish Beach to Fishing Cove. **Mileage:** 71. **Drive Time:** 3 hours. **Route:** Cabot Trail and White Point Road.

Stopovers & Side Trips: From here the Cabot Trail loops in and out of 367-square-mile **Cape Breton Highlands National Park** (the park's daily family entrance fee is $6 per family). At **Sea Spray Cycles** (902-383-2732) in Smelt Brook, you can rent mountain bikes ($19 per day) and a bike rack ($3.80), then pedal into the highlands or along the shoreline.

At Cape North take a side trip north to Nova Scotia's most isolated coast. From St. Lawrence Bay **skipper Dennis Cox** cruises uninhabited, cliff-rimmed coastline in search of humpbacks and minkes; the cetacean-sighting success rate is better than 95 percent (902-383-2981; $19 per person; $15 for kids 12 to 15; $9.50 kids 6 to 11; kids under 6 free). Beyond Pleasant Bay, the Cabot Trail switchbacks up MacKenzie Mountain to the highland plateau.

From **Boarsback Ridge,** a 5-mile hike suitable for children 10 years and older winds 1,100 feet down the steep valley of the Fishing Cove River to cobbled Fishing Cove, which offers the park's only coastal wilderness camping, as well as fishing for brook trout.

Bedtime: Camp at **Fishing Cove** ($11 for a backcountry permit from the Ingonish visitor center; 902-285-2691).

Day Three

Fishing Cove to Margaree Valley. **Mileage: 42. Drive Time:** 2 hours. **Route:** The Cabot Trail to Egypt Road.

Stopovers & Side Trips: Watch for moose in the barrens atop **French Mountain,** and then stop at the roadside **Cap Rouge scenic viewpoint** and look for the black fins of pilot whales slicing gulf waters. Turn right off the Cabot Trail onto the Chéticamp Island Road and unwind at **St. Pierre Beach,** which is strewn with seashells and lapped by shallow 75-degree F waters. Farther south, the **Margaree** is one of North America's finest salmon rivers, with thirty-three pools in 20 fishable miles of crystalline water. **Dave MacDonald** of the Normaway Inn, 2 miles off the Cabot Trail on Egypt Road, can set you up with a guide ($75–$99 a day), tackle ($15 a day), and license ($32.50 for a

weeklong permit). You can also rent mountain bikes at the Normaway ($18 per day) and head into the hardwood hills that shelter the valley.

Bedtime: Normaway Inn (doubles, $64–$84; 800-565-9463 or 902-248-2987).

Day Four

Margaree Valley to Roberta. **Mileage: 106. Drive Time:** 3 hours. **Route:** Cabot Trail to Highway 105 to Bras d'Or Lakes Scenic Drive.

Stopovers & Side Trips: Baddeck, a yachting center on Bras d'Or Lake, was the summer home of kite-enthusiast Alexander Graham Bell. Go fly a borrowed Parks Canada kite (or make your own sled kite) at the **Alexander Graham Bell National Historic Site** (902-295-2069).

Loch Bhreagh Tours (902-295-2016) and **Amoeba Sailing Tours** (902-295-1426) will take you past Bell's rambling estate, **Beinn Bhreagh** ("beautiful mountain" in Gaelic) on a nearby headland. **Island Eco-Adventures** in Baddeck (800-707-5512 or 902-295-3303) rents hybrid bikes ($23 per day) for customized self-guided rides, and also leads guided day trips ($11.50 an hour, minimum 4 hours). Kids 10 and older can handle the 4-hour Baddeck River loop with a swimming stop at **Uisge Ban** (ISH-keh ban) **Falls.**

Bedtime: The **Diana Resort,** 2 miles west of Roberta, has three two-bedroom cottages and eight motel units ($75–$85 for cottages; $50 for motel rooms, including breakfast; 902-345-2485).

Day Five

Roberta to Sydney. **Mileage:** 115. **Drive Time:** 3 hours. **Route:** Bras d'Or Lakes Scenic Drive to Highway 4 to East Bay, then southwest along the north shore of East Bay on Highway 223 and along the coast of St. Andrews Channel. At North West Arm, take Highway 125 to Sydney.

Stopovers & Side Trips: Half-day paddles ($30 per person) with **Kayak Cape Breton** (902-535-3060) include instruction in a sheltered bay and a short paddle to a lake island. For the best ocean swimming hereabouts, drive 8 miles east of St. Peters on Highway 247 to the uncrowded, miles-long sandy beach at **Point Michaud.**

Super Natural Sailing Tours departs Johnstown for 2½-hour excursions on a 50-foot catamaran. A marine biologist entertains everyone with food-chain demonstrations; just try getting your kid up on deck to see a cormorant colony when he can stay in the cabin and watch a starfish extrude its stomach to scarf down a mussel ($20 adults; $9 for children 6 to 12; children under 6 free; 902-535-3371).

Bedtime: You can camp and swim on the Mira River at **MacKeigan's Bay Beach Park** ($12 for tent sites; 902-727-2369); to get there, take Highway 327 about 12 miles south of Sydney.

—David Dunbar

15

For my far-flung and busy tribe, summer brings the year's only real chance for a good old-fashioned reunion. The main aim of our vacations is to get that easy summertime rhythm going—lots of outdoor day-tripping, a little lazing around just reading or catching up on family news, and plenty of cookouts. And for us the simplicity, privacy, and flexibility offered by a housekeeping cabin on a backwoods lake is the best way to cop some quality time. Once we've got that

Renting a Houseboat or Lakeside Cabin On the Waterfront

mother lode of groceries stashed away, there's plenty of time for everything— for hikes, bike trips, and the like with everyone on board; for the kids to perfect their "cannonball" and "flying squirrel" form through long practice off the dock; for Uncle Bob to offer sailing lessons on his Sunfish to all comers; even for me to sneak off alone into the green world for a few hours.

We plan to make houseboating this year's venture; it's a lock, we figure, to offer the same kind of experience—only this time we'll be mobile. One of the reasons we're looking forward to trying it is that even landlubbers like us can jump right in: Novice skippers can manage these crafts, since on-board training and a ship-to-shore radio are part of the deal.

Herewith are six of the land's best places to rent yourself a summer home-away-from-home.   —IAN WILKER

CABINS

The Upper Saranac and St. Regis Lakes Area
Adirondack Park, New York

First settled as a tuberculosis treatment center in the late 1800s, Saranac Lake is a low-key Adirondack retreat ringed by cabins and small houses left over from that era.

Cabins range from $700 to $1,500 per week; a typical rental is a four-bedroom lakeside cottage at Upper Saranac Lake that sleeps eight and rents for $1,100 per week, including use of canoes and rowboats. Contact **Century 21 Wilkins Agency** (518-891-0001); most rentals usually include use of watercraft.

If you want someone else to do the cooking, try **Northbrook Lodge,** set on a 12-mile peninsula on Osgood Lake in the town of Paul Smiths (518-327-3379). The central lodge is a former Adirondack Great Camp estate; seven cabins big enough for four face the lake. From mid-June to mid-September, weekly rates range from $420 to $540 per person and include meals and use of canoes.

Mountain bikes rent for $15 per day from **Barkeater Bicycles** in Saranac Lake (800-254-5207), which provides maps. A recommended trail is the 40-mile Bloomingdale Bog Trail, a flat, easy cruise with panoramic views of the Adirondacks.

From the town of Saranac Lake, try the hike to **Mount Baker** (2,452-foot elevation), a favorite for families because it's not too steep and runs about 2 hours round-trip. For a more challenging climb, head to **Ampersand Mountain** (elevation, 3,352 feet), 8 miles from Saranac Lake. The 6½-mile round-trip trail leads to an open, deforested summit with 70-mile views. Get trail maps from the **Chamber of Commerce** (518-891-1990).

Kids enjoy the **Adirondack Park Agency Visitor Interpretive Center** in Paul Smiths, which houses in-

Houseboating on Lake Powell

For the past 20 years, my family has spent 2 weeks of the summer aboard a houseboat on Lake Powell in Utah. I'm 19, so I've been doing this my whole life.

My grandfather owns a time-share in a 33-footer. Every July, for his birthday, some twenty members of my dad's side of the family convene—including my parents, my younger sister, and me. It sounds remarkable that one boat can sleep so many people. But what we do, like the majority of boaters on Lake Powell, is camp on the beaches at night and cruise by day aboard the boat, which is a boxlike cabin atop three huge pontoons. The roof of the cabin is a big deck where we eat meals, barbecue (though there's a kitchen below), read, and play games.

The best part about being on Lake Powell is that you can be as active or inactive as you want, which is how both the young and old in our family can stay entertained. When I was a kid, I spent every waking moment in the water (which is actually crystal-clear, not muddy). We usually rent a speedboat so we can water-ski and run reconnaissance missions in search of each night's campsite. Now that I'm older, I spend a lot of time Jet Skiing, too. My grandparents are content to putt around and check things out.

The sights are spectacular: The 186-mile-long lake with sheer sandstone cliffs meanders for 1,900 miles—longer than the entire West Coast of the U.S. Dunes cascade down from rifts in the walls of red rock, forming pockets of soft sand beaches. There's also Rainbow Bridge, a natural rock formation that spans an astonishing 275 feet over an inlet.

Launch from either **Wahweap** (520-645-2433) or **Bullfrog** (801-684-2233), the two marinas (90 miles apart; you can also call Central Reservations at 800-528-6154). At either marina you can rent a houseboat; they range in size from a 36-footer to a 59-foot Admiral, and cost $723–$1,376 for 3 days, $1,445–$3,984 for 7 days. You might want to bring along some playthings—Jet Skis ($209 per day), motorboats ($209–$261), skiffs ($65), canoes ($41), and water skis ($19) are all available at the marinas. For houseboats smaller than 56 feet, bring your own towels and bedding or rent a set from the marina ($18 for a sleeping bag, two towels, and a washcloth). The larger boats are equipped with everything you'll need except, of course, food. The only city for hundreds of miles is Page, Arizona (population 8,000). If you stock up on supplies there, you'll only need to make occasional trips to the marinas for ice and gas.

Then take off down the main channel—which looks more like the ocean than a lake, with waves and gusty winds. (Boardsailors will want to bring their gear.) Hug the towering cliffs and explore coves that cut inland for miles, telescoping down to just hundreds of feet wide. Once inside, you're shielded from the wind and the rest of the world.   —ZAC KORTH

197

jured birds of prey such as red-tail hawks, and offers daily guided hikes. The staff naturalist drops in at private beach campfires, offering tips on stargazing.

Guided fishing trips for lake trout, brook trout, and landlocked salmon can be arranged through **McDonnell's Adirondack Challenges** (518-891-1176) or **Middle Earth Expeditions** (518-523-9572). **Hickok's Boat Livery** also rents canoes ($12–$16 per day; $72–$96 per week; 518-891-0480).

—ANNE MOORE

Cape Breton Island
Nova Scotia

Ringed by ocean water, Nova Scotia is nevertheless a land of lakes, where waterfront cottages offer visitors a blissfully quiet vacation. Head straight to Cape Breton Island, a lake- and mountain-filled island off Nova Scotia's eastern coast.

Cottages here book up quickly, so reserve as far in advance as possible. Try **Kayak Cape Breton Cottages** in West Bay, whose 12 wooded acres house two two-bedroom cedar-log cabins that sleep five and a one-bedroom boathouse, all with fully equipped kitchens and easy access to the gravel beach. Weekly rates run C$390 in May, June, September, and October, and C$440 in July and August. Rates are based on two-person occupancy; there is a surcharge of C$9 per extra person. Canoes and kayaks (half-day, C$20; full-day, C$35) as well as mountain bikes (C$10 per day) are available (902-535-3060). There are also morning kayak lessons available for C$30; you can add a tour to your lesson for C$40, or a whole day of kayaking for C$60.

The **Dundee Resort** (902-345-2649) rents out 38 one- and two-bedroom cottages overlooking Bras d'Or; they have complete kitchens, decks, and barbecue units (one-bedroom cottages, C$110 per night; two-bedroom units, C$130 per night). They also have a tennis court and swimming pools.

To rent a private home, check the want ads in the Halifax newspapers, the *Chronicle Herald/Mail Star* (902-426-2811) or the *Daily News* (902-468-1222). Rates are comparable to commercial cottage rentals.

Hike or bike the 185-mile **Cabot Trail**, where you'll see bald eagles and pods of whales offshore. **Cape Breton Highlands National Park** has twenty-seven trails into wilderness areas of tundra and bogs. **Island Eco-Adventures** (800-707-5512) rents mountain bikes (C$25 per day) and will deliver them to your door, as well as canoes (C$25 per day). **The Outdoor Store** (902-295-2576) rents kayaks (C$9 per hour; C$39 per day) and offers guided tours.

—ANNE MOORE

Lake Michigan
Washington Island, Wisconsin

Among the lakefront communities that line Lake Michigan, Washington Island, Wisconsin, with its defiantly laid-back pace and Scandinavian heritage, stands out.

Lakeside cabins and homes rent weekly (two bedrooms, $550, three bedrooms, $850; both include full kitchen, 1½ baths, and laundry facilities). You can also book a two-bedroom, 1½ bath inland cabin for $525 a week.

Housing styles range from rustic rock-and-cedar cabins to A-frames. To book one, call **Island Realty** (414-847-2626).

Gibson's West Harbor Resort (414-847-2225) rents one three-bedroom and four two-bedroom beachfront cottages with kitchens and the use of a canoe ($55–$60 per night; $265–$290 per week).

The island's protected bays make for good sailing, sailboarding, kayaking, and canoeing, but most rental properties do not include watercraft, and watercraft rentals are not state of the art. You'll be better off bringing your own gear.

Sand Dunes Beach is a good stop for small children because of its smooth sand and gradual drop-off. **Schoolhouse Beach** is the place for teens: It's rocky, but the quick drop makes it a natural spot for boating.

Washington Island, heavily wooded with birch and evergreens, has more gentle terrain, ideal for bike touring with younger children in tow. Rentals are $12 per day at the ferry landing, but again, don't expect state of the art: They're single-speed Schwinns.

—ANNE MOORE

HOUSEBOATS

Shuswap Lake
British Columbia

Picture a poorly-scrawled "H" with about 620 miles of shoreline and you have houseboat heaven: Shuswap Lake. Head up quiet Anstey Arm and send the kids searching for Indian pictographs around Marble Point. Or try cliff-diving at Copper Island on Shuswap Arm. You can moor just about anywhere at nightfall; much of the lakeshore has been designated a provincial park. Choose among **Waterway Houseboat Vacations'** fifty-six boats (six different models) that sleep ten to eighteen; all boats include waterslides, gas barbecue, and steering from the bridge. Cost: $1,029–$3,468 per week. Phone: 800-663-4022.

—DEBRA SHORE

Voyageurs National Park
Minnesota

The lakes of Voyageurs National Park offer dozens of nooks and crannies, island beaches, and secret coves. Embark near the southeast corner of the park, about 1½ hours from International Falls. Head through Namakan Narrows and up Namakan Lake to the Wolf Pack Islands where your kids can scout for a family of otters. Then cruise to Kettle Falls, dine at the historic hotel, and hike to the damtender's cabin, one of just two places in the continental U.S. where you can look south into Canada. You need to tie up on shore at night but the park makes it easy with dozens of designated campsites (look for the houseboat icon). **Voyagaire Houseboats** gives you a choice of thirty boats (eight models) sleeping six to twelve, some with waterslides, hot tubs, and upper deck command bridges. Cost: $975–$3,850 per week. Phone: 800-882-6287.

—DEBRA SHORE

199

Offbeat Trips

We're Doing What?

16

Been there, done that" may well be the credo for your kids' generation: To wrestle their attention away from GameBoy and Goosebumps, your travel itinerary will require a little imagination. A standard vacation at a theme park or resort may cause their eyes to roll—but if your kids can be the first on the block to pilot a riverboat, rappel down a 600-foot granite spire, or track wildlife by radio, they'll lose that world-weary pose in a hurry.

Sylvan Rocks Climbing School
Black Hills, South Dakota

A rock-climbing vacation adds a whole new meaning to family bonding—you and yours will be literally hitched at the waist. The classrooms of Sylvan Rocks Climbing School are the Needles of South Dakota's Black Hills, otherworldly granite spires with forgiving surfaces, and hundreds of easy summits. Package programs—all with a four-to-one climber-to-guide ratio—promise a steep learning curve to ensure that everyone from rank beginners to mountain-rescue trainees learn the ropes safely. For a break from tackling the area's cracks and crevasses, you can explore the sights of the history-rich Black Hills: Mount Rushmore, Crazy Horse Memorial, Jewel Cave, and Flintstone's Bedrock City theme park are all within a half-hour's drive.

Highlight: After 3 days of instruction, half of the school's clients are able to summit nearby Devils Tower, where the spaceship landed in *Close Encounters of the Third Kind*.

Your Kids Will Be First To: Belay their own parents.

Ages: 13 and up

Cost/Lodging: For a 5-day family climbing immersion, combine the 2-day basic package for absolute beginners ($200 per person for a family of four) with the 3-day novice package for people who have some rock-climbing experience ($300 per person for a family of four). Cost includes instruction and equipment. Meals and lodging are not included, but the staff will help guests find campsites or hotels in Hill City, South Dakota.

Information: Sylvan Rocks Climbing School and Guide Service, P.O. Box 600, Hill City, SD 57745; 605-574-2425.

Yellowstone Wildlife Safari
Jackson, Wyoming

Wildlife biologists call Yellowstone's Lamar Valley the American Serengeti. Stomping grounds for hundreds of pronghorn, bison, elk, moose, and bighorn sheep, this region is the focus of a weeklong safari offered by the Great Plains Wildlife Institute. You and your kids can indulge your Marlin Perkins fantasies while helping your guides—all working wildlife biologists—gather information for ongoing research projects. Depending on the month, that might include counting wild horses, checking in on the spring lambs, watch-

Air Conditioning Included

Heading way north may call up notions of a Will Steger–style schlep across some frozen wasteland, but summer weather and family-oriented outfitters actually make far-north odysseys more than feasible.

Only a sliver of ripstop nylon separates you and your clan from 186,000 caribou on **Arctic Treks'** High Arctic Spring Caribou Basecamp trip in the Arctic National Wildlife Refuge. After a 300-mile bush-plane flight from Fairbanks, you set up camp near the south flanks of the Brooks Range. Husband-and-wife guides Jim Campbell and Carol Kasza know all the right day hikes in the foothill valleys and coastal plains to get you close to the caribou, as well as to migrating songbirds and seabirds.

It's a nonpampered, share-the-camp-chores outing in spectacular wilderness. **Departure:** May 31–June 6. **Cost:** $2,400 per person (families get a 10 percent discount). **Phone:** 907-455-6502.

Or, book your brood berths aboard the 120-passenger *Marine Discovery* and you'll cruise to an iceberg factory (Greenland's Jakobshavn Glacier), spot multiple species of whales, and see murres and kittiwakes by the thousand. **Nature Expeditions International**'s Northwest Passage trip is a 9-day jaunt up the west coast of Greenland and across to Arctic Canada, with stops to view Inuit ruins. **Departure:** August 18–26. **Cost:** $1,995 per person (in a four-person cabin), including round-trip air from Ottawa. **Phone:** 800-869-0639.   —BOB HOWELLS

ing the bison rut, or tracking trumpeter swans. Along the way, you'll stop for hands-on lectures about the local flora and fauna, a sight-seeing float down the Snake River, and photo ops set against the Grand Tetons.

Highlight: Checking in on the gray wolves recently reintroduced to Yellowstone.

Your Kids Will Be First To: Strap a radio collar on a porcupine.

Ages: 12 and up

Cost/Lodging: $1,485 per person, including lodging and most meals. Winter safaris cost $1560 per person, double occupancy. Group sizes are kept under

ten per trip; depending on the time of year, your family could have a guide all to itself.

Information: Great Plains Wildlife Institute, P.O. Box 7580, Jackson Hole, WY 83002; 307-733-2623.

Breteche Creek Ranch
Cody, Wyoming

Cowboys writing poetry? Bird-watchers rounding up steers? Breteche Creek Ranch is a dude ranch of a different stripe. In addition to the normal lineup of trail rides, campfires, and cattle drives, it offers some decidedly uncowboylike touches: fly-fishing instruction, bird-watching,

Surfin' Camp U.S.A.

If you and the kids are dying to learn how to surf but just don't know where to begin, you could take the approach pioneered by Keanu Reeves in *Point Break:* Buy a goofy-looking board and wander around Malibu until Patrick Swayze shows up to teach you. Or, you could go to surf camp.

Be prepared to spend long days in the water—paddling, turning turtle, dropping in, and, hopefully, standing up— then swap surfing stories around the nightly campfire. All camps listed below provide wetsuits, leashes, boards, wax, all meals, and tents. Just bring your sleeping bags and pads.

Club Ed Surf School and Camps of Santa Cruz sets up class on Manresa State Beach south of town, a primo summer break. If the waves don't deliver there, you'll travel by van to reliable breaks like Pleasure Point or Cowell's Beach farther up the coast. Club Ed uses video coaching and includes a field trip to the Santa Cruz Surfing Museum at Steamer's Lane, where you'll see a photo of Ed's grandmother surfing back in 1915. The camp is limited to just fourteen students, but families can also customize a mobile surf camp, in which three to five people share a well-stocked motorhome and two instructors, and cruise the coast looking for that perfect wave. Club Ed Surf Camp; 800-287-7873 or 408-459-9283; $690 per person for 7 days/6 nights.

Summer Fun Surf Camp in San Clemente has sessions geared especially for kids 10 to 18 (parents are the only adults allowed). At nearby San Onofre State Beach, home of some of California's gentlest waves, beginners start out on soft foam boards, then transition to fiberglass as their skills progress. In the evenings you'll watch surf videos and listen to visiting pro surfers. Summer Fun Surf Camp; 714-361-9526; 5 days/4 nights $495 per person, 7 days/6 nights $695.

If all that California sun sounds too warm for you, sign on for a cold-water surf camp with **Adventure Surf Unlimited,** which runs weeklong camps along the Oregon coast at Nehalem State Park and Cape Lookout State Park. This is the most rugged of the surf camps, but after a day in that chilly water you'll camp in state park campgrounds with hot showers. Adventure Surf Unlimited; 617-648-2880; $659 per person. —ANDREW RICE

geology hikes, whitewater rafting trips, night astronomy classes, fireside lectures on Plains Indian mythology, and workshops in photography, writing, and poetry.

Guests stay in rustic wood and canvas tent-cabins along the ranch's namesake creek. The nearest electricity is at the main ranch office, 2 miles down the valley, but propane gas provides for hot showers, lights, and meals in a central lodge area.

Highlight: Close encounters with Shoshone National Forest's megafauna—grizzly bears, black bears, elk, bighorn sheep, and bald and golden eagles abound.

Your Kids Will Be First To: Write their own lonesome-cowboy poetry.

Ages: 8 and up, to really enjoy the horses.

Cost/Lodging: Weeklong sessions are $975 for adults, $825 for kids 12 and under, plus a 15-percent gratuity.

Information: Breteche Creek Ranch, P.O. Box 596, Cody, Wyoming 82414; 307-587-3844.

Dolphin Discovery Camp
Roatan, Honduras

Your kids will be happily in over their heads with this immersion-by-submersion program dedicated to the Atlantic bottlenose dolphin. Held at Anthony's Key Resort on Honduras' largest Bay Island, the 6-day program for kids is overseen by the nearby Institute for Marine Sciences, a center for marine biology research and home to a number of captive dolphins. Camp sessions involve snorkeling, dolphin feeding and training, and marine experiments. In addition to horseback riding and glass-bottom boat excursions, there'll be scavenger hunts, sand-sculpting, and nature hikes. Parents, meanwhile, will dive, dive, dive along the Bay Islands' famous barrier reefs.

Highlight: Two class sessions are set aside for the ultimate immersion—snorkeling with the dolphins.

Your Kids Will Be First To: Know what Flipper is really saying on all those reruns.

Ages: 8 to 14

Cost/Lodging: Dolphin Discovery Camp rates are $500 per child when they share a room with an adult, including three meals daily. A weeklong dive package at Anthony's Key Resort is $750–$825 per adult (double occupancy), including meals, three daily dives, two night dives, and accommodations in a family-size bungalow.

Information: American Wilderness Experience Inc., P.O. Box 1486, Boulder, CO 80306; 800-444-0099.

Family Dino Camp
Fruita, Colorado

Millions of years ago, this part of Colorado was a watering hole for dinosaurs. Today it's an ideal destination for kids who've graduated from "Barney & Friends" but still can't get enough of *Jurassic Park*. Sponsored by the non-profit Dinamation International Society, the Family Dino Camp is a 5-day exploration of the Mygatt-Moore Quarry of western Colorado and the dinosaurs that once lived there. You and your kids split up for some classroom training (while you attend a lecture by a noted paleontologist, your kids paint the plaster casts of fossils), but come together again for lab visits, picnic lunches near dinosaur tracks, and river hikes to study fossils. On the climactic excavation day, kids who aren't ready for an actual prehistoric boneyard get to dig in a special quarry laden with fossil replicas they can "discover" and take home. Of course, any discovery in the real quarry has to go to a museum.

Highlight: The thrill of the find (in 1993, a 14-year-old girl uncovered the quarry's first egg—an armored dinosaur's).

Your Kids Will Be First To: Spot a *Mymoorapelta maysi* in a lineup.

Ages: 6 and up

Cost/Lodging: $850 for adults, $575 for children ages 6 to 12. Cost includes one room per family at a nearby hotel, two dinners, four lunches, ground transportation, instruction, and equipment.

Information: Dinosaur Discovery Expeditions, Dinamation International Society, 550 Crossroads Court, Fruita, CO 81521; 800-344-3466.

Ellinwood Ranch
Arizona

Saddle everyone up for an authentic working ranch experience on this 33,000-acre spread in the shade of the Mogollon Rim. Here, the rugged Hellsgate Canyon wilderness is home to the Hunts, who let families join in to drive the herd from pastures of grama grass through plains of yucca and prickly pear and, depending on the month, rope and brand new calves. If you get saddle-weary, check out the Indian petroglyphs near Muddy

Grand Ideas, Indeed

Call it cross-generational bonding, old-fashioned mentoring, or just doing neat stuff with the grandkids—more and more outfits are bringing disparate generations together on outdoor jaunts. Not surprisingly, Elderhostel lurks behind many of them, such as Let's Talk Wolf: Intergenerational Wolf Discovery at the International Wolf Center in Ely, Minnesota. The syllabus of the 6-day (August 3–8) immersion into wolfdom includes learning to howl to the center's resident wolves and talks by the center's "Alpha" wolf, a human who lives with the pack. Cost is $365 for adults; $310 for kids 9 (minimum age) to 12. Book through **Elderhostel**, 617-426-8056. Elderhostel (with Canyonlands Field Institute) also runs a 6-day raft trip on the San Juan River in southern Utah for grandparents and kids 8 to 14 that includes time for nature hikes, storytelling, and epic water fights. The river's mellow enough that kids can run stretches solo in inflatable kayaks. The $415 per-person cost includes 1 motel night and 4 under the stars. Trips run from mid-June to mid-August; contact Elderhostel.

Grandtravel does nothing but intergenerational trips, typically by bus with, naturally, lots of stops. On the 10-day American Indian Culture trip through New Mexico, Colorado, Utah, and Arizona, the stops include a raft-run of the Animas River, a Navajo-guided jeep tour of Canyon de Chelly, and visits to both the real Grand Canyon and its virtual surrogate, the IMAX Theatre. The trip runs June 22 to July 1 for ages 12 to 17, and August 10 to 19 for ages 7 to 11. Rates are $3,185 per person, all-inclusive, double-occupancy. Call **Grandtravel**, 800-247-7651.

—BOB HOWELLS

Springs, or practice rope tricks in the corrals. Western fare and campfire stories are served up nightly. Accommodations are by way of roomy tents, though your kids may take their bedrolls outside to sleep under the stars.

Highlights: Roping and branding the spring calves like a true buckaroo; taking a dip in secluded swimming holes.

Your Kids Will Be First To: Rope a dogie.

Ages: 8 to 16

Cost/Lodging: An 8-day package costs $1,105 for adults, $1,055 for kids 8 to 16 and seniors. Groups are met at the Phoenix airport; 2 nights of pre- and posttrip lodging and meals are included in the price.

Information: American Wilderness Experience Inc., P.O. Box 1486, Boulder, CO 80306; 800-444-0099.

Erie Canal Boat Cruise
Skaneateles, New York

The trouble with your average road trip is that it's a challenge to absorb the scenery at 70 mph. Not so on a 33-foot Erie Canal cruise boat, where anything over 7 miles an hour is pushing the envelope. But your kids won't be bored if you let them chart the course themselves through the miles of waterways that run from Albany to Buffalo. They can plot the way through the busy towns of Syracuse and Rochester, set their fishing lines at Cayuga Lake, drop through the spectacular double lock at Seneca Falls, check out the museums on Lake Ontario, or get out the binoculars for a troll through the Montezuma National Wildlife Refuge. No experience is required: Each canal lock is manned, and a 3-hour orientation is enough for most people to take the helm with confidence.

Highlight: Every boat comes with a bike (you can arrange for extra bikes for a small fee) so your kids can blow off steam on the bike trails that parallel parts of the canal.

Your Kids Will Be First To: Captain their own ship.

Ages: 5 and up

Cost/Lodging: The 33-foot cruiser rents for $1,500 a week and accommodates a family of four, with a private berth for two and two bunks in the galley. Larger boats are also available for chartering.

Information: Mid-Lakes Navigation Company, P. O. Box 61, Skaneateles, NY 13152; 800-545-4318.
—LAURA BILLINGS

17

I f you'd asked what I thought of humpback whales when I was 8, I probably would have told you they have bad breath. On a family salmon-fishing trip out of Juneau, we came upon a group of feeding humpbacks who breached the surface and smashed their huge bodies on the gray water. One whale came up right in front of me and gave me a spray of salty blow-hole breath in the face.

Alaska

The Ultimate Adventure

In Alaska, such intimate encounters with wild things are quite common, and children can learn firsthand about animals and places they otherwise might see only on television or in zoos.

Now I travel the state with my children, Robin, 5, and Julia, 2. They point out with wonder many things I overlook. We once sat on a dock for hours, watching a mother sea otter play with her pups, thanks to Robin's persistent fascination. And who would have guessed there could be so many ways to have fun in a Forest Service campsite?

Following are six Alaska itineraries recommended for active families with children of various ages. Each includes unspoiled wilderness and wildlife viewing that you can get to without the expense of chartering a bush plane or a boat.   —CHARLES P. WOHLFORTH

Glaciers, Whales, and Country Inns

The relatively undiscovered village of **Gustavus,** at the north end of southeast Alaska's Inside Passage and accessible only by ferry or aircraft, makes a good base for exploring one of the richest wild areas in Alaska. Gustavus is so quiet you often feel as if you're the only visitor, but the headquarters of **Glacier**

Bay National Park and Preserve, one of Alaska's most visited attractions, lies just 10 miles down the road.

In **Glacier Bay,** a 65-mile-long set of fjords, you'll find a few short hiking trails and a campground at the park headquarters. The outfitter **Alaska Discovery** offers sea-kayaking day trips ($119 per person; 10 percent discount under age 18; minimum age 12; 800-586-1911). Its 8-day paddle into the park proper ($1,890 per person; 10 percent off under age 18) is only for fit older teens and adults. To get to the many immense glaciers and the whales and other wildlife deep in the bay, take the park concessionaire's tour boat ($150, half price for kids 12 and under; 800-451-5952).

There's at least as much to do in and around Gustavus itself. **Icy Strait,** just south of Gustavus off Point Adolphus, is one of the most reliable places in Alaska to see humpback whales and to catch halibut ranging into the hundreds of pounds. You can charter a small boat with any of several local skippers (around $200 per person, slightly less without the fishing). Or take the daily excursion boat, the *Auk Nu,* run by the park concessionaire (3-hour cruise, $78 per person), which also functions as the passenger ferry linking Gustavus to Juneau ($85 round-trip). Kayakers obviously can get closest of all to the whales; Alaska Discovery leads a 3-day kayaking trip off Point Adolphus from a base camp for $550 per person (there's a 10 percent discount for kids under 18).

There are four country inns in Gustavus, and a number of cabin rentals and B&Bs. The **Gustavus Inn** ($135 per adult, half price under age 12, all meals included; 800-649-5220), an old farmhouse, has bicycles for guests to use, and makes arrangements for sea kayaking, whale-watching, and fishing. **Puffin's Bed and Breakfast** offers simply furnished one-room cabins with baths ($85 per night for two; $20 each additional person; $10 kids 2 to 11; 907-697-2260).

—CHARLES P. WOHLFORTH

Hiking the Kenai Peninsula

There are several excellent multiday hikes suitable for families in the spectacular virgin country of the Chugach National Forest. The most famous of these hikes is the **Resurrection Pass Trail,** a 39-mile National Recreation Trail linking the villages of Hope and Cooper Landing that takes 3 to 5 days for good hikers. It's also suitable for mountain biking and horseback riding after July 1.

The starting point is 4 miles south of **Hope,** a tiny seaside town of white clapboard Gold Rush buildings and so few people that Polaroids of all the residents are posted on the wall of the bar. The trail climbs from here through coastal forest into the Chugach Mountains.

At about the halfway mark along the hike you reach the pass, well above treeline in a valley of alpine tundra and wildflowers. On the downhill stretch to Cooper Landing, a series of three lovely fish-filled lakes nestle in the mountains' shoulders, and there are four Forest Service cabins available to rent ($25 per night plus an $8.25 reservation fee; call 800-280-2267). Along the way you have an excellent chance of seeing plenty of wildlife—moose, bears, wolves, Dall sheep, and mountain goats.

Inside Skinny

Alaska for Less

Alaska can cost a lot. Lodgings typically run well over $100 for a standard motel room, and meals cost more than in the Lower 48. Getting into the wilderness may require expensive small-airplane flights and boat rides, and guided trips can be out of reach for many families. Nevertheless, there are a number of tricks for holding down your expenses:

✦ **Getting There.** Take the **Alaska Marine Highway** ferry (800-642-0066) to Haines, 780 miles by road from Anchorage. The ride is spectacular for adults and fun for kids, and the ferry is the best way to get to southeast Alaska's small towns. The foot-passenger fare from Bellingham, Washington, is $240 for adults, $120 for kids under 11, free under 2; $568 extra for a vehicle under 15 feet (from Prince Rupert, B.C., it's C$118 for adults, C$60 for under 11; C$273 extra for a vehicle). Cabins run an extra $227–$392; you can save the extra cost by camping on deck. (Remember to bring duct tape to hold down your tent.)

✦ **Lodging.** High hotel prices have produced a bumper crop of B&Bs in every Alaska town. If you don't mind sharing a bathroom, you can get a good room for $75 a night even in expensive areas. Most towns have agencies that can tell you which places welcome children. In southeast Alaska, call the **Alaska Bed and Breakfast Association** (907-586-2959). In Anchorage, try **Alaska Private Lodgings** (907-258-1717), which books G Street Bed and Breakfast, an old house near downtown that caters to families. In Juneau, **Blueberry Lodge B&B** (907-463-5886) sits in a wonderful natural setting near the water. The cheapest lodging is, of course, a tent; there are places to camp virtually everywhere.

✦ **Meals.** Pack picnics, cook on a camp stove, or find rooms with kitchenettes—anything to avoid eating three meals a day in restaurants. Hotels of converted apartments, such as the **Parkwood Inn** in Anchorage (studios with kitchens, $90–$100; 907-563-3590) are convenient and can save you some money.

—CHARLES P. WOHLFORTH

211

HIRED HANDS

Alaska Wildland Adventures (800-334-8730) offers eight trips this summer (most for kids 12 and older), including a 10-day, van-based camping trip for $1,695–$1,895 per person. But one trip caters to families with children ages 6 through 11: The Family Safari includes a float trip on the Kenai River and a look at an Iditarod champion's racing kennel, and finishes with 2 nights at Denali Backcountry Lodge near Mount McKinley. The 7-day trip costs $2,595 for adults and $2,295 for kids, not including airfare to Anchorage.

Nature Expeditions International (800-869-0639) leads a 9- to 15-day trip that covers more of Alaska; you'll go to Glacier Bay, Barlett Cove, and Kenai and Denali national parks, among other places. Recommended for ages 10 and up, the trips costs $2,690 for 9 days, $3,790 for 15 days, not including airfare.

Alaska Discovery (800-586-1911) takes children as young as 12 on some of its 3- to 12-day southeast Alaska sea kayaking trips ($495–$2,600; 10 percent off for kids under 18 and groups of four or more). —*C.P.W.*

The riverside sportfishing town of **Cooper Landing** has many good places to stay, ranging from rustic cabins to motel rooms to the **Kenai Princess Lodge,** a luxury hotel operated by Princess Cruise Lines (907-595-1425). Take a float trip down the Kenai River with a company such as **Alaska Wildland Adventures** (day trips, $95; ages 7 to 11, $55; 800-334-8730). This is among some of the best places in Alaska for king and red salmon fishing.

—CHARLES P. WOHLFORTH

A Trip through the Klondike

Stories of raw and rugged adventure during the Klondike Gold Rush of 1896–97 are still the inspiration for many a trip to Alaska. You can visit the towns the stampeders left behind and the wilderness they crossed, all essentially unchanged; along the way stop to hike, canoe, bike, and sea kayak. But don't go unless your kids can handle long hauls; the trip can take as long as 12 days and cover 1,200 miles, with drives covering up to 240 miles in a single day.

The route goes from the port of Skagway over White Pass into the Yukon Territory to Dawson City, the site of the Klondike strike in 1896. Then the loop continues west, back into Alaska and back to the ocean in Haines.

Fly by way of Juneau or take the Alaska Marine Highway ferry (800-642-0066) to **Skagway,** where the National Park Service has preserved the historic Gold Rush district. Here you can ride the spectacular narrow-gauge railway built over White Pass around 1900 (adults, $75; 12 and under, half price; call 800-343-7373).

The **Wind Valley Lodge** (907-983-2236) is a good standard motel; the

Where the Wild Things Are

Grizzly Bears: Number in the wild in Alaska: 25,000–38,000. Best places to find them: Denali National Park, Katmai National Park, Kodiak Island. How close can you get? Stay at least a few hundred yards away unless you're in a vehicle or at a guided bear observatory. Chances a child can see one: Fair. Brown bears blend into their surroundings and can be hard to pick out at a distance.

- -

Humpback Whales: Number in the wild in Alaska: 750, summer only. Best places to find them: Resurrection Bay outside Seward, Frederick Sound outside Petersburg, Point Adolphus near Gustavus. How close can you get? Federal law prohibits vessels from forcing the humpbacks to change course, but sometimes the whales will surface nearby. Chances a child can see one: Fair to Good. Patience and quick reactions are needed to catch a glimpse of one when it briefly surfaces.

- -

Sea Otters: Number in the wild in Alaska: 100,000–150,000. Best places to find them: Small boat harbors all over southeast and south-central Alaska, Kenai Fjords National Park, Prince William Sound. How close can you get? It's illegal to harass or handle otters, but in a small boat you can sometimes get within a few feet. Chances a child can see one: Excellent. Sea otters are ubiquitous in coastal Alaska and seem almost to enjoy the presence of humans.

- -

Bald Eagles: Number in the wild in Alaska: 50,000. Best places to find them: Almost any coastal area in south-central or southeast Alaska; Homer and Haines are especially good. How close can you get? Bald eagles are generally seen at a distance, and are protected by federal law from being disturbed. Chances a child can see one: Good. Eagles are easy to see in flight, but can be hard to pick out when sitting in a tree.

- -

Caribou: Number in the wild in Alaska: 960,000. Best places to find them: Denali National Park, Dalton Highway north of the Brooks Range, Arctic National Wildlife Refuge. How close can you get? Caribou tend to flee from people. They may wander closer if you stay in a vehicle. Chances a child can see one: Fair to poor. Caribou often are seen at a distance and patience is required to wait for them to come to you.

—CHARLES P. WOHLFORTH

Golden North Hotel is a wonderfully funky old place little changed in 100 years (907-983-2294); both places charge about $75 for a double room.

From Skagway, drive along the **Klondike Highway** to Dawson City, 426 miles north. (**Avis** in Skagway charges about $50 per day/$349 per week for a midsize car; call 800-331-1212.) There are a number of Yukon Territory campgrounds all along the route; a good stop is **Tatchun Creek**, about halfway, just north of the town of Carmacks, for a day hike down to

One for the Road: The Kenai Peninsula by Car

There are few places left in the world that can still be classified as pristine wilderness but are as easy to reach as the Kenai. The peninsula contains a national park and forest; a river that runs with the biggest sport-caught chinook salmon in the world; ocean habitat for whales, puffins, otters, and sea lions; and several small towns. Before you go, check with the **Alaska Public Lands Information Center** (907-271-2737).

Day One

Anchorage to Seward. Mileage: 128. Drive time: 2½ hours. Route: South from Anchorage on the Seward Highway.

Stopovers & Side Trips: The **Seward National Scenic Highway,** chipped into the toe of the Chugach Mountains, is the most spectacular in Alaska. To your right, look for beluga whales chasing salmon in the gray waters of Turnagain Arm; on the cliffs to the left, watch for Dall sheep. There are several well-marked trails into the mountains on the left side of the highway. At **Girdwood,** 37 miles from Anchorage, you can explore the **Alyeska Resort** (907-754-1111) and take the tram (adults, $12; ages 8 to 17, $10; under 7, $7) to the restaurant and mountain-top walking trails. At **Crow Creek Mine** in Girdwood, you can pan for gold ($5 for adults, $3 for kids; 907-278-8060), or just explore the mine ($3 for adults, children under 12 free).

Bedtime: Camp on the pebble beach on Ballaine Avenue in Seward (tent-camping with showers, $6; 907-224-3331), where you can fish for salmon right outside your tent. The kid-friendly **Farm Bed and Breakfast** (doubles and cabins, $65–$95; 907-224-5691), set on 40 acres just out of town, rents rooms and cabins.

Day Two

Seward to Cooper Landing. Mileage: 55. Drive time: 1 hour. Route: Back the way you came on the Seward Highway, then turn left onto the Sterling Highway at Tern Lake.

Stopovers & Side Trips: Take a boat trip to **Kenai Fjords National Park** with Kenai Fjords Tours (6-hour trips, $99 per person, under 12, $49; 8½-hour trips, $109 per person, under 12 $49; 800-478-8068) for a look at glaciers, otters, sea lions, puffins, and probably humpback whales. Or book a guided sea-kayaking excursion from Seward with **Adventures & Delights** ($95 per day; no kids under 16; custom tours for families of four with younger children, $395 plus $95 each additional person; 800-288-3134). In Cooper Landing, fish for red salmon, or take a river float; call **Alaska Rivers Co.** (half-day float trips from $39 per person; fishing from $75; 907-595-1226).

Bedtime: The 180-site **Russian River Campground** ($11 plus $8.25 reservation fee; call 800-280-2267) may be full in sum-

Five Fingers Rapids on the Yukon River. Plan to spend 2 full days seeing the historic sights in **Dawson City**. During the Gold Rush, this was the second-largest city on the West Coast, after San Francisco. Dawson City also is a good place to start a float trip on the Yukon, Klondike, or Stewart rivers. A provincial campground is located just across the Yukon from town (you can take the free ferry). The **Triple J Hotel** has rooms (doubles, $85–$115; 403-993-5323) and cabins ($107) right in town.

The gravel **Top of the World Highway** leads west from Dawson City back to the U.S., traversing treeless mountain peaks. Back on the U.S. side, 79 miles from Dawson City, the road meets the gravel **Taylor Highway** in

mer; just east on the highway, **Gwin's Lodge** ($99–$119; 907-595-1266) has cabins for rent and good meals.

Day Three
Cooper Landing to Homer. Mileage: 140. Drive time: 2½ hours. Route: Follow the Sterling Highway.

Stopovers & Side Trips: The towns of Ninilchik, Deep Creek, and Anchor Point are known for their fishing streams and provide beach access on Cook Inlet (check with the **Alaska Department of Fish and Game;** 907-262-2737). In Homer, visit the **Pratt Museum** (907-235-8635), with superb displays on marine natural history. Homer also has great mountain biking and hiking over trails through fields of wildflowers, as well as good sea kayaking; for rentals, check with **Central Charter Booking Agency** (doubles, $70 per day; singles, $60; 800-478-7847).

Bedtime: You can camp on the beach at **Homer Spit Campgrounds** ($3 a night for tent-camping), or you can book a B&B through **Homer Alaska Referral Agency** (907-235-8996).

Day Four
Homer to Halibut Cove by boat. Route: Take one of the boats from the Homer Spit harbor.

Stopovers & Side Trips: To get out on the water and across Kachemak Bay to **Gull Island**, sign on with **Rainbow Tours** (about $15 per person; 907-235-7272); their trip to the **Alaska Center for Coastal Studies** is especially good for kids (daylong trips, $55 for adults, $43 for children).

Bedtime: The **Quiet Place** ($150 per couple plus $75 each additional person; 907-296-2212) in Halibut Cove has cabins perched above the water and rents sea kayaks and boats (sea kayaks, $35 single; $55 double per day; motorboats, $65–$75 per day). You can't camp in the village, however (it's all private property).

Day Five
Homer to Anchorage. Mileage: 225. Drive time: 4 hours. Route: Take the Sterling Highway to the Seward Highway.

Stopovers & Side Trips: About 80 miles up the road from Homer, the town of **Soldotna** provides access to the **Kenai River,** spawning ground of the world's largest king salmon. The headquarters of the **Kenai National Wildlife Refuge** (907-262-7021), also in Soldotna, has a visitor center and information on canoe routes that lead through the rivers of the refuge.
—CHARLES P. WOHLFORTH

the Fortymile country, which to this day remains a wild haven for small-time gold miners. There also are two **BLM campgrounds** (907-883-5121) near two of the put-ins for the Fortymile River.

A detour north on the Taylor leads 65 miles to the village of **Eagle**, a Gold Rush town with five museums but fewer than 200 residents. Getting there takes several hours over dirt roads, 144 miles from Dawson City, but it's worth it to see the wonderful historic buildings. There's a comfortable motel, a cafe, a campground, and a visitor center (907-547-2233).

From Eagle, you've got about 600 miles to cover to get back to Haines. It's best to do it in three stages: Stop at one of the inexpensive motels or camp out in **Tok** (173 miles), then stop again at Canada's awe-inspiring **Kluane Lake**, another 242 miles.

The final stop, **Haines** (207 miles), is a charming and offbeat seaside town with some of Alaska's best wilderness guides and territory for sea kayaking, rafting, mountain biking, hiking, and climbing. Call the visitor center (800-458-3579) for referrals. Haines also is the center of Tlingit Native culture. The **Halsingland Hotel** (doubles, $49–$89; 907-766-2000), part of an Army fort built at the turn of the century, is a fun, creaky old place to stay.

In Haines, you're back on the ferry system, just 12 miles from Skagway by water. If you rented a car in Skagway, you can drop it off here for a $100 charge or take it back to Skagway yourself on the ferry for $25. —CHARLES P. WOHLFORTH

Sea Kayaking
Prince William Sound

The locals say Prince William Sound hasn't fully recovered from the massive lube job provided by the *Exxon Valdez* back in 1989, but first-time visitors remain awestruck by the sound's sheer beauty and scale: stark fjords, lushly forested islands, mountains, tidewater glaciers, and 200-foot waterfalls. There are more miles of coastline here than in all of California—and so many bald eagles you stop looking up after a while. The kids can gather mussels at low tide, and troll a line for pink salmon and rockfish while paddling. The sound is protected by the Chugach Mountains and the Kenai Peninsula on three sides, so the water is usually calm. As you approach calving glaciers through the ice fields, it sounds like a thunderstorm and feels like paddling through a frozen margarita.

There are an enormous number of critters afloat and aloft around Prince William sound: Orcas, minke and humpback whales, porpoises, sea otters, harbor seals, and sea lions are likely to surface. Some of the black bears are habituated, so cook away from camp and hang your food. You'll see more birds than you can keep straight, including three kinds of terns, sea ducks, and trumpeter swans.

A few words of caution: Although the air temperature in June—the warmest, driest month—may hit 70 degrees Fahrenheit, the water maxes out at 50. Tipping over is not an option, and any help in emergencies is a long way off. Stay a half mile away from glaciers: When a hunk of ice the size of a small apartment building breaks off, you want to be riding a gentle swell, not a breaking wave.

The easiest access to the waters of the western sound is the town of Whittier, southeast of Anchorage. Take the **Alaska Backpacker Shuttle** ($30 round-trip; 800-266-8625) from Anchorage to Portage, then the **Alaska Railroad train** from Portage to Whittier ($16 round-trip; 800-544-0552). Two outfitters that will get you out on the water in style: **North Star Alaska** (800-258-8434) runs 4-day trips for $950 and 5-day trips for $1,200; **Anadyr Adventures** (800-865-2925) offers a range of trips, from overnights for $275 per person to 10-day trips for $2,750. If you're an experienced paddler, **Prince William Sound Kayak Center** in Whittier rents boats (907-276-7235).

Put in at the town dock and head out to the east, passing cliffs where a colony of black-legged kittiwakes have set up shop. Hug the shore and camp at the small, protected cove at **Decision**

Point 8 miles out—or at **Shotgun Cove,** 5 miles out, if you get a late start. The next day, round the point and head southwest into **Blackstone Bay.** Here you have a 2-mile open-water crossing of the bay to Tebenkof Glacier. Two miles up is **Thirteen Mile Beach,** with a waterfall you can paddle up to at high tide, good hiking, and usually a lot of sea otters around. Protected forest camps at **Seventeen Mile Beach** are 4 miles farther on. Spend 2 days here, doing day paddles up to Blackstone Glacier and around Willard Island. Returning the way you came, curse yourself for not bringing more film.

Before you go, be sure to pick up maps and get current travel information. Trails Illustrated puts out a good map of Prince William Sound (call 800-962-1643 to order). **Alaska Public Lands Information Center** (907-271-2737) and the **Chugach National Forest** (907-783-3242) will provide you with information about forest-service campsites, cabins, and maps.

—BILL HEAVEY

Kachemak Journey

You can get away from the road system in a marine wilderness rich with wildlife across from Homer in Kachemak Bay, which is south of Anchorage on the Kenai Peninsula. Any of the several tiny communities makes a good base, or you can link them together in a backcountry journey, as follows.

Passenger ferries, excursion boats, and water taxis crisscross the bay daily in the summer. **Rainbow Tours** (907-235-7272) will take you to **Seldovia** for $40 round-trip, $25 for ages 12 and under. On the way you'll see otters, eagles, puffins, probably seals, and maybe even whales. Seldovia is a good place to bike on miles of deserted roads, fish for salmon or halibut, hike, or just wander around.

You can get breakfast at The Buzz coffee shop and take the daily van to **Jakolof Bay,** the only place connected to Seldovia by road. Jakolof Bay makes Seldovia look like a metropolis, but there are a couple of places to stay here. Call Marcia or Tom at the **Jakolof Ferry Service** for information about cabin rentals ($50–$70; 907-235-2376).

Back in Seldovia, **The Buzz** (907-234-7479) also rents mountain bikes ($20 a day) to ride the old logging roads into the countryside. A good route is the Rocky River Road, which threads 20 miles through the mountains across the tip of the Kenai Peninsula to the remote fjords.

Two outfits guide sea-kayaking trips through Kachemak Bay. **True North Kayak Adventures** (907-235-0708) offers all-day guided paddles for $125 per person as well as multiday trips (ask about discounts for parties of four or more). **Trips,** at the same phone number, is a custom adventure-travel booking service in Homer that can take care of all the details of a Kachemak Bay journey.

The Jakolof Ferry Service can take you back to Homer or to **Halibut Cove,** a town Dr. Seuss could have invented, with no roads, and docks and boardwalks serving as sidewalks. The town's biggest business is fine art. With fewer than a hundred year-round residents, there are fourteen professional artists and three galleries.

Most people come to Halibut Cove on a day trip from Homer aboard the *Danny J* passenger ferry (907-235-7847) to eat at the Saltry, an exceptional seafood restaurant. But you could stay overnight at the lovely **Quiet Place Lodge,** whose five one-room cabins sit on pilings above the floating post office ($150 per person, half price for kids 6 to 12, under 6 free, all meals included; 907-296-2212). The lodge also can help you arrange for kayak and boat rentals, or you can go hiking on the 25-mile network of trails in Kachemak Bay State Park. It would be easy to spend an entire summer here, but, eventually you'll have to catch a boat back to reality.

—CHARLES P. WOHLFORTH

18

Short of Disneyland, families have it best in Hawaii, particularly in the summer months when the *keikis* (kids) are out of school and the whole state pitches in to observe local holidays like King Kamehameha Day (June 11). Your kids will love the magnificent *aina* (land) and *wai* (water), but what they may well remember best is playing at the beach alongside Hawaiian children or surfing with real beachboys. Within a few days,

Hawaii

Everything under the Sun

words like *aloha* and *mahalo* (thanks) will creep into their language, and they'll feel more like *kamaaina* (locals) than tourists. They might even learn to like poi.

Royal Hawaiian Hotel
Oahu

Claim to Fame: Despite the fact that Waikiki Beach is an urbanized tourist magnet with hotels crammed onto nearly every beachfront inch, it's still paradise. Your oasis is the elegant Royal Hawaiian Hotel, a Moroccan-style, all-pink palace on the beach that dates back to 1927 and has the attentive feel of a big-city hotel, albeit one where everything is pink—rooms, towels, lobbies. In the main building, the rooms are spacious, with colonial-style furniture; in the Royal Tower, all rooms have ocean views with private lanais.

Because guests here have charging privileges at three other Sheraton hotels in Waikiki, you'll feel like you have the run of the place. Teens especially love the casual, urban ambience of Waikiki, where pedestrians stroll the sidewalks carrying surfboards, and movie theaters are just around the corner. All four hotels share the free (with lunch available for $6.50) Keiki Aloha program and Ho'okipa activity center

at the Sheraton Waikiki, adjacent to the Royal, where kids 5 to 12 are taken on trips to attractions like the Honolulu Zoo and Waikiki Aquarium. Kids 4 and under eat free with adults.

Sports On-Site: The beachboys at Aloha Beach Services, two doors down, give surfing lessons ($25 per hour) or rides on outrigger canoes ($5 per person) or catamarans ($10 per hour). The gentle, near-shore break is great for boogieboarding; rent a board for $5 a day, or buy one at any ABC Store for about $20–$40. For snorkeling, pick Dream Cruises; its 100-foot yacht comes equipped with a waterslide and floating trampoline (3½-hour cruise with lunch; adults, $60; age 4 to 17, $30; under 4, free; call 808-592-5200).

Farther Afield: Rent a car and make a loop of the island, beginning with an early visit to **Hanauma Bay**, 10 miles from Waikiki in Oahu's southeastern corner. This snorkeling magnet is mobbed by 9 A.M., so get there by 8 and you'll see dinner plate–size parrot fish and butterfly fish in waist-deep water. Keep the ocean on your right side as you drive around Koko Head to **Kailua Beach Park** on the windward side, where **Kailua Sailboards & Kayaks** (in the shopping center on Kailua Road) rents kayaks ($28 per day; doubles $39) and windsurfing rigs ($30 per day; $39 for a 3-hour lesson).

Kids over 7 will enjoy the relatively flat, hour-long hike just south of Laie along the muddy, ferny banks of Kaluanui Stream that takes you to **Sacred Falls**, a thrilling 80-foot stream tumbling through a cleft in the Koolau Mountains. Pull into the marked parking lot and take the 1.3-mile trail to the dirt path. It's another 0.7 miles to the falls. Be sure to drop a leaf in the water to appease the resident *mo'o* (legendary giant lizards who are said to live at the bottom of deep lakes and swamps) before jumping in. For tougher, guided hikes into the mountains, the **Hawaii Nature Center** (808-955-0100) and **Sierra Club** (808-538-6616) lead groups every weekend for a nominal charge.

Booking Information: Rates at the Royal run $290–$490 per night for a double or $475 for a junior garden suite. There is no charge for kids under 18 staying in the same room as their parents. Call 800-325-3535 for additional information.

Another Option: On the north shore, the **Turtle Bay Hilton** (ocean-view doubles, $175–$215; under 17 free with parents) is a bit worn, but is quieter than Waikiki. Call 800-445-8667 for reservations and information.

Hyatt Regency
Kauai

Claim to Fame: As the northernmost Hawaiian island, Kauai is the first stop for the world's howling winds and crashing waves, and thus has some of the most amazing eroded landscapes on the planet.

The Hyatt Regency Kauai in Poipu on the south side is a handsome place where you'll find the best beach, spa, bar, and pool complex on the island. The waterslide, river-current pool, action pool with basketball and volleyball, and hidden Jacuzzis keep kids 5 and up busy, and parents with smaller kids love the shallow, sand-bottomed lagoon. Classes on poi-pounding and lei-making are offered by a local *hula halau* (school), and Camp Hyatt Kauai ($45 per day for kids 3 to 12, including lunch), stresses history and ecology through nature treks and guided hikes of the resort's archaeological sites.

Sports On-Site: Rent snorkels and fins ($5 per day) and kayaks ($7.50 per hour) at the poolside kiosk. Free guided hikes are offered every other Monday morning to prehistoric native Hawaiian settlements alongside the property.

Farther Afield: A 3-hour horseback tour with **CJM Country Stables** ($71; 808-742-6096) explores **Mahaulepu**, the craggy, untraveled southeastern corner of the island. Or rent bikes from **Outfitters Kauai** at Poipu Plaza ($20–$33 per day; 808-742-9667) and ride past **Poipu Beach Park,** which has fine snorkeling on the rocky sides, to the **Spouting Horn,** a startling gusher that funnels waves from an undersea lava tube into a narrow crack in the rocks. Farther west, Joshua Rudinoff of **Kauai Coasters** leads a morning bike ride that descends 12 miles and more than 2,500 feet along the rim of stark, red-cliffed **Waimea Canyon** ($65; minimum age 12; 808-639-2412). Nearby, at **Kokee State Park,** there are great hikes along

HIRED HANDS

Ocean Voyages (800-299-4444) offers customized 7-day island-to-island all-inclusive sailing trips aboard a 50-foot sloop; you decide when to go and where to stop. Rates start at $4,995 for a family of four.

- -

REI Adventures (800-622-2236) leads a 7-day Kauai Island Paradise trip that includes sea kayaking along the Na Pali coast, snorkeling among spinning dolphins and sea turtles, and hiking and mountain biking in the Kokee highlands. Departures are June 22–28 and August 3–9; cost is $1,195 per person; recommended minimum age is 14 (no discounts for kids).

- -

American Wilderness Experience (800-444-0099) accepts travelers of all ages on its 10-day Land of Aloha Three Island Adventure. Highlights include hiking on Kauai along the Na Pali coast and the rim of Waimea canyon; swimming and snorkeling, plus hiking in Haleakala crater on Maui; and exploring Kilauea Iki crater and the Waipio Valley on the Big Island. Departures are June 22, July 6 and 27, and August 17; cost is $1,595 (no discounts for kids).

trails that hug the ridge overlooking the Na Pali Coast or descend into muddy, boggy Alakai Swamp. With its 486 inches of annual rainfall, Alakai is famous as the wettest place on earth.

Paddling the **Na Pali Coast** on the north shore, an hour's drive from Poipu, is completely *ono* (great, bitchin', wicked, cool) in summer, when winter's 30-foot waves have stopped smashing into the coastline. For families with kids 16 and up, **Kayak Kauai** leads an all-day, 15-mile paddle ($130 per person; 808-826-9844) past hanging valleys, stark cliffs, and sea caves that you can paddle into. Kids under 16 can take a tour with **Captain Zodiac** (adults, $58–$120; $10–$20 discount for kids 4 to 12; 808-826-9371) that explores the coastline in rubber motorcraft. Just south of Princeville, on **Anini Beach**, rent windsurfers from **Anini Beach Windsurfing** (3-hour lessons, $65; rental, $50 per day; 808-826-9463).

Booking Information: Double rooms at the Hyatt Regency Kauai (800-233-1234) go for $365–$415 per night, or $485 for a Regency Club room with continental breakfast, free evening cocktails, and a dedicated concierge service.

Another Option: The **Kiahuna Plantation**, also in Poipu, sits on 35 oceanfront acres with manicured gardens. One-bedroom units ($175–$400) come with kitchens. Call 800-462-6262.

Kona Village
The Big Island

Claim to Fame: Great. You came all the way to the Big Island, only to find a smashed-up parking lot of jagged lava that stretches north from Keahole-Kona Airport for miles. Don't sweat it; there are wonderful resort oases hidden

Say Aloha to Kids' Camps

The idea of a family vacation is, of course, to do things as a family. But even the most dedicated parents need some time to themselves, as do their kids. While kids' programs at many resorts are just glorified baby-sitting services, in Hawaii they're something special. Programs emphasize Hawaiian history, culture, and geography with a whole range of activities—nature walks, sand-volcano building, tide-pool exploration, petroglyph walks, native Hawaiian storytelling, and Hawaiian arts and crafts like lei-making, poi-pounding, and leaf-painting.

At the **Maui Prince Hotel** (800-321-6284) in Makena, kids 5 to 12 can join the Prince Kids Club, with bamboo-pole fishing, scavenger hunts, and Hawaiian arts and crafts (half-day, $20; full day, $40 including lunch). For an additional $20, special items can be purchased such as a disposable camera and photo album with T-shirt and tote bag, or a beach package that contains a straw mat, sunscreen, towel, T-shirt, and a tote bag.

Maui's **Kapalua Bay Resort** (800-367-8000) offers Junior Golf Clinics from the end of March through August, Family Tennis Clinics, and individual lessons for kids 4 to 17. It also has an on-site art school that offers weekly kids' classes in the visual and performing arts, including painting, photography, and drama (about $10–$20 per class). Parents can join their kids in ballet, yoga, and piano classes. Kamp Kapalua features activities like a sand-castle contest, swimming and snorkeling, and nature hikes ($25 for one kid; $45 for two, 9 A.M. to 1 P.M., including lunch).

On Oahu, the **Hilton Hawaiian Village** (800-445-8667) conducts kids' wildlife tours of its lagoon filled with flamingos, carp, and penguins, stressing interesting facts about the water, plants, rocks, and foliage of Hawaii. Kids receive a Wildlife and Ecology certificate and a souvenir photo taken at the penguin pond. The Rainbow Express Young Explorers Club offers Hawaiian arts and crafts, nature walks and wildlife feeding, and fishing expeditions ($32 per day, including lunch).

The **Princeville Resort** (800-782-9488) on Kauai has an in-house theater that screens locally filmed movies like *South Pacific* for its Keiki Aloha program (free from June 15–August 31; otherwise $40 per day). On Friday nights, kids get dinner and a movie for $10.

On the Big Island, **Camp Menehune** ($45 per day for kids 5 to 12) at the sprawling Hilton Waikoloa Village Resort (800-445-8667) emphasizes special events like Indiana Jones Day and Olympic sports. Its Coconut Club for teens 13 to 17 has free sports—water polo, beach volleyball—and social activities like the Splash Bash ($10).

At the **Mauna Kea Beach Hotel and Hapuna Beach Prince Hotel** (800-882-6060), also on the Big Island, the program for kids 5 to 12 (half-day, $20; full day, $40) includes T-shirt painting, treasure-hunting, swimming, and fishing.

Down the road at the **Orchid at Mauna Lani** (800-845-9905), the Keiki Aloha program offers hula lessons, storytelling, trips to a petroglyph park, and coconut-leaf weaving for kids 5 to 12 ($50 per day). —JIM GULLO

among the lava fields, the water is spectacularly blue and alive, and you can use up every last calorie having fun in the out-of-doors.

Your base is Kona Village, 5 miles north of the airport on the site of an ancient Hawaiian fishing village. Secluded and unpretentious, the Village has comfortable thatch-roof huts along a small beach, great restaurants, and only one television and VCR in the whole place. Your kids can learn how to throw fishing nets, hook carp in the resort's pond, and paint coconuts in the free Na Keiki in Paradise program (for ages 6 to 12).

Backpacking Maui's Haleakala National Park

The Hawaiian Islands are famous as repositories of rare and unique life-forms and landscapes, but Maui's Haleakala Crater—7½ miles long, 2½ miles wide, and 3,000 feet deep—is unlike any other place on earth. Throughout the crater, you'll see interesting adaptations like Hawaiian snow, a lichen that was the first plant to grow on lava and begin the process of breaking down the rocks to soil.

With older kids, enter via the Sliding Sands Trail on the crater rim at 9,800 feet. The first day is the most strenuous: The trail plunges more than 3,000 feet, and if you can't get reservations for the cabin at Kapalaoa, it's a 10-mile hike to the campground at Paliku (permit required; first-come, first-served). But, once there, you can stay 2 nights and explore this least-visited side of the crater. Hike out via the Halemauu Trail—it's much easier. From Paliku it's 7½ miles to the campsite at Holua; from there you've only got another 4 miles to the parking lot at Halemauu. With smaller children, it's best to do this hike as an in-and-out from the Halemauu parking lot; the daily mileage is lower, with less-drastic elevation changes.

Things to Do: From the tropical oasis of Paliku, hike to Kawilinau (formerly called the Bottomless Pit), a 65-foot-deep spatter vent, and take note of Pele's Paint Pot, a natural mosaic of colored ash and lava. Near Holua you can walk the Silversword Loop, one of the best growing areas of the threatened silversword. A beautiful succulent that's native only to Haleakala Crater, it grows for years before shooting up a beautiful purple flower—then it dies.

Local Wisdom: You'll need warm sleeping bags (night temperatures drop into the 30s or 40s) and sturdy hiking shoes, as the hard, ropy lava here can destroy sandals or tennies. You'll also need a good tent with a fly, as rain falls heavily in places.

The Way There: From the airport at Kahului, it's 40 miles and 10,000 vertical feet to the rim of the crater along the Haleakala Highway; just follow the Haleakala signs. Check in at park headquarters for permits; then head for the trailhead, which starts farther up the road at the Visitor Center.

Resources: For maps and trail information, or to enter the lottery for the backcountry cabins (3 months in advance), contact **Haleakala National Park** at 808-572-9306. Permits are required for all overnight stays, and visitors are limited to 3 nights in the crater per month, or 2 nights at any one campsite.

—ANDREW RICE

Sports On-Site: Explore the bay with snorkels, kayaks, Sunfish and Laser sailboats (free to guests) from the Beach Shack, or go diving ($85 for one tank) or take a snorkel sail ($55). The hotel won't let you stray far from its shores with its gear, so you might want to rent a kayak from **Ocean Safaris Kayak Tours** in Kailua-Kona (singles, $30 per day; doubles, $45; 808-326-4699). From Kona Village paddle north for miles of unobstructed lava coastline with the best blue water and underwater formations in Hawaii. Arrange to have someone pick you up at Kiholo Bay, about 8 miles up the coast, or plan for a tough return paddle into the teeth of the wind and current.

Farther Afield: Hawaiian Walkways (800-457-7759) leads a 4- to 6-mile hiking tour ($110 per person; $90 kids 12 and under) from Anaehoomalu, near the Waikoloa Resort, to the **Kona Coast State Park** on the Ala Kahakai Trail, a shoreline trail through petroglyph fields. **Hawaii Volcanoes National Park,** about 2½-hours from Kona, also has eerie, venting trails and the bizarre Thurston Lava Tube. Call the **eruption hot line** (808-967-7977) to see where the lava is flowing.

Waipio Valley on the Hamakua coast is a carved-out bowl surrounded by sheer cliffs and ocean. Explore it on horseback with **Na'alapa Trail Rides** (2½-hour tour, $75; kids 8 to 14, $65; 808-775-0419), which takes you deep into the valley for views of Hiilawe Falls and taro fields. For a killer paddling trip, **Ocean Safaris Kayak Tours** (808-326-4699) offers a new overnight excursion along the coast from Waipio Valley to Pololu Valley

(starting at $450 per person for 3 days; minimum age 10).

Booking Information: Kona Village rates ($625 per day for two adults) include three meals daily and airport transfers. Kids' rates run $170 for 13 and up; $115 for age 6 to 12; $60 age 2 to 5; $25 for infants. Call 800-367-5290.

Another Option: In the town of Volcano, the **Kilauea Lodge** (two-bedroom cottage, $175 for a family of four, including breakfast; 808-967-7366) is a comfortable inn near Hawaii Volcanoes National Park.

Embassy Suites
Maui

Claim to Fame: Maui gives you the choice of all-in-one-resort convenience, with the option of escaping to some remote and dazzlingly lovely corners where you can kick back in peace, away from the crowds.

In west Maui, the Kaanapali Resort is a stretch of high-rise hotels fronting a 3-mile strip of manicured sand. Check out the Embassy Suites, a big, pink pyramid on the far-north side of the beach. Accommodations are one-bedroom suites equipped with kitchenettes and big-screen TVs with cable and VCR; full breakfast is included. There's a 1-acre pool, a fitness center, and golf and tennis nearby. Kids 4 to 10 can enroll in the Beach Buddies Children's Program ($20 per day including lunch and a T-shirt) and learn how to count in Hawaiian, take nature walks, and go beachcombing.

Sports On-Site: Grab snorkels, seacycles, sailboards, or kayaks at the beach activities desk (charges vary) and head south inside the barrier reef. To the north are rocky coves and the rugged seaside cliffs of the Kapalua Resort.

Farther Afield: Take a 45-minute catamaran cruise from Lahaina across the Auau Channel to **Club Lanai,** where you can spend the day snorkeling, kayaking, or mountain biking. The $79–$89 tariff includes lunch and equipment; call 808-667-4000.

You can hike into the crater of **Haleakala,** the dormant volcano (see "Backpacking Maui's Haleakala National Park"), or traverse it on horseback with **Pony Express,** which leads a daily 7½-mile trip down into the crater ($120 per person; 808-667-2200).

Explore Maui's desolate southwestern shore on a 3-hour kayak tour with **South Pacific Kayaks and Outfitters** ($55; 808-875-4848) that paddles around **Puu Olai,** a shoreline cinder cone, to **Oneloa Beach** (also known as Big Beach).

Booking Information: A one-bedroom suite at Embassy Suites runs $265–$335 per night for up to four people; call 800-669-3155.

Another Option: The **Silver Cloud Upcountry Guest Ranch,** on the slopes of Haleakala in Kula, is a B&B with stunning ocean views ($95–$135 per couple, plus $15 per child 5 and up, for a bunkhouse with kitchenette; call 808-878-6101).

Molokai Ranch
Molokai

Claim to Fame: If you're having trouble deciding what kind of vacation you want—a tropical beach getaway, a safari, mountain biking, horseback riding, or camping—the answer is simple: Go to Molokai. At Molokai Ranch, a 53,000-acre complex stretching from up-country ranchland to the ocean, you can have it all. Families stay in two-unit tents mounted on wooden platforms with solar-powered water and lights and self-composting toilets, or in two-person yurts right on the beach.

Sports On-Site: There are daily jeep tours of the ranch's 350-acre wildlife park where zebras, giraffes, elands, and barbary sheep roam through a landscape reminiscent of Africa's savannah. You can also take a guided horse trek; hike or bike more than 30 miles of trails; sea kayak and snorkel among green sea turtles, angelfish, and anemones; or attend a *paniolo* (Hawaiian cowboy) rodeo.

Booking Information: Prices are $154 per adult per night, $85 for each additional person (full price in two-person yurts), including airport transfers, all meals, and one activity per day. Kayaks, surfboards, mountain bikes, and snorkel gear can be rented from the ranch's Outfitters Center. Extra cots and sleeping bags are available for an additional $30. For more information and reservations, call 800-254-8871.

—JIM GULLO

19

Thirty-four years later, we still talk about it in mythical terms: The Trip to England. I was 16 and my sister Becky 14 when our midwestern family boarded the S.S. *United States* and sailed for Southampton. We saw 500-year-old cathedrals, funny little cars that drove on the wrong side of the road, and people with strange accents who were entirely ignorant of the Chicago Cubs.

Going Abroad

It's a Big, Big, Big, Big World

For a clean-cut suburban Hoosier kid, it was a life-changing experience. Horizons irrevocably broadened, I applied to Stanford instead of settling for the small Indiana college I'd been thinking about. (To my astonishment, I was accepted.) I developed a passion for travel that has taken me to every continent, shaped my career, and enriched my life beyond measure. It all started, I'm convinced, with that family trip to England. Every kid should be so lucky.

We can help. Listed below are twenty international trips, all fully outfitted and guided, all family-friendly in their physical demands and logistics. Most, in fact, are specifically tailored for kids, with special programs and staff. Sure, these trips are expensive, especially when you add international airfare. So put off the new minivan for a few years and drop the personal trainer. Instead, spend that money on something really important, something your kids will still be talking about in the year 2031.

AFRICA

To a child, an African vacation is a 2-week trip to the world's biggest zoo, a special kind of zoo where the animals have the run of the place while the humans are confined in steel boxes. The appeal of wild animals—name a kid who doesn't adore Simba, Bambi, and Bagheera—makes Africa perhaps the ultimate international destination for kids.

In East Africa, **National Audubon Society's** quickie 12-day Kenyan safari includes the obligatory visit to Masai Mara Game Reserve, plus a stay at Shaba National Wildlife Reserve. A Young Explorers program for kids 8 to 17 includes a lecture by Philip Leakey (son of Mary and Louis) and a visit to the home of Karen Blixen, a.k.a. Isak Dinesen, author of *Out of Africa*. **Born Free Safaris'** 15-day Hakuna Matata Family Safari takes in Masai Mara and Amboseli parks, plus Tanzania's Ngorongoro Crater. There's plenty of kid stuff: camel rides, giraffe feeding, baby-animal orphanages, and even a tree-house hotel. Families are grouped according to their kids' ages.

At $1,950 for adults, **Journeys International's** 13-day Tanzania Family Safari is only about half the price of the other trips listed here ($1,450 for kids under 12). The price is kept low by the lack of internal plane flights, stays in modest lodges, and the use of local guides. (However, this summer's trip will be accompanied by Journeys' owners, who are bringing along their kids.) The itinerary includes 2 days each in the Serengeti and Ngorongoro Crater.

Luxo-outfitter **Abercrombie & Kent** runs a 15-day Kenyan Family Safari that hits the traditional wildlife high spots: the Masai Mara Game Reserve, Amboseli and Aberdare parks, and Samburu. Kids are given the opportunity to hand feed giraffes, explore an ostrich farm and a baby-animal orphanage, and visit Masai and Samburu village schools. Although somewhat expensive for adults, the A&K trip is discounted for teens. (Most outfitters charge adult rates for age 12 and above.)

Micato Safaris' 14-day Family Safari visits Masai Mara and Samburu, as well as several off-the-beaten-path wildlife reserves. In addition to the usual giraffe feeding and ostrich-farm visit, Micato kids visit with Masai students at Sister Jenny's school in the bush.

In Southern Africa, **Family Explorations** offers a 21-day safari through Namibia and Botswana. High spots include visits to Etosha National Park, Victoria Falls, and 1 week exploring the Okavango Delta.

The Details: National Audubon Society, 212-979-3066; adults, $4,195; kids 8 to 17, $1,995–$2,295; departure, July 5. **Born Free Safaris,** 800-372-3274; adults, $3,899; kids under 12, $2,350; seven departures, June 6–August 8. **Journeys International,** 800-255-8735; adults, $1,950; kids under 12, $1,450; departure, June 27. **Abercrombie & Kent,** 800-323-7308; adults, $4,305; kids under 18, $2,805–$2,935; four departures, July 4–August 15. **Micato Safaris,** 800-642-2861; adults, $3,575; kids under 12, $2,555; five departures, June 23–August 18. **Family Explorations,** 800-934-6866; adults and kids, about $150 per person per day; departure dates can be customized for individual families.

AUSTRALIA

From a child's perspective, Australia must seem straight out of Lewis Carroll: animals with pockets, a sun that moves backwards across the sky, cowboys who ride camels. **Abercrombie & Kent** and **Journeys International** offer similar family itineraries that include Sydney, the outback, the Great Barrier Reef, and the Queensland rain forest. On both trips, kids can ride boats, horses, camels, and mountain bikes, snorkel, explore caves, climb Ayers Rock, and feed baby kangaroos. The upscale A&K trip, at 15 days, is a bit longer and a lot more expensive, and features a 3-day stay at a beach resort on Hayman Island. Alternatively, Journeys' kids stay 2 nights at a working cattle ranch in the outback.

The Details: Abercrombie & Kent, 800-323-7308; adults, $4,872; children under 18, $2,712–$4,702; departure, August 9. **Journeys International,** 800-255-8735; adults, $3,395; kids under 15, $1,745; departure, August 2.

EUROPE

For many kids, the rich cultural heritage of Europe—its treasures of history, art, music, and architecture—can be described in one word: Boooooring. (My mom still smugly reminds me of a comment I made during our trip to England: "What's so great about Stonehenge?")

Europe needs to be jazzed up, disguised as a bike trip or a rock-climbing school or a boat cruise. Distracted by all the fun stuff, your kids might just absorb a little culture by osmosis.

A bike trip is great for kids; it keeps them focused and wears them out. **Backroads** offers a low-mileage (30 miles per day average) 8-day family bike trip in France's Dordogne River Valley. Kid-size bikes are available for rent, as are enclosed Burley bike trailers to haul the toddlers. Cyclists stay overnight in European-style car-camp-grounds, which are typically equipped with showers, laundry facilities, and swimming pools—not to mention swarms of French and German kids. Backroads offers discounts ranging from 10 to 40 percent for kids traveling with two adults.

For a less strenuous trip, try **Brooks Country Cycling**'s 8-day bike-and-barge trip in the flatlands of Holland. A refurbished canal barge serves as a floating lodge while guests cycle past castles and windmills, usually along car-free bike paths. Shipboard quarters are a bit snug, but if you're 4 feet tall, who cares? Discounts for kids run from 10 to 75 percent.

If you like a challenge, **Adventures to the Edge**, a Colorado guide service with a family connection in Switzerland, can customize a family hiking/climbing vacation in the Swiss Alps for kids as young as 7. A typical trip might include a 5-day hut-to-hut hike—including a glacier walk—from Champex to Chamonix, followed by 2 days of rock-climbing lessons on the granite Aguilles of Chamonix.

Maybe your kid is more bird-watcher than needle-climber; The **National Audubon Society** runs an 8-day island-hopping cruise through the Stockholm Archipelago, a traditional haven for Swedish family outings. The restored ex-ferryboat has bikes and fishing poles on board. And if your kids think Grandma's house is really old, wait till they stay in Gripsholms Vardshus and Hotel, which dates back to 1609.

The Details: Backroads, 800-462-2848; adults, $1,198; kids under 18, $719–$1,078; departure, July 8. **Brooks Country Cycling**, 212-874-5151; adults, $934–$998; kids 10–75 percent off; departures, weekly all summer. **Adventures to the Edge**, 800-349-5219; group rate with two adults, two kids, $5,035; custom departures. **National Audubon Society**, 212-979-3066; adults, $2,580; kids 7 to 16, $1,290; departure, June 1.

THE GALÁPAGOS ISLANDS

If Africa is the anti-zoo—animals roaming free, people in cages—the Galápagos might be called the unzoo. Everybody roams free. Because the islands' wildlife—tortoises, seals, sea lions, iguanas, and blue-footed boobies—are harmless and have no fear of humans, the odds are very good for nose-to-snout encounters right out of *The Jungle Book*. If your child loves the water, so much the better, since most trips include daily swimming and snorkeling. But slightly hyperactive kids may feel a bit cooped up on the small ships that are the only way to reach the islands.

Discovery Tours, operated by the American Museum of Natural History, will run an 11-day family Galápagos trip this summer that welcomes kids as young as 7. Discovery's ultramodern 90-passenger mini-cruise ship will call at ten islands, with plenty of time allotted for numerous shore excursions and day hikes. A special Youth Coordinator will arrange all kinds of activities to occupy kids while the adults attend the regular shipboard lectures offered by various museum experts. Discounts for kids 15 and under range from about 10 to 25 percent.

If you're looking for a more intimate experience, **Wilderness Travel** offers Galápagos cruises from 8 to 13 days aboard your choice of two 12-passenger sailing yachts. Sit-on-top kayaks are available for coastal exploring. Wilderness has no family program as such, but does make an effort to steer families with children under 12 to specific departures. There are no special discounts for children, however.

Mountain Travel–Sobek offers 10- and 13-day cruises on a variety of 8- to 14-passenger sailing and motor yachts. There are no special family programs, but $200 discounts for kids 18 and under are available on the most economical ship, the *Beagle III*, which has shared baths but no air conditioning.

If your child has a special interest in zoology, consider the 11-day Galápagos trip offered by **Nature Expeditions International**, which specializes in wildlife-oriented trips all over the world. The company puts a special emphasis on education, with daily on-board lectures and expert Ph.D. trip leaders.

The Details: Discovery Tours, 800-462-8687; adults, $3,210–$4,030; kids 7 to 15, $2,260–$3,595; departure, July 1.

Wilderness Travel, 800-368-2794; adults/kids, $1,850–$3,495; 27 departures, June through August. **Mountain Travel–Sobek,** 800-227-2384; adults, $1,895–$2,595; kids, $1,695–$2,595; eight departures, June through August; the *Beagle III* will depart June 16, July 21, and August 18. **Nature Expeditions International,** 800-869-0639; adults/kids, $2,490; departures on July 3, August 7.

COSTA RICA

Got kids who are budding environmentalists? There's no better place to take them than this hotbed of biodiversity, which has 2,000 species of trees, 1,500 species of orchids, 850 of birds, and 35,000 different kinds of insects. You'll see monkeys, sloths, peccaries, tree frogs—maybe even a jaguar. Best of all, Costa Rica is very accessible—relatively close to home, with the world's most progressive national park system.

Family Explorations has two Costa Rican itineraries and a choice of family togetherness quotients. The 9-day Discovery trip includes Arenal Volcano, Monteverde Cloud Forest Reserve, and a 4-day cruise along Costa Rica's Pacific coast. There's a full-time leader for separate children's activities. The 9-day Adventure itinerary substitutes the Carara Biological Reserve for the cruise and dispenses with the kids' programs. On both trips, children under 12 get a 15- to 45-percent discount. **Journeys International's** Natural Wonders Week is a whirlwind 8-day tour of Tortuguero National Park,

Arenal, and the dry tropical forest in Guanacaste. Departures can be customized, or you can join a multi-family group departure on July 19. Kids' discount is 35 percent.

Abercrombie & Kent's 10-day family tour includes a nature walk in the Monteverde Cloud Forest, a river float trip (minimum age 6; day care available for kids 5 and under), bird-watching lessons, tours of a butterfly farm, local school visits, and a rain forest canopy ride. Kids under 12 get a 20-percent discount. **Natural Habitat,** a nature-trip specialist, offers a 10-day family program to Arenal, Monteverde, and Carara. Kids under 12 get a discount of about 20 percent.

The Details: Family Explorations, 800-934-6866; adults, $1,750–$1,800; kids under 12, $1,000–$1,500; Discovery departure, July 8; Adventure departure, August 15. **Journeys International,** 800-255-8735; adults, $1,525; kids under 12, $990; departure June 19, or custom anytime. **Abercrombie & Kent,** 800-323-7308; adults, $2,515; kids under 12, $2,065; departure, July 18. **Natural Habitat,** 800-543-8917; adults, $1,895; kids under 12, $1,495; departure, August 1. —DAVID NOLAND

20

Ask any good trail dog: When slopes get steep and rocks get slick, full-time four-paw drive is a very nice option. But a hyperactive nose and ceaseless imagination are just as crucial. Dogs live to smell. And the outsideworld is one giant snifforama. This point struck home one day as I

Come Along, Little Doggie

watched Lucy, my young Labrador re-cliner, stop abruptly along a trail she had trod at least 300 times. Transfixed, Lucy dropped her snout and inhaled deeply, as if savoring a fine cabernet. Lucy has sniffed a billion rocks. But she'd never had a good whiff of this particular one. That is precisely what makes back-country trips with a canine companion so rewarding. Over time, people begin to take wild places—even new ones—for granted. But for a dog, every scramble into the bush is the first time, part 844. That glint in the eye at every switchback can render wet trails drier, evil winds friendlier, lonely places homier. But for successful backcountry tromping you need to abide by some basic rules, most of which Lucy and I learned the hard way:

✦ Don't overdo it at first. Older dogs probably have spent too many evenings watching zebras on the Discovery Channel to take on a 27-mile backpack trek. Just like people, dogs need to build up muscle strength and footpad-toughness for long hikes. Pick a short trail not too far from home and let her build her stamina.

✦ Practice commands. Working on voice control will pay big dividends later, when you might be hiking on trails filled with people, llamas, horses, and other dogs. If the dog is on a leash, a well-learned "wait" command is key. An untrained dog will clear an obstacle such as a deadfall or rock in a stream, and then plunge ahead, pulling you off balance right when you're teetering on top of it.

✦ Make it a habit to carry water for two or three. Dogs often drink more than people, and you won't always be near streams or other convenient water stops, particularly in midsummer.

✦ Let your dog shoulder some of the burden. Dogs in good condition can carry 30 percent of their body weight. A proper-fitting pack is essential (see "Canine Couture"). Don't forget to re-move it before your dog crosses streams or other obstacles.

✦ Create a designated sleeping spot for your dog inside the tent with a roll-up mat or burlap bag as a bed away from home.

✦ Be patient, or failing that, learn to embrace your dog's unsinkable zeal for all things outdoors. Five minutes after discovering her irresistible rock on our walk that day, Lucy spotted another one behind me, raced to sniff it, and hog-tied my legs with her leash. I stumbled and fell, smacking my head on a stump. Cursing, I looked up and saw Lucy's upside-down snout, nose working madly. I could almost read the delight in her eyes. "Dufus." Sniff. Sniff. Sniff. "Excellent!"

—Ron C. Judd

Finding a good place to unleash your dog in the wilds can sometimes be risky business, given the hundreds of differing rules for thousands of public lands. We polled dog owners for a few legally sanctioned canine favorites.

Boulder
Colorado

Boulder's hardy hikers, climbers, and bikers rave about the 33,000 acres of public open space and 131 miles of trails around the city—most of which are open to dogs on voice control. Residents note that the Third Flatiron, Boulder's most famous climbing rock, has been summitted by more than one four-legged climber. **Information:** City of Boulder Mountain Parks, 303-441-3400.

The Sky Lakes Wilderness
southern Oregon

South of Crater Lake National Park, Sky Lakes' 110 miles of trails lead through spectacular glacier-carved lake basins, and the Pacific Crest Trail cuts north–south for 30 miles through the 7,113-acre wilderness. Dogs are permitted off leash (voice-control rules apply), and hikers are advised to avoid the mosquito-plagued month of July. **Information:** Rogue River National Forest, 541-858-2200.

Pasayten Wilderness
North Cascades, Washington

This high, dry, 530,000-acre wilderness in the North Cascades is crisscrossed by 740 miles of trails, all of which are open to dogs under voice control. But don't let the pooch stray too far as a large lynx population lives here. **Information:** Okanogan National Forest, 509-996-4003.

Tilden Park
Berkeley, California

Here's one for the day-tripping crowd. Tilden, which allows dogs off leash on trails and in fields, has fast become the favorite escape of Bay Area dog owners. This large East Bay park has miles of hiking trails with expansive bay views, and even a lake for dog-paddling. **Information:** Tilden Park, 510-562-7275.

—RON C. JUDD

FIRST AID FOR FIDO

What can you do when you're miles from the nearest vet and your dog gets a seed in his eye or a cut on his paw? Never leave home without *A Field Guide: Dog First Aid* by Randy Acker, D.V.M., and Jim Fergus. This 4 x 6 inch spiral-bound pocket guide covers symptoms and treatments for a slew of problems your pup can get into in the big outdoors ($15, plus $4 shipping and handling, Wilderness Adventures Press; 800-925-3339).

—LAURA BILLINGS

DIGS FOR DOGS

To avoid getting the sniff-and-circle routine from hotel clerks when you unpack the Pit bull, we recommend the following guides: Frommer's *On the Road Again with Man's Best Friend*, by Dawn and Robert Habgood ($14.95, Howell Book House/Macmillan Publishing; 800-428-5331), profiles inns, hotels, B&Bs, and resorts that roll out the canine welcome mat; regional titles cover the Mid-Atlantic, New England, and the West Coast. *Vacationing with Your Pet!* by Eileen Barish ($19.95, plus shipping and handling, Pet-Friendly Publications; 800-496-2665), covers some 20,000 pro-dog lodgings in the U.S. and Canada. Just out from the same publisher: *Doin' California with Your Pooch!* and *Doin' Arizona with Your Pooch!*   —LAURA BILLINGS

NEWS FROM THE FIELD

The Roving Reporter position at the travel newsletter "DogGone" is staffed by Sparky, a Beagle who confers his "tails-up seal of approval" upon destinations featured in this bimonthly. For travel tips on hotels, national parks, resorts, and restaurants that actually welcome your dog, plus first-paw accounts of great trips, subscribe to "DogGone" ($24 per year, including a one-time personalized travel consultation; call 407-569-8434 for more information).   —LAURA BILLINGS

CANINE COUTURE

You'd never want to be caught up a long trail without the proper rain slicker, boots, or mess kit. Neither would your favorite quad-pod friend. Here's what's new in canine adventure gear.

Dog Packs: Most serious dog hikers consider them essential, because they allow Butch to pack his own grub, sup-plies, and family vacation guides. **Wolf Packs'** handmade packs come in a number of sizes, and range from the simple **Cordura Trekker Reflector** ($54.50), to the full bells-and-whistles **Banzai Explorer** ($69.50), which has ballistic-cloth sides to ward off prickly brush, and fleece-padded buckles (call 541-482-7669). **Caribou's Woofer I, II,** and **III** packs ($24–$30, 800-824-4153), with rounded corners to avoid snares, are good no-frills choices. **Wenaha's Explorer II** ($64.95; 206-488-2397) comes in two pieces: a harness consisting of straps and webbing, and a separate saddlebag that attaches with Velcro. **Mountainsmith**'s durable, saddle-style dog's backpack comes with wide polypropylene webbing to prevent chafing; a chew-resistant, double-layer Cordura bottom; and room enough for him to carry up to a third of his weight safely ($62–$82, Mountain-smith; 800-426-4075).

The Portable Bowl: Raise your hand if you've ever tried to rehydrate Old Jake by squirting water from a water bottle toward his confused jaws. Solve the problem with a collapsible nylon water bowl/supper dish. We particularly like the big, bombproof **Oasis Bowl** by Ruff Wear, a 2½-quart Cordura model sold by **Wolf Packs** ($15.50; 541-482-7669). It folds up nicely, dries quickly, and in a pinch, serves as an emergency dork rain hat. Or try the **Travel-N-Pet Bowl,** which inflates to 8 inches around, 3 inches high at feeding time, then deflates easily to fit in your pack ($6, **P.S. I Love You**; 212-727-2390).

Seat Savers: Getting a trail-soaked dog back home can wreak havoc on

Canine Summer Camp

For some, family travel means packing the sunscreen, the car seat, and the baby wipes; for others, it means packing the flea powder and the retractable leash. Hundreds who share that special breed of puppy love converge each year at **Camp Gone to the Dogs,** one of a growing number of travel retreats for the four-legged. Held on the grounds of Vermont's Putney School, the weeklong camp is designed entirely around entertaining your pet. Campers can sign up for doggie swimming lessons, the doggie steeplechase, and the weenie retrieve. There is also doggie square dancing, leash- and bandanna-decorating classes, and a "Senility Agility" competition. And dogs even get to catcall at a climactic hoochie-poochie fest—the doggie swimsuit contest. Small children aren't allowed (they tend to spook unfamiliar dogs), but teenagers are welcome. Camp dates are in late June and early July; the cost is about $700, including accommodations for you and your dog in a dorm room or nearby B&B or cabin. Call 802-387-5673.   —LAURA BILLINGS

your car. **Auto Seat Savers (Kramer Products**; 541-683-6539) are urethane-treated nylon slipcovers sized to fit full bench seats ($59.95) or bucket seats ($34.95). They come in four colors to match dogs and interiors.

Bowser-Boost: When your terrier scrambles around the car like a greyhound around a racetrack, give him what he really needs—a view. **O'Donnell's booster seat** has a lambswool interior to keep his perspective heightened and a seat-belt slot to keep his perch in place ($54.95, O'Donnell Industries; 800-635-9755).

Booties: Dogs putting in heavy-duty miles—or walking through inhospitable terrain such as snow or hot sand—suffer from the same foot failures we do, and then some. Cracked pads are a common problem. Better booties have tough Cordura shells, fleece-padded liners and Velcro tighteners. **Wolf Packs' Summer Pad Protectors** ($14 for all four wheels) have a dual layer of tough ballistic nylon on the soles and come in ten colors and four sizes (541-482-7669). If you think your dog would die of embarrassment and chew booties off, consider **"Musher's Secret Paw Wax,"** a sled-dog product from **Eco Pak Canada** ($12 for 200 grams; 514-953-1218).

Life Jackets: We know what you're thinking—the dog swims better than you do. But a boat spill far from shore or in cold, fast water can leave even a strong-swimming dog in peril. The **Pet PFD** from **Boundary Waters** ($18; 800-223-6565) is cheap insurance. It'll keep a dog afloat, and comes equipped with a grab-loop for hoisting him back to safety.

Jackets: We suspect any self-respecting trail dog would not be caught dead in one, but fleece-lined jackets are available from **Boundary Waters** for dogs of all sizes. The **Ultrex shell** offers wind and water protection ($34.95; 800-223-6565). —RON C. JUDD

Backcountry Grooming: Your Rottweiler's coat is developing dreadlocks on your wilderness trek, and you're miles from the nearest garden hose. Rub him down with **Petkin Doggywipes,** designed to keep your dog's coat clean and moisturized (three boxes for $14.95, plus $4.95 shipping, **Petkin Pet Care Systems**; 800-738-5461).

—LAURA BILLINGS AND RON C. JUDD

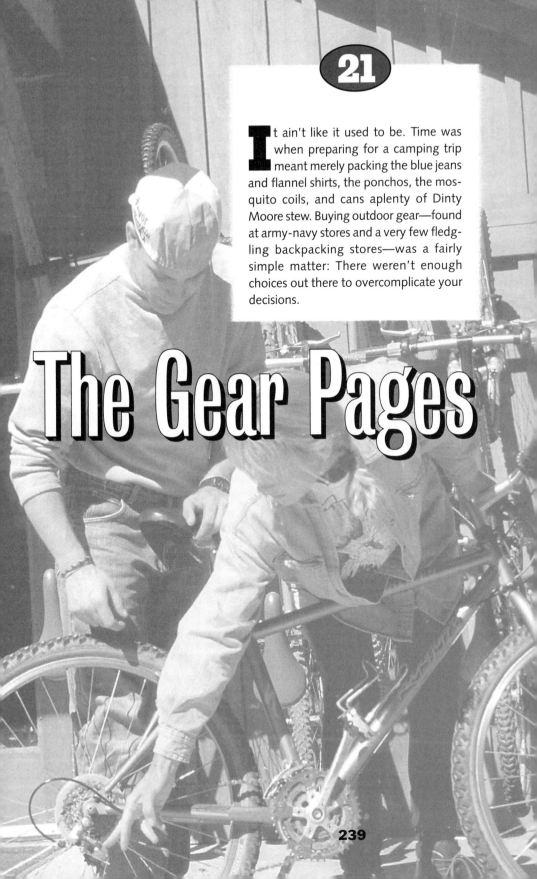

21

It ain't like it used to be. Time was when preparing for a camping trip meant merely packing the blue jeans and flannel shirts, the ponchos, the mosquito coils, and cans aplenty of Dinty Moore stew. Buying outdoor gear—found at army-navy stores and a very few fledgling backpacking stores—was a fairly simple matter: There weren't enough choices out there to overcomplicate your decisions.

The Gear Pages

These days your typical outdoors store displays a mind-numbing array of high tech apparel, equipment, and gadgetry of all manner. It can all cost a lot of money, and the usefulness of some of it to ordinary folk is highly debatable—most families do not need GPS receivers, $3,000 full-suspension bikes, or the same technical outerwear a world-class alpinist would wear on her assault of Everest.

However, though there may be something lamentable about the bells and whistles of all this commerce, a simple truth lurks beneath: Most of today's gear makes getting outside easier, safer, and *much* more comfortable—just more fun, no matter how you slice it. Switching a 50-pound load from a 1970s-vintage external-frame pack to, say, a Dana Designs Terraplane is like trading up from a horse-drawn cart to a Land Rover.

So while a healthy skepticism will do you well as you parse your way through choices, we encourage you to make some investments in your family's outdoor quality-of-life. Herewith some of our favorite gear.

GIMME SHELTER

Tents: If car-camping is as backcountry as your family gets and you're looking for one cavernous tent for the whole gang, **Quest's Odyssey V** tent ($375) is a roomy, tall tent that will sleep a family of five comfortably. It's a classic umbrella-type design, with awnings over the three big mesh windows and door to keep out rain while still allowing good ventilation. Another good choice is **Eureka's Shadowdance 10** with a net enclosure ($660). This tent has a bug-proof front porch, so you can sit and watch the RVs cruise by without being eaten alive.

For bikers, trekkers, and other backcountry travelers, tents best-suited for family camping need to be a little larger than ordinary backpacking tents, so there's room for everyone to crowd in when it rains. But they still need to be light enough to carry. One tactic is to buy two reasonably sized tents so that parents and kids have their own sleeping quarters; if you go this route, there are few better tents than **Sierra Designs's Comet CD** ($365). This roomy tent is a good hangout for Dad, Mom, and two small children, and at 7 pounds, it's easy to carry. The **North Face's** new **Cumulus** ($395) is another three-person-plus tent that offers roominess and durability. Also light is **EMS's Thunderlite** ($200) that weighs just 4 pounds, 11 ounces, and is a good second tent for the kids. But if you choose to buy a single tent that can sleep the whole family, **REI's Camp Dome 6** ($249) is the size of a small house and tall enough for 6-footers to stand upright. **Eureka's Mountain Pass XT 4** ($290) has two covered storage areas for keeping boots and packs out of the rain. And campers on a budget will appreciate **Camp Trails's Escape 4** ($199), which has big, easy-access doors and great ventilation, although its fiberglass poles make it a little heavy (13 pounds). **L.L. Bean's #4 Geo Backcountry** ($280) also isn't light at 12 pounds, 2 ounces, but it's roomy and sturdy. Just tell the kids that carrying a tent is character-building.

Sleeping Bags & Pads: When buying a sleeping bag, your main choice is whether to go with down or synthetic insulation. Down is generally warmer for its weight and lasts longer, while synthetic bags are less expensive and easier to care for (they're washable). Synthetics also dry much faster than down—if you're going to be around the water a lot, this is the way to go.

One excellent synthetic bag is **The North Face's Cat's Meow** ($170–$180), redesigned for 1997 with new Polarguard 3D insulation. The women's version is cut a little shorter overall and wider at the hip. In a down-filled bag, **Sierra Designs's** new **Sundance** ($199) won't bust the budget yet has technical features like a snug-fitting hood and a water-repellent polyester shell. A roomier bag is **Mountain Hardwear's Two Bit Bag with Crazy Legs** ($175) which has an expandable Lycra knee section. Less packable but perhaps more fun and comfy is **Slumberjack's Romeo & Juliet** ($119), a double-bag wide enough for couples. For youngsters, **Slumberjack's Aurora Junior** ($69) is a warm bag that fits kids up to young teens and stuffs down compactly for easy carrying. Slumberjack also makes the traditionally styled **Trapper** sleeping bag ($50)—a roomy, rectangular-cut bag with the requisite plaid flannel liner, good for car-camping. And for little tykes, **Tough Traveler's Baby Bear** ($85) wraps 3-year-olds in a semi-mummy–shaped bag. To keep bags grime-free while being slept in by clammy bodies slathered in mosquito repellent and sunblock, use **Cotton Mummy Bag Liners** ($20–$29) by **Design Salt.**

Nothing is worse than following a hard day's hike with a hard night's rest on lumpy, rocky ground. **Cascade Designs's** self-inflating **Therm-a-Rest Staytek Long** pad ($63) will cushion all but the biggest bumps, yet is light and packable. Lighter still is **Casa Artiach's Skin-Mat Mid Regular** ($63), which has a sticky polyurethane shell so sleeping bags don't slide off. **Slumberjack's Standard Camper** ($60) is a wide, durable self-plumper with its own mesh carrying pouch. And **Basic Designs's Ergomat** ($45) is contoured for comfort and has independent air chambers that can be adjusted for more support. It also has a built-in pillow—and if that isn't enough head cushioning, **Basic Designs's Super-Size Pillow** ($21) will make you think you're back in your own bed. Car-campers, if they so desire, can forget sleeping on the ground: Set up a couple of **L.L. Bean's Allagash** folding cots ($42), made by Byer of Maine. These have sturdy hardwood side panels, four galvanized wire legs that double as carry handles, and a durable polyester cover.

Perhaps no modern camping invention, though, is as welcome as the chair kit, which converts most self-inflating pads into a handy chair for relaxing around camp. **Crazy Creek's Therma-Lounger** ($51) goes with you wrapped around your pad. **Cascade Designs's Therm-a-Rest Sport Seat** ($19) is a light, self-inflating cushion that's useful in the stadium as well. Much less compact but very plush is **Byer's Deluxe Maine Lounger** ($46), a compact, durable chair for the outdoors with a polyester back and soft poly-filled cushion on a flexible, hardwood slat and frame, or a folding camp chair ($36) from **B-West.** Pair one of these with a **Coleman** electronic-ignition two-mantle lantern ($30) and you'll be ready to read the kids some Jack London stories.

Where to Find It: B-West: 800-293-7855; Basic Designs: 800-328-3208; Byer: 800-338-0580; Camp Trails: 888-245-4985; Casa Artiach: 800-569-4110; Cascade Designs: 800-531-9531; Crazy Creek: 800-331-0304; Design Salt: 800-254-7258; EMS: 603-924-6154; Eureka: 888-245-4984; L.L. Bean: 800-341-4341; Quest: 800-875-6901; REI, 800-426-4840; Sierra Designs: 800-736-8592; Slumberjack: 800-233-6283; The North Face: 800-447-2333; Tough Traveler: 800-468-6844.—DOUGLAS GANTENBEIN

THE OUTDOOR KITCHEN

Stoves: Ah, dinnertime. Hungry kids are unhappy kids, so you want dinner ready quickly. It's then that you'll appreciate **Peak 1**'s **Backpacker Stove** ($40). It's fueled by a butane/propane canister, so there's no white gas or priming to fool with. Click the built-in igniter, and you'll have a quart of boiling water in under 4 minutes. Traditionalists, meanwhile, can't miss with the **MSR WhisperLite** ($52.50), a reliable white-gas stove that is hot, quiet, and allows simmering so you don't burn the stew. To cook for a mob, it's hard to beat **Coleman**'s three-burner propane **Guide Series** stove ($90)—as long as you've got the car around to haul it. It works off disposable bottles or bulk propane and puts out enough BTUs to accelerate global warming.

Cookware: Cascade Designs's **Evolution II** cookware has a non-stick coating both inside and out, so it's always easy to clean up. Get the family-size set ($37), which has 1½- and 2-liter pots and lids, a potlifter and scrubber pad.

Carry condiments and utensils in **Outdoor Research**'s handy **Compact Outdoor Kitchen Kit** ($29), which comes equipped with just about everything you need to do your Martha Stewart Goes Hiking routine. And for a traditional look at mealtime, **Pioneerware**'s sixteen-piece enameled "campset" ($50) has enough place settings for a family of four.

Water Filters: Keeping a family going on the trail also means lots of water for hydration. But *giardia* and other waterborne nasties can result in a mass visit to the doctor once you get home. So take along a **PUR Hiker** ($55), an effective, easy-to-use filter that will keep everyone tanked up. **MSR**'s **MiniWorks** ($65) offers slightly more effective filtering and greater convenience, but is harder to pump. A great camp accessory is a plastic, 5-gallon **waterbag**—fill it with purified water when you make camp, and you'll be set for the rest of the evening. You can find them at most outdoor stores for under $10.

Where to Find It: Cascade Designs: 800-531-9531; Coleman: 800-835-3278; MSR: 800-877-9677; Outdoor Research: 800-421-2421; Peak 1: 800-835-3278; Pioneerware (call GSI Outdoors): 800-704-4474; PUR: 800-449-2837.
—DOUGLAS GANTENBEIN

FOR WILDERNESS WALKERS

Packs: Three- to five-year-olds can hike under their own power, albeit for maddeningly short intervals. A perfect kids' knapsack is the **Tough Traveler Ruffian** ($63), a comfy soft pack with a fleece-lined pouch inside. **Kelty's Zip-On Kid Pack** ($40) has 1,600 cubic inches of space (it expands to 2,000), and also zips to a Kelty child-carrier so Mom and Dad can take the load.

Six- to eight-year-olds can start carrying their own jacket and Walkman, and they'll be comfortable doing it with **Lowe Alpine's Contour 25** ($40), a 1,500-cubic-inch pack with a zippered inside pocket.

Jansport's Scout ($90) is an adjustable-frame backpack that can accommodate fast-growing kids between 9 and 11. It's a comfortable, ruggedly built pack with five sewn-in pockets. Jansport also has a line of accessories (like a first-aid kit and camera pocket).

Eastern Mountain Sports's EMS 3000 ($100) is a moderately capacious pack (3,000 cubic inches) that lets young teens carry bulky but light items such as clothing and sleeping bags. Older teenagers will love **CirqueWorks's** cutting-edge **Descent 3.6** ($319). All black with a red/orange logo, the great-fitting Descent also has the best snowboard strap system on the market.

For an adult carrying a family-size pile of gear, **Dana Design's Terraplane** ($429) is the pack that sets the standard for comfort and durability. With 6,000 cubic inches of space, it holds

REI: The Great Indoors

Don't get dirty. Three little words, passed on daily from parents to kids for at least a millennium. But they might be in danger of extinction at REI's new mondo Seattle flagship store, where explorers both big and little can climb on rocks and hike on trails without coming near any actual soil. On any given day, visitors to the 80,000-square-foot virtual world for outdoor adventurers will find:

✦ A crowd of parents and youngsters upstairs in the REI Jansport kids' camp, where junior rangers can climb a nonskid mountain, fish in a foam-rubber stream, or prance through an impact-resistant simulated old-growth tree stump. (No simulated poison-oak rash—yet.)

✦ A gaggle of mountain bikers testing brakes, shocks, and tires on a single-track trail that winds through the store property, at one point passing a two-story waterfall that swells when it rains.

✦ Several extremely nervous backpacking-kitchen newbies learning how to properly prime a white-gas stove (soak in gas, ignite, stand back, not necessarily in that order) on a flameproof rock covered by a fume hood.

✦ One or more people—apparently unable to find suitable quantities of rain outside in Seattle—testing rain parkas and hats in a glass-walled shower booth sponsored by (surprise!) Gore-Tex.

✦ Any number of hikers tromping over a short simulated hiking path, complete with actual ankle-twisting rocks and a couple of nasty, cartilage-shredding roots.

✦ A dozen climbers testing their mettle—and REI's latest climbing harnesses—on what's being billed as the world's tallest freestanding indoor climbing rock (which locals point out looks alarmingly like either a seven-story petrified yam, or Lyndon LaRouche). —RON C. JUDD

enough for a week, while its superb suspension makes even 70-pound loads tolerable. At a more reasonable price, **The North Face's Renegade** ($250) is a roomy pack with a suspension system that allows a wide range of fit adjustments. **Eureka's Nova** ($260) has useful features like a well-padded hip belt and a top pocket that converts to a fanny pack.

Kelty's Kangaroo ($60) is a soft, front-carrying pack that's perfect for lugging the littlest hikers. For older infants, **Tough Traveler's Stallion** ($158) has big-pack features like padded, adjustable shoulder straps.

Footwear: Good generals know they must look after the troops' feet. So should you. For adults, **Merrell's** new **M2 Ventilator High** ($130) is a perfect summer boot—light and comfortable with an over-the-ankle design, a rugged polyurethane footbed for support, and mesh panels to keep your feet cool. **Salomon's Adventure 7** ($155) offers a bit more support and weather-resistance and also has sticky soles for traction. For wet weather and light packs, you'll appreciate the Gore-Tex liner in **One Sport's Skyline GTX** ($135). **Hi-Tec's** new **Trilogy** ($75) is a light, all-leather hiker that has good impact protection and a durable outsole. And **Timberland's Midweight Backpacker** ($180) has long-lasting all-weather construction and a comfortable flex for trail hiking. For kids, **Nike's Air Skarn** ($60) offers good traction and foot stability in a comfortable, cool-looking, low-cut shoe. For more support, **Vasque's All-Leather Kids Klimber** ($55) has an over-the-ankle design and an unusual adjustable insole that lets you peel off layers as your

youngster grows, giving you more wear out of the shoe.

Where to Find It: CirqueWorks: 800-313-0427; Dana Design: 406-587-4188; EMS: 603-924-6154; Eureka: 888-245-4984; Hi-Tec: 800-521-1698; Kelty: 800-423-2320; Jansport: 800-558-3600; Lowe Alpine: 303-465-3706; Merrell: 800-359-3050; Nike: 800-344-6453; One Sport: 800-826-1598; Salomon: 800-225-6850; The North Face: 800-447-2333; Timberland: 800-445-5545; Tough Traveler: 800-468-6844; Vasque: 800-224-4453.

—DOUGLAS GANTENBEIN

FOR WATER SPORTS

Waterproof Bags: There's nothing quite like shimmying into your sleeping bag after a hard day of paddling, only to find (yech!) that it's damp. Whether the vessel is a raft, canoe, or kayak, whatever you pack—clothes, cameras, food, tent—may very well end up wet.

Waterproof bags are well worth the investment. Consider bags made of waterproof nylon rather than vinyl. While vinyl on vinyl tends to stick, nylon bags slide against each other, making it easier to pack them into the hull. Experienced kayakers also recommend buying several medium-size bags, which are easier to cram into the hull's nooks and crannies than one huge bag would be.

Some bags have waterproof zippers—but those familiar old turn-down closures work just as well and tend to be a bit more economical.

For convenience, nothing beats **Seal Paks** ($22) by **Cascade Designs:**

Small waterproof bags with a waist belt, big enough to hold your water bottle and sunglasses case. The **Large Seal Pak** ($31) has an 8-liter capacity—enough space for one person's camera gear, lunch bag, and scrunched-up sweater. For more room, check out the huge variety of bags made by **Seattle Sports, Voyageur,** and **Northwest River Supplies**. The **River Pack 4.2** ($50), Seattle Sports' largest bag, has shoulder straps and will haul enough gear for a multiday trip. Bags with blow-up air pockets, such as Voyageur's nylon **Shutterdry** camera bag ($45–$60), keep your gear both dry and safe from bumps.

Footwear: Think of your footwear as helmets for your feet: If you do wind up in the water, ricocheting off boulders in the feet-first position, you'll appreciate a little sole asylum. Despite the fact that the first sport sandal was designed by a river guide and sandals are almost synonymous with rafts, these days some outfitters ban them. Sandals come off, they complain, and guides spend too much time retrieving them for clients. This faction also insists that a sandal doesn't protect the toes and sides of your feet the way, say, a pair of old Keds does. (But Keds squish when wet and take forever to dry.)

Enter the latest in river gear, the water shoe. Not to be confused with the flimsier "water sock" introduced a decade ago, water shoes stay on in big water, protect the entire foot, and dry quickly—though some models lack the traction and support of a good sport sandal. The **Teva Wet Climber** ($80) and **Rockport's HydroSport XCS** ($100) are a bit pricey but provide the best traction. Other options include the new

Hi-Tec Piranha ($50) for good value in a solid shoe, and the new **Adidas Equipment Water Moccasin** ($65) with a super-fast-drying upper and sticky sole.

In fact, sport sandals have legions of loyalists. Among the most loyal are

---

What Every Bug-Catcher Is Wearing

If you can see it, hear it, and pinpoint its location, then surely you can catch it. A bug, that is. New from **Wild Planet** (800-247-6570) are the necessities for budding entomologists.

✦ **The Live Insect Collector** ($9). Catch 'em, then identify 'em with the accompanying manual.

✦ **The Trail Light** ($7). An adjustable lamp that attaches to any size head, arm, or bike.

✦ **Explorer's Watch** ($9). A six-in-one Survival Watch with digital time display, compass, thermometer, alarm, stopwatch, and signal mirror.

✦ **Supersonic Ear** ($24). Enjoy the insect-tracking potential of this "Powerful Listening Device," but don't take it too close to Yosemite Falls.

kids, who appreciate a sandal's barefoot feel without a bare foot's vulnerability to cuts and abrasions. The newest sandal models self-bail, which speeds the already-speedy drying process and, in addition to Velcro, straps come with buckles or ratchets for added hold. Wearers should be prepared to endure one indignity, however: that so-called Teva tan. Check out the new **Nike Tiyo** ($65) and the **Merrell M2 Blackwater** ($85); both have all the right features—like neoprene cuffs and cinches—to keep the sandal locked on the foot.

Personal Flotation Devices (PFDs):

Most outfitters will provide life jackets, but too often they're more than a little funky after a summer of blended sunscreen and sweat, and the PFDs provided to children are often adult size small. If your family is around water a lot, consider buying your own. Coast Guard–approved PFDs are rated in terms of the amount of flotation provided. Type II PFDs have extra flotation in the front and a large collar, and will float a "swimmer" face up. Strong swimmers might prefer a Type III PFD; it provides the same amount of flotation, but is more comfortable and easier to maneuver in. The **Extrasport Basic Kids** ($50 for Type II and Type III), **Stearns Heads-Up** ($20, Type II) and **Perception Wave** ($42, Type III) all are excellent PFDs for children. Kids' small torsos make it essential that they use a crotch strap to keep the jacket from riding up around the head. Popular adult models are the **Extrasport Rogue** ($79), **Stearns Adult River Rafting Vest** ($50), **Lotus Designs Rio Grande** ($80), and the **Stohlquist Silhouette** ($90). The obvious is worth repeating: Life jackets are only effective when worn.

River Accessories: The glare on the water can be intense, so make sure that the whole family is wearing sunglasses. So certain are most raft companies that a big wave will knock your glasses off that they require eyeglass retainers. **Croakies** or **Chums** cost $3.50–$6 and can be found at most sporting goods stores. Candid snapshots of everyone getting splooshed by waves will keep the memories of your raft trip alive. Let the kids take their own pictures with a dunkable **Kodak Fun Saver Weekend 35** one-time-use camera (about $15) or **Fuji's Fujicolor Quicksnap Waterproof Plus** (about $17), both recyclable with 27 exposures. Finally, no river trip would be complete without the end of the day (sometimes daylong) water fight. Come well armed. **Super-soaker** water guns sold at most toy stores have an effective range of 30 feet, but real water-fight aficionados prefer the quick-loading **Hydro Stik** sold by **Northwest River Supplies** ($17–$18.50). Then again, maybe it's best to just pull out the corn cob pipe and read aloud a few chapters of *Huckleberry Finn*.

Where to Find It: Adidas: 800-423-4327; Cascade Designs: 800-531-9531; Chums: 800-222-2486; Croakies: 800-443-8620; Extrasport: 800-633-0837; Fuji: 800-755-3854; Hi-Tec: 800-521-1698; Kodak: 800-242-2424; Lotus Designs: 704-689-2470; Merrell: 800-359-3050; Nike: 800-344-6453; Northwest River Supplies: 800-635-5202; Perception: 800-595-2925; Rockport: 800-343-9255; Seattle Sports: 800-632-6163; Stearns: 800-783-2767; Stohlquist: 800-535-3565; Teva: 800-433-2537; Voyageur: 800-843-8985.

—STEVE SHIMEK

FOR CYCLISTS

Mountain Bikes: One of the best bikes for kids is **Specialized**'s **Rockhopper 24** ($250). It has serious bike features such as eighteen-speed gearing and comes in frame sizes for both boys and girls. For even younger cyclists who can manage changing gears, **Schwinn**'s **Thrasher 2.4** ($209) is a mini-mountain bike with six speeds, a durable steel frame, and good stopping power with its cantilever brakes. For very young children, a simple, inexpensive bike is the **Schwinn Tiger** (for boys; **Tigress** for girls; both $110), which has a rear coaster brake and handlebars that adjust as your youngster grows. For adults, **Marin**'s **Bear Valley** ($649) comes fully equipped with Shimano's smooth-shifting STX component group and a Rock Shox Quadra 5 to absorb life's ruts and bumps. Another solid midprice bike is **Diamondback**'s **Topanga SE** ($530), which has a mix of Shimano components, a Rock Shox Quadra 5 fork, and a comfortable Avenir saddle. If you don't need the extra weight and expense of a suspension, take a look at **Cannondale**'s **M500** ($596). It has a light, handmade frame, a mix of Shimano components with grip-shifters, and sure-stopping Dia-Compe brakes. Another alternative is the hybrid bike, which combines the low gears and easy maneuvering of a mountain bike with a more upright position. **Trek**'s **750** ($560) is a fine around-town/camp/cabin cruiser, with easy-to-use grip-shifts and a comfortable frame.

Helmets: Take a cantaloupe and drop it from chest level. The fruit lands with a sickening thud, oozing seeds and juice from the gash in its rind. Take another cantaloupe, strap it into a bike helmet, and drop it from the same height. This one lands intact. Now imagine that cantaloupe is your head in a bike crash. This demonstration is a favorite of the Youth Bike League, which conducts bike safety assemblies at schools nationwide to impress upon kids the importance of wearing a helmet.

Every year, 560,000 Americans are treated in emergency rooms for bicycling injuries; 1,000 die. Eight out of ten cycling deaths are a result of brain injury. According to a *New England Journal of Medicine* study, helmets reduce the risk of head injury in a bike crash by 85 percent. At last count, thirteen states have enacted mandatory helmet laws for minors: Alabama, California, Connecticut, Delaware, Georgia, Massachusetts, Oregon, Pennsylvania, Maryland, New Jersey, New York, Rhode Island, and Tennessee.

When buying a helmet, look inside for a certification sticker from either the American National Standards Institute, the American Society for Testing Materials, or the Snell Memorial Foundation. To fit your helmet, make sure it sits level on your head—straight over the brow—and that the chin strap is tight, with only a finger's width of space between strap and chin. The helmet shouldn't move when buckled.

Kids even like wearing **Bell Sports**'s cool-looking **Jumpstart Pro** ($30). This youth-size helmet has twelve vents and great-looking finishes like black Graffiti and purple Shooting Stars. Younger children will benefit from **Specialized**'s **Bike Bug Youth** ($35), which has extended cov-

The Outdoor Medicine Chest

The Wilderness Medical Society conducted a study that was published in the *Journal of Wilderness Medicine*. Researchers polled backpackers coming down off trails in Yosemite National Park and discovered that 14 percent had to cut short their hike because of injury. Half of those—blisters, infected insect bites, or minor cuts— were easily treatable. The moral of this story: A good first-aid kit can save your vacation. More importantly, it can save your life. Things to consider in a first-aid kit are: (1) the number of people that the kit will have to support; (2) the length of your trip; (3) unique features of the environment (e.g., black flies in Maine); and (4) whether there are children in your party. Children, after all, aren't simply extremely short adults. Aspirin occasionally can be harmful for some children; child's-strength acetaminophen or ibuprofen is usually recommended as an alternative. Packing a thermometer (a digital model is easier to read in a tent) is crucial, since temperature is often a barometer of how sick your child is. A number of companies do the packing for you—two sell specialized family kits. **Atwater Carey Ltd.**'s (800-359-1646) kit for parents and older children can be supplemented with prepackaged essentials for the juvenile set. **Adventure Medical Kit**'s (800-324-3517) Family Spirit includes the youngsters' package, so there's no need for a supplement; The booklet *Caring for Children in the Outdoors*, by Barbara Kennedy, M.D., is highly recommended. And for big jobs, **Outdoor Research**'s Family Camping Medical Kit ($68) has enough supplies to last for an extended tour; call 800-421-2421.

erage and cute bug graphics. For adults, **Giro**'s **Air Blast RL** ($60) is an excellent all-around skull shield for road or trail riding. It has nine vents to keep you cool, a good fit thanks to Giro's head-hugging Roc Loc system, and a removable visor. Protect both your head and your dignity with **Specialized**'s **Sub 6** ($65). Not only is it the lightest SNELL-approved (a head-injury rating) hardshell helmet on the market, it also thankfully comes in plain blue or white.

Apparel: For some bikers, a T-shirt and a loose pair of shorts are fine. But once you've ridden with "real" bike clothes, you'll see how much more comfortable they are. And safer, too, if you wear a garment made with IllumiNITE, a new highly reflective material that's also windproof and highly water-resistant. **Performance**'s **IllumiNITE Jacket** ($100) has mesh side panels for ventilation and two zippered front pockets. It's also available as a vest ($70). In warm weather, no adult with a sense of humor should be without a **Looney Tunes jersey** from **Giordana** ($70). These come with a variety of cartoon characters, including Yosemite Sam, Roadrunner, and Wile E. Coyote. For comfort in the saddle, **Bellwether**'s **Double Short** ($69) combines biking-short features like a Microsuede chamois pad with Cordura outers that wear like iron and look like ordinary shorts. For a sleeker look, there's no better bicycling short than **Pearl Izumi's Stretch Ultrasensor Shorts** ($75). These are made with fast-drying polyester and have a superb fit. Younger riders will find **Cannondale's Junior Jams** ($25) appealing. These cotton flannel jams have a knee-length cut and are designed to fit well during cycling. Match the shorts with **Cannondale's Kids Jersey** ($45), which is made of quick-drying and comfortable Polartec Bipolar. Finally, a top-flight all-around bike shoe for both roads and trails is **Nike's Pedali Combo** ($85), which is compatible with any SPD-type pedal.

Bike Luggage: Adding a few packs to your bike turns it into a perfect touring vehicle for extended trips from your cabin or camp. One of the handiest is **Jandd Mountaineering's Rac Pac II** ($60). It secures to any rear luggage rack and holds up to eight cans of soft drinks or mineral water. The top expands for awkward loads like long loaves of French bread. There also are zippered storage pockets on each side, and D-rings for a shoulder strap. Fit it to **Blackburn's Mtn. Rack** ($40), a sturdy, easy-to-mount luggage rack that fits mountain and road bikes. For a handlebar-mounted bag, **Overland's Touring Bag** ($70) has a clear plastic map pocket for keeping on course and side pockets for sunglasses or sunscreen. Taking a longer trip? One of the best sets of bike luggage is **Performance's HP series**. Available in large size for a rear rack ($80 per pair) or compact for front or rear mounting ($70 per pair). These sturdy bags are made of Cordura rip-stop and have big mesh side pockets for things you want kept handy, internal pockets for organization, and an easy-mount system for securing them to your bike. The large model also has a zippered rear pocket.

Trailers are becoming increasingly popular for bike tours. **Burley's d'Lite** trailer ($380) hauls youngsters or extra gear and folds for storage. For luggage only, **the Yak** from **B.O.B** ($229) hauls up to 70 pounds. Its single-wheel design is more maneuverable than double-wheel trailers, and also works on single-tracks. To carry your littlest traveler, the three-wheel **Baby Jogger II** ($248–$268) in the 16- or 20-inch wheel size, can be converted into a bike trailer with a trailer-conversion kit ($193).

Accessories: Few activities known to humankind have generated as many add-ons, accessories, and widgets as bicycling. Many are even useful, while a few fall into the order of must-have. For many people, one of the latter is a backpack-type hydration system. One of the best is **Camelbak's M.U.L.E.** ($73), which combines a big, insulated 2.7-liter fluid back and easy-uptake bite valve with a pump pocket and several zippered and mesh pockets for carrying keys, your wallet, and other necessities. Another good design is the **Gregory Arroyo** ($83), which has four side compression straps as well as a main compartment that can hold a cycling jacket and tools. For a no-frills way to carry liquids, **Cascade Designs's Quack Pack** ($44) comes with a 2-liter bottle in a simple backpack style.

For the bike, a cycling computer keeps track of your speed and mileage. **Cat Eye's Mity 2** ($24) is a rugged, compact computer with an easy-to-read display that gives you average speed, top speed, elapsed time, trip mileage and total mileage.

Should you have a flat, the **Mt. Zefal Graph Mini Pump** ($24) has an easy-to-pump design and a built-in pressure gauge so you get the correct inflation instead of just a guess. **Park Tool**'s **Mini Tool Kit** ($30) has tire patches, tire levers, wrenches, and a chain tool, and folds up to fit into a seat bag.

For safety, outfit your bikes with a **VistaLite VL300X** rear light ($15) that has five LEDs and is visible to 2,000 feet. To light your way and to alert approaching traffic, **Specialized**'s **PreView Xe** ($18) is one of the brighter low-priced headlights on the market. It runs on four AA batteries.

Fat-tire trails teem with pebbles, dirt, and low-hanging tree branches—all of which can wind up in your eyes. Invest in a good pair of sport sunglasses to protect you and yours from these trail hazards, and specify that you want a shield. These wrap around your face and grip the head. When buying for kids, look for lenses made of lightweight and shatter-resistant polycarbonates. Adults can choose between these lenses and glass (better optics and, when well made, just as durable). And when outside, get in the habit of wearing shades for protection from UV rays. Knock-off glasses with cheap tinted lenses can do more harm than good by causing the eye's lenses to open, leaving them vulnerable to UVs. These companies offer UV protection for both adults and kids: **Bollé, Nikon, Revo, Vuarnet-France Optical, Suncloud,** and **Ray-Ban.**

Where to Find It: Baby Jogger: 800-241-1848; Bell Sports: 800-456-2355; Bellwether: 800-321-6198; Blackburn: 800-456-2355; B.O.B.: 805-541-2554; Bollé: 800-554-6686; Burley: 800-311-5294; Camelbak: 800-767-8725; Cannondale: 800-245-3872; Cascade Designs: 206-583-0583; Cat Eye: 800-522-8393; Diamondback: 805-484-4450; Giro Sport Design: 800-969-4476; Giordana: 800-729-4482; Gregory: 800-477-3420; Jandd Mountaineering: 800-727-7172; Marin: 800-222-7557; Nike: 800-344-6453; Nikon: 800-645-6687; Overland: 800-487-8851; Pearl Izumi: 800-877-7080; Performance: 800-727-2453; Ray-Ban: 800-472-9226; Revo: 800-843-7386; Schwinn: 303-473-9609; Specialized: 408-779-6229; Suncloud: 800-578-8767; Trek: 800-369-8735; VistaLite: 800-456-2355; Vuarnet-France Optical: 800-348-0388; Zefal: 800-727-2453. —DOUGLAS GANTENBEIN

FOR ROAD-TRIPPERS

Car Racks & Carriers: How to get it all packed? For durability and flexibility, it's hard to beat a setup like **Yakima**'s **Q rack system,** which includes a tower set ($115), clips ($40), crossbars ($39), and RocketBox (13.2 cubic feet, $399). The box is particularly valuable if you have a small vehicle and plan a long trip—its yawning maw can swallow just about anything that won't fit in the trunk. To carry a bike, you'll also need a **SteelHead bike mount** (about $100). A similar, slightly more economical system is available from **Thule,** which includes gutter-mount towers ($92), bars ($35), and an Adventure box (16 cubic feet, $350). Thule's Adventure box fits on Yakima racks as well. For bikes only, **Rhode Gear**'s Euro Shuttle ($140) enables you to mount bikes vertically, like a roof rack, but still fit them on the trunk. In stand-alone units that fit a variety of roof rack systems, **Packasport**'s massive **System 115**

($925) is just the thing for extended trips. This rack provides 30.5 cubic feet and is more than 7 feet long and nearly 4 feet wide. A different approach is taken by **The Kanga Company,** which makes affordable soft rooftop carriers. Their 15-cubic-foot **RoofPouch** ($150) is big enough to hold most things that won't fit in the trunk, and is made of totally waterproof polyester.

Optics: When you're standing atop Glacier Point looking out over Yosemite Valley, you're going to wish you had the best optics to enjoy and take home the view. **Canon**'s new **ES6000** ($1,699) is expensive but spiffy, with an "eye control" feature that tracks what the user is looking at through the viewfinder, automatically centering and focusing the image. The ES6000 also has a color viewfinder, a 20:1 optical zoom lens (40:1 digital zoom), and a variety of editing effects. Other first-rate camcorders for vacation shooting include **Sony**'s **CCD-TRV30** cam-corder ($1,099). Composing your shot is made easier thanks to a flip-out, 3-inch LCD monitor that lets you watch the action in color while shooting. It shoots in less than one lux of light, has a twelve-power zoom, and comes with a wireless remote. **Sharp**'s **VL-E39U Viewcam** ($1,000), meanwhile, uses a 3-inch full-color screen as a full-time viewfinder. Special glass makes it usable under almost all lighting conditions. Finally, for budget-minded filmmakers, **Samsung**'s **SCX-915** ($599) has a 12:1 zoom lens, programmable auto-exposure, and fade control.

Still-photo types will appreciate the auto-focus capability and all-around ease-of-use of **Nikon**'s **N6006** ($563 for body only). Pair it with a **Sigma 28-200** F3.8–5.6 zoom lens ($451) to get just about any shot you'll come across on vacation. For even simpler vacation picture-taking, **Pentax**'s **IQZoom 90-WR** ($385) is a weather-resistant point-and-shoot camera with a 38–90mm zoom lens, a sophisticated auto-focus system, and an easy-to-handle contoured body.

Olympus's new **Stylus Zoom 105** ($436) is billed as the smallest, lightest weatherproof camera on the market to come with a 3:1 zoom, red-eye reduction, auto-focus, and built-in flash. And though expensive for a point-and-shoot, **Minolta**'s slick little **Vectis 40** ($598) has a surprisingly powerful 30–120mm zoom lens and uses the new Advanced Photo System film. APS film yields improved picture quality, lets you change film midroll, and gives you a choice of print formats.

For just taking a closer look at things, **Canon**'s **10 X 25A compact binoculars** ($219) fold for easy storage and are built to take the kind of abuse you can expect on vacation. For even sharper viewing, especially in low light, **Steiner**'s **Rocky 10 X 28 binoculars** ($649) have razor-sharp optics with special coatings for high light transmission. They're also designed for rough wear, encased in an armored coating to keep out dust and moisture, and the folding rubber eye-cups are kind to eyeglass wearers.

Where to Find It: Canon: 800-652-2666; The Kanga Co.: 800-347-9793; Minolta: 201-825-4000; Nikon: 800-645-6687; Olympus: 800-622-6372; Packasport: 800-359-9870; Pentax: 800-877-0155; Rhode Gear: 800-456-2355; Samsung: 800-767-4675; Sharp: 800-237-4277; Sigma: 516-585-1144; Sony: 800-222-7669; Steiner: 800-257-7742; Thule: 800-238-2388; Yakima: 888-925-4621.   —Douglas Gantenbein

ANY QUESTIONS?

Ask Outside Online

You're clearly a tough nut to crack: You've been all the way through the scores of vacations outlined in this book, and yet you want more. Maybe you need to know what climbing gear to buy for those budding wall rats of yours. Perhaps you're looking for a really beautiful campground near the big city where you live. Or maybe you and yours have just been everywhere and done all that.

Don't worry, we're not stumped. Dial yourself into Outside Online, at **http://outside.starwave.com.** You'll find archived feature stories from the award-winning pages of *Outside* Magazine, an enormous database of information on America's national parks from the National Parks Foundation, and travelogues that will whet your appetite for the wild. Best yet, you can put all questions about where to go and what you'll need while you're out there into the able hands of Outside Online's Adventure Advisor and Interactive Gear Guy.

Every week the Adventure Advisor provides detailed answers to selected questions about journeys both close-to-home and far-flung. Archived on the site are two years' worth of vacation ideas, trip itineraries, and outfitter recommendations—you can browse through it all and pose your own stumper if you want to. The Gear Guy's Q&A is set up in the same way; we guarantee he'll be able to help you sift through the ever-more-confusing array of outdoor gear on the market.

Set forth here are some examples of what you'll find in the archives at Outside Online. Happy surfing!

Hiking Mount Robson's Berg Lake Trail

Q *We are going to be in British Columbia this summer and would like to backpack the Berg Lake Trail at Mount Robson Provincial Park. We are wondering about maps and temperatures in July for day and night, and the number of hikers on average during weekdays and weekends. We are trying to decide how long to allow for both the hike and sight-seeing when we arrive at Berg Lake. We are hiking with our family, whose members range in age from 13 to 49. Could you advise us on the campfire rules and regulations? Your input would be a great help.*

A Here's the lowdown: The main route to Berg Lake from the Mount Robson Provincial Park visitor center, on Highway 16, is a moderately strenuous, 13-mile trek through the Valley of a Thousand Falls—with great views of 12,972-foot Mount Robson along the way. From the lake, it's another 1.3 miles to the Continental Divide, which marks both the Alberta/B.C border and the border of Jasper National Park. Expect to share the wilderness with heaps of other hikers in July, regardless of whether you go midweek or on the weekend. This is by far the most popular trail in the park and it sees heavy use from backpacking families, school groups, and solo trekkers. In fact, hiker numbers have skyrocketed so dramatically over the past few years that park officials are now limiting the number of tents allowed on the Berg Lake Trail system to seventy-five per night.

The upshot for this summer is that you'd be wise to call ahead and reserve a site at one of the seven backcountry campgrounds along the trail; most have in the neighborhood of seven tent sites, with the Berg Lake Campground sporting a generous twenty. Camping costs $2.80 per person per night (kids under 12 are free); there is also a reservation fee of $8.40 per tent if you reserve by phone (800-689-9025).

As for temperatures, you'll probably see daytime highs in the mid-60s to mid-70s, but bring plenty of warm clothes, as temps can drop into the 30s at night. Bring a camp stove or two, as campfires are not allowed anywhere along the Berg Lake Trail. If you've got extra time on your hands afterward, consider ditching the crowds on a more low-key overnight hike to Mount Fitzwilliam, in the east corner of the park. You don't need a backcountry permit—just self-register at the trailhead—and keep your eyes peeled for caribou, goat, wolverine, and, yes, grizzlies. For maps and route suggestions throughout the park call the visitor center at 250-566-4325.

To Shower or Not to Shower: Camping near Bend

Q. *My wife and two sons (ages 12 and 11) and I are camping up the California coast. Then we're heading into central Oregon for 3 to 4 days. We are camping in a tent but like the convenience of a shower. Where would be a good place to stay in the Bend area?*

A. There's nothing like a hot shower, I'll admit, but why sacrifice true, usually RV-free camping for a little running water when there are plenty of lake and riverside campsites to be had in central Oregon? Besides, a good scrub with cold, fresh water will really get you going in the morning.

Yes, the reality is that most campgrounds in the Bend area are a little on the primitive side, which is a good thing. If you've got an open mind, there are a few that might work for you.

Take Big River Campground, on the Deschutes River in the eponymous national forest, for instance. About 25 miles southwest of Bend off U.S. 97 and Forest Road 42, it has eleven sites along the river, each with a picnic table and fire pit, and there are launching facilities nearby ($5 per night; no reservations). Call the Bend/Fort Rock Ranger District at 541-388-5664 for more details.

If you're not sold on shower-less camping, there's always Lava Lake Campground on the shores of beautiful (you guessed it) Lava Lake, about 40 miles south of Bend off Cascade Lakes Highway (otherwise known as County Road 46). This one is plush by Oregon standards: forty-three sites, vault toilets, picnic tables, as well as a coin-operated laundry and showers at the adjacent Lava Lake Lodge. Mini-golf, however, is sadly not available. Bring your fishing rods and canoe if you've got 'em, and your camera. Mount Bachelor and The Three Sisters are in the background, making it a primo spot for those inevitable family photos. They don't take reservations, but it will cost you about $10 a night. The Bend/Fort Rock Ranger District has more info.

For other suggestions, I recommend picking up a copy of *Pacific Northwest Camping* (Foghorn Press, $19.95). It's crammed full of about a bizillion (exaggeration alert) campgrounds, so if my ideas don't fit the bill, you're bound to find something that'll fly with the family.

Summer Day Hikes in Yellowstone

Q. *My wife and children (ages 6 and 3) and I will be spending a week in Yellowstone this summer. Would you kindly recommend some day hikes that would offer us some solitude?*

A. In order to avoid the crowds that throng to Yellowstone in the summer, you'll need to follow a few basic rules. First off, know that Old Faithful, Mammoth Hot Springs, and The Grand Canyon of the Yellowstone are prime tourist destinations. If you're planning to take the well-traveled pilgrimage to these areas, be prepared to sacrifice solitude for awe-inspiring—albeit crowded—views.

That said, we recommend planning your day hikes in the less-trammeled corners of the park. Head to the Monument Geyser Basin Trail, near Madison Junction, for a short 2-mile (out and back) walk that's perfect for kids. The first half of this hike follows the Gibbon River before climbing a hill to a thermal area with steam vents, sulfur caldrons, and mud pots. To find the trailhead, drive 8.6 miles northeast from Madison Junction to the parking area on the west side of the road (just south of the first bridge after Beryl Spring). Look for a small sign for "Monument" at the turnoff.

If you're not quite sure how far your kids can hoof it, try a hike (or two) around the Lost Lake and Lost Creek Falls area, where you'll find several short-hike options. A half-mile round-trip trail to Lost Creek Falls offers spectacular views from both the base and top of the falls. The trail to Lost Lake (1.6 miles round-trip) begins from the same trailhead and gently winds its way up forested hillsides to the long, narrow lake full of water lilies and ducks. Leave your car in the Roosevelt Lodge parking area at Tower Junction. The trailhead for both hikes is just behind the lodge and is hard to miss.

Because Yellowstone is grizzly country, it's a good idea to check for trail closures with rangers before heading out. For more information about the park, call 307-344-7381. Pick up a copy of *Day Hikes in Yellowstone National Park* (Day Hike Books, $7.95; 800-541-7323). For good nuts-and-bolts information, see the Wyoming section of the National Park Foundation's "Complete Guide to America's Parks" on Outside Online or at http://www.goparks.org.

Buggy but Crowd-Free on Lake Superior

Q. *My wife, two teen-age kids, and I are planning a camping trip (we're tenters) on the north shore of Lake Superior* *in early August. What are your recommendations for great places to camp, preferably public sites, when traveling from Duluth to Sault Sainte Marie, Ontario? Can I make camping reservations in Minnesota and Ontario? Also, how are the insects?*

A Well, if you're willing to lose the car for a few days and strike out with your backpacks (which is quite character-building for the teenagers), I recommend heading north out of Duluth and spending a couple of days on the Superior Hiking Trail, a 200-mile stretch of wilderness between Two Harbors and the Canadian border.

For a good taste of the trail, try the 20-mile section between Silver Bay and Little Marais with its great views of the lake from the top of the 1,500-foot Sawtooths and its old-growth cedar groves in Tettegouche State Park. Particularly exciting for acrophobes is the wobbly, stomach-turning suspension bridge over the Baptism River.

And, for your tenting convenience, there are primitive campsites near water sources every 5 miles or so. If this doesn't fit into the family plan, plenty of spur trails and access roads to U.S. 61 break up the through-hike into perhaps more tolerable (and teen-friendly) day hikes. For camping information (for reservations at Tettegouche State Park, call 800-246-2267; otherwise, reservations aren't necessary), shuttle details, and maps, call the Superior Hiking Trail Association at 218-834-2700.

Consider it a warm-up to the even more remote—and I mean remote—camping opportunities on Lake Superior's rugged north shore. Destination: Pukaskwa National Park, a 765-square-mile swath of wilderness.

To get there, take U.S. 61 north to Thunder Bay, Ontario, where you'll take Highway 11/17 past Sleeping Giant Provincial Park (good spot to overnight; call 807-977-2526) to Nipigon. From there, follow 11/17 along the lakeshore, tenting at Rainbow Falls Provincial Park (807-824-2298) and Neys Provincial Park (807-229-1624) before making a right turn toward Pukaskwa at the Hattie Cove access road (Highway 627). Entrance at the park kiosk will run you $7 a night (plus a $4.20 registration fee).

If you arrive late, stay overnight at the drive-in Hattie Cove Campground ($10.50–$12.60 per night), before setting out on the 36-mile Coastal Hiking Trail. The hike along this out-and-back route gets steeper and tougher as you go, but the vertigo-inducing cliffs and sand beaches will keep your mind off your achin' dogs.

Camp at designated backcountry sites along the trail—each about 4 or 5 hours apart and reservable in advance (call the park at 807-229-0801, ext. 242). Water's available at most sites, but you'll need to boil or filter it before drinking. Keep your eyes open for resident moose, bears, wolves, and woodland caribou, especially in late August when the park has quieted down.

While June is the buggiest time up north, August isn't pest-free, by any means. Bring the bug juice and prepare to do some swatting.

For more ideas, check out "The Flatland's Private Big Blue" in the Destinations section of *Outside*'s September 1995 issue.

Paddling
Coastal New England

Q *My wife, teenage kids, and I are interested in learning to kayak. We are fit runners, bikers, swimmers, and hikers.*

What resources are available in our area? We're looking for a beginners' tour for up to a week.

A Geographically speaking, you're in great shape. You can either make the short drive north to the Essex/Gloucester area on Cape Ann, a fast-growing playground for novice and veteran paddlers that's perfect for day trips or overnighters, or head farther afield to the Maine coast, home to a virtual sea kayaking explosion in recent years and plenty of outfitter-run multiday trips.

In Essex, the folks at Essex River Basin Adventures run 3- or 5-hour guided paddles for $35–$75 per person, including all equipment and shuttle service. Most of their trips head out toward Hog Island and northeast to Crane's Beach and Plum Island, an 11-mile stretch of barrier-beach dunescape that's one of the East Coast's best spots to see migratory shore birds. To the southeast is Thacher Island, a 52-acre patch of dry land one-third of which has been designated a national wildlife refuge.

Even if you opt for a longer paddle, keep Cape Ann in mind for an overnight trip. Stay at the Camp Ann Campsite, a campground with about 250 sites, overlooking the Annisquam River estuary in Gloucester ($16 per couple per night, plus $6 each additional adult and $1 each additional child 16 and under; 508-283-8683) once you've learned the basics and are ready to strike out on your own.

If you don't mind the drive, consider signing on with the Maine Island Kayak Company. Based on Peaks Island in Casco Bay, they offer a whole slew of multiday tours and clinics, including a $250, 2-day fundamentals course that covers equipment, strokes, safety and rescues, wind and waves, tides and currents, weather analysis, route selection, and chart and compass reading. Or, get the basics down while paddling a 5-day circle route through Downeast's Jonesport Archipelago ($750 per person, including all meals and equipment). Although there's no minimum age for paddlers, they suggest you weigh at least 100 pounds or so in order to ensure your ability to maneuver the kayak. Keep in mind that they've got plenty more to choose from, so call them at 800-796-2372 for a detailed trip itinerary.

If you're in the mood for some serious family bonding, try Maine Island Kayak Company's 3-day Family Fun trip. Here parents and kids 10 and up paddle together in double kayaks, exploring Maine's unique islands, protected inlets, tidal pools, and lighthouses at a leisurely pace ($345 per adult; $230 per child riding double). Departure dates are July 8, August 4, and September 5.

And, finally, before you don the spray skirts and life jackets, check out our write-up of Sea Kayaking Cape Ann in the Destinations section of *Outside's* October 1995 issue.

A Family Vacation in Jamaica

Q *My wife and I would like to take a trip to Jamaica in August with our two daughters (ages 9 and 2). We'll stay 7 to 10 days and are interested in a recommendation on where active families should stay. My wife and I would like to scuba dive at least once, but as a family we enjoy hiking/walking, biking, and playing around at the beach. Any suggestions would be great! Thanks.*

A I recommend the family friendly Franklyn D. Resort near Runaway Bay on Jamaica's north coast. With plenty of kid-oriented programs, plus free daytime nanny service available for kids under 16, this upscale but not uncomfortably stuffy resort is a good choice for parents with sun-seeking kiddies. Call 800-654-1337 for rates and more information. For other suggestions, contact the experts at Rascals in Paradise, a California-based travel agency that specializes in family vacations (800-872-7225).

Taking Young Children around the World

Q *Hi, we're looking for some good guidebooks or advice on traveling with kids. We're planning a year-long trip with a 10- and a 5-year-old. Our itinerary includes Australia, New Zealand, Southeast Asia, India, Nepal, Europe, and hopefully South Africa. Any advice?*

A A good idea while planning your trip is to pick up Lonely Planet's *Travel with Children* for $11.95 in any major bookstore. This publication sums up almost everything you need to know about taking your children around the world: places to eat, places to stay, what to pack, medical treatment, basic health rules, cultural interaction, and various travel tips and stories. Rest assured it's not that difficult. According to *Travel with Children*, "From about the age of four on, travel with children becomes a real pleasure. It is still hard work, but also very rewarding as your children now form their own impressions and relationships, and can tell you what they are experiencing." For more information, call Lonely Planet at 800-275-8555. Have fun!

Mountaineering Courses for Teenagers

Q *I'm a 16-year-old student and interested in getting into mountaineer-*

ing. I wanted to take a trip to learn the basics and to do some climbing in the process.

A You have a couple of options. For a short trip that'll cover the basics of mountaineering and glacial skills in 5 days, sign on with REI Adventures' Mount Shasta Climbing Seminar and Summit Attempt that tackles the U.S.'s second-highest volcano. Starting on Shasta's lower slopes, you'll be briefed in alpine techniques, rope-team skills, ice axe use, and crevasse rescue en route to the summit at 14,161 feet. Trips run during summer breaks, with four departures from late June through Labor Day. It costs $720 per person ($620 for REI members); you're on your own for round-trip travel to Shasta City, California.

Also in the summer is REI's 7-day mountaineering course on Mount Rainier. With much the same focus as the Shasta trip, the Rainier program is led by crackerjack climbers from Rainier Mountaineering, Inc., and is open to climbers of all abilities. Start saving now: the trip is $1095 per person ($925 for REI members), including all food and accommodations. Airfare to Seattle is extra. REI sets a minimum age of 14 for Shasta and 15 for Rainier if you're accompanied by an adult; 18 if not. For details and departure dates, call REI Adventures at 800-622-2236.

If you've got more time on your hands, say 3 to 4 weeks, go whole hog and commit to a mountaineering course with either the National Outdoor Leadership School (NOLS) or Outward Bound. The operative word for both is "course," as these are much more demanding than plush, guided trips. Instead of being a guest, you're a student, which can only mean one thing: You learn by doing, and that goes for everything from setting belay routes yourself, to making fajitas over the camp stove, to pitching your tent. NOLS runs a whole bunch of month-long excursions through the Wind River Range in Wyoming, the North Cascades in Washington, and Alaska. The minimum age, however, is 17. Courses run all summer beginning in late June; $2700 for the Wind River Range trip, and $2800 for the North Cascades and Alaska trips. Call 307-332-6973.

Outward Bound's main mountaineering staples include 2- and 3-week courses in the High Sierras, the North Cascades, and British Columbia's Coast Mountains. Minimum age is 16 and trip costs are $1,695 for the 2-week programs, $1,995 for 3 weeks. In addition, Outward Bound offers mountaineering courses for 14- to 16-year-olds as part of their Adventure Program in both the High Sierras and the North Cascades ($1,795 for 2 weeks, and $2,195 for 3 weeks). Call the Pacific Crest Outward Bound School at 800-547-3312.

Customized Bike-Touring Maps

Q *Is there a map that has the best bike touring routes through the U.S.A.?*

A Sadly, there's not a single map of all the best routes, but there is an organization that can help. The Montana-based Adventure Cycling Association has mapped out over 20,000 miles worth of on- and off-road preset routes throughout the U.S., specifically designed for touring cyclists. Their maps come complete with down-to-the-foot mileage accuracy, don't-miss diners, and convenient campgrounds along the way. All you need to do is figure out where you want to ride, how long you have, and whether or not you want to camp or inn-hop, and the Adventure Cycling Association will provide you with the most intensely-detailed route maps you can imagine.

If you want to go whole hog and pedal clear across the country, Adventure Cycling can help you out with that, too. They have three ready-made east-west routes mapped out—the Northern, Southern, and the TransAmerica Trail—as well as a route along both coasts. Cross-country route maps range in price from about $78.95 to $92.95, and individual, regionally-specific maps start at $9.50. For more details, call the Adventure Cycling Association at 406-721-1776.

Biking with Small Children: Child Seats or Bike Trailers?

Q *What is the best way to bring your 18-month-old child along with you on a bike ride? Is the child trailer better than the child seat? I've looked at Burley's trailer and Rhode Gear's child seats and still can't decide which way to go. Please help!*

A I've never hauled a kid on a bike, but I've hauled plenty of gear and I'm a firm advocate of trailers. Much more stable than loading up the frame, and easier on your components. In the case of carrying a youngster, I'd be convinced it's safer, too, If the unthinkable happens and you crash, your child is lower to the ground in a trailer at least partially encased by metal tubing.

If you go with a trailer, then, the two best choices probably are the Burley d'Lite ($380; $265 for the solo model) or the Rhode Gear Chariot ($350). They're very similar in design and features; shop around and compare them on the basis of ease-of-use and rollability. —DOUGLAS GANTENBEIN

259

INDEX

FROMMER'S COMPLETE TRAVEL GUIDES

*(Comprehensive guides to destinations around the world, with
selections in all price ranges—from deluxe to budget)*

Acapulco/Ixtapa/Zihuatenejo
Alaska
Amsterdam
Arizona
Atlanta
Australia
Austria
Bahamas
Barcelona, Madrid &
    Seville
Belgium, Holland &
    Luxembourg
Bermuda
Boston
Budapest & the Best of
    Hungary
California
Canada
Cancún, Cozumel & the
    Yucatán
Cape Cod, Nantucket &
    Martha's Vineyard
Caribbean
Caribbean Cruises & Ports
    of Call
Caribbean Ports of Call
Carolinas & Georgia
Chicago
Colorado
Costa Rica
Denver, Boulder &
    Colorado Springs
England
Europe

Florida
France
Germany
Greece
Hawaii
Hong Kong
Honolulu/Waikiki/Oahu
Ireland
Israel
Italy
Jamaica & Barbados
Japan
Las Vegas
London
Los Angeles
Maryland & Delaware
Maui
Mexico
Miami & the Keys
Montana & Wyoming
Montréal & Québec City
Munich & the Bavarian
    Alps
Nashville & Memphis
Nepal
New England
New Mexico
New Orleans
New York City
Northern New England
Nova Scotia, New
    Brunswick & Prince
    Edward Island
Paris

Philadelphia & the Amish
    Country
Portugal
Prague & the Best of the
    Czech Republic
Provence & the Riviera
Puerto Rico
Rome
San Antonio & Austin
San Diego
San Francisco
Santa Fe, Taos &
    Albuquerque
Scandinavia
Scotland
Seattle & Portland
South Pacific
Spain
Switzerland
Thailand
Tokyo
Toronto
Tuscany & Umbria
U.S.A.
Utah
Vancouver & Victoria
Vienna & the Danube
    Valley
Virgin Islands
Virginia
Walt Disney World &
    Orlando
Washington, D.C.
Washington & Oregon

FROMMER'S DOLLAR-A-DAY BUDGET GUIDES

(The grown-up guides to low-cost travel)

Australia from $50 a Day
Berlin from $50 a Day
California from $60 a Day
Caribbean from $60 a Day
Costa Rica & Belize from
    $35 a Day
England from $60 a Day
Europe from $50 a Day

Florida from $50 a Day
France from $70 a Day
Greece from $45 a Day
Hawaii from $60 a Day
India from $40 a Day
Ireland from $45 a Day
Israel from $45 a Day
Italy from $50 a Day

London from $60 a Day
Mexico from $35 a Day
New York from $70 a Day
New Zealand from
    $50 a Day
Paris from $70 a Day
Washington, D.C., from
    $50 a Day